BODE:
GO FAST, BE GOOD,
HAVE FUN

BODE:
GO FAST,

VILLARD ⓥ NEW YORK

BE GOOD, HAVE FUN

Bode Miller
with Jack McEnany

Published in the United States by Villard Books,
an imprint of The Random House Publishing Group,
a division of Random House, Inc., New York.

VILLARD and "V" CIRCLED Design are registered trademarks
of Random House, Inc.

LIBRARY OF CONGRESS CATALOGING-IN-PUBLICATION DATA
Miller, Bode.
  Bode: go fast, be good, have fun / Bode Miller with Jack McEnany.
    p. cm.
  ISBN 1-4000-6235-7
    1. Miller, Bode. 2. Skiers—United States—Biography. I. McEnany, Jack. II. Title.

  GV854.2.M55A3 2005
  796.93'092—dc22   2004054954
  [B]

Printed in the United States of America on acid-free paper

www.villard.com

9 8 7 6 5 4 3 2 1

First Edition

Book design by Mary A. Wirth

To Jo and Woody,
for giving me love and freedom
and leaving the rest to me

—Bode

Contents

Prologue   ix

1. Tamarack   3

2. The Feral Life   29

3. The End of the Beginning   69

4. The Anti-Preppie   83

5. Go Fast   109

6. Go Faster   143

7. Have Fun   179

8. Be Good   187

9. The Essential Raw Material   203

10. Running My Mouth, Ain't I'm a Dog   211

Acknowledgments   217

Prologue

"The most important thing in the Olympic Games is not to win but to take part, just as the most important thing in life is not the triumph but the struggle. The essential thing is not to have conquered but to have fought well."

That's the Olympic Oath, and I believe the last line pertains only to games, because being conquered literally is to be avoided at all costs, even by exceedingly good sports. This I think we can all agree on. The rest of the oath sounds noble enough, but I ask myself: Who but an American Green Party politician or a Chicago Cubs fan could go through life doing his best and never winning? That's got to suck.

I can't say I thought much about the oath during the opening ceremonies at the Salt Lake City Olympics in 2002. I never memorized it, of course; I'd never even learned the Pledge of Allegiance in school. Life, the Olympics, and competition in general are exactly as the oath describes, but if you're squishy on the subject of winning, well . . . don't expect much.

I was in Salt Lake City to have fun and to win, which is my attitude in every race I run. Not for the medals, but for the moment. If I win a medal it adds to the fun, but not by much. That said, if I don't win anything at all, I still have fun. Otherwise it would have been a long, hard road.

See it from my perspective: the U.S. Ski Team right out of high school, a pretty hot first gig—lots of international travel, and I never had to wear a pin that says ASK ME ABOUT OUR HOT APPLE PIE. I was planning this when other kids were dreaming of being astronauts. I never had a grand strategy using the byzantine FIS point system or the Jedi Mind Trick. I'm just happy to have gotten here, happy to go out to rip and win.

Most of the media, and all of the ski media, are generous to me for the most part. But not entirely. Do a Google search on "Bode Miller" and "outhouse," and see how many hits you get: a lot. I don't want to know the number, so don't tell me.

I keep my distance from the quizzlers when I can. Not that I don't like them, because I often do, but it's extra work, which I always avoid. Besides, newspapers depress me, television is stupefying, and radio is full of bad music and people who talk more than they think. I have a monitor at home to watch DVDs, and satellite radio that plays nothing but what I want. We got no stinking cable, no damn broadband connection either. We be info-low-tech here, by careful design. It keeps me sane.

In hotels, I watch C-SPAN if I can get it. And even there, it seems like every time I turn on Book TV I get some old wheezer bragging about clever generals and the horrible beauty of war. It always raises this question: Is history more reliable than the news? I say probably not.

Don't get me wrong. The press work as hard as anyone I know without calluses on their hands. They're notoriously early risers. I'm up at six-thirty every morning, no matter what went on the night before, and as I make coffee, I usually notice movement out the frosty window of the RV—I have to scrape it with a thumbnail to see outside—and in the barren gray light there's always some sorry bastard with a notebook in his hand, lightly stamping his feet to keep warm while waiting for me to do what, I do not know.

Do they know what they want? A story, of course. Reporters will tell you that they want information that no other reporter has, and that's why they call it news. I can't imagine that there's anything that I care to share with the media that I haven't already discussed ad nauseam. I like the technical discussions we have after a race. I wish they'd publish more of that—the hill, the gear, and the conditions.

Pop culture, especially sports television, is getting dangerously close to *The Running Man*. Professional sports today are too much about the players and not enough about the game. Reporters are often more interested in what I did the night before a race than in the race itself. Après press conferences often remind me of when I was a kid and the ski patrol chased me. The media give me that same eerie sense of being pointlessly pursued by someone who can never really catch me.

I'm interesting for all the wrong reasons. I don't choke, and I don't distract easily. I do fall, as does everyone, and ski off-course, and I even missed a start at the Nationals last year because I didn't hear my wake-up call. The media love that stuff. Big wins, big crashes, big fuckups. The Bode Show is what the coaches used to call it. Not that reporters don't appreciate a well-run race, because they do. But I've had difficulty conveying one small, simple truth: when I ski, I enjoy myself. I never come away feeling like a fifth woulda-coulda-shoulda. I do my best and then, after a beer and big-ass steak, I sleep like a baby.

Not that I don't consider what went wrong. There was a down-hill race in Vail in 2001 that I fretted hours over afterward. I was having this magic run on the long boards and loving it. Victory flitted above me as I zoomed faster and faster, deciding whether she should land or not. Maybe my shoulders weren't big enough, or I hadn't washed my hair, or she just couldn't catch me. In the midst of this stupid fucking reverie, with next to no gates to go, I hooked a tip. And that was that. Victory flew off and sat on somebody else's head. Share the love.

I want to win all the races I run, but I really wanted that down-hill. My mind was ready; my feet were not. It was fall 2004 in Lake Louise before I actually won a downhill or a super-G. Patience.

I fall a lot less now. Flachau, Austria, in 2004, for instance, two races in a row. The next season in Beaver Creek, Colorado, I won the first two races and DNF'd on the next two. One second I'm beating the shit out of the course, the next I'm pointless and time-less. Life goes by fast on its own, never mind on two slippery slats at seventy-five miles per hour.

Falling doesn't bother me; I don't slip into a trough of despair over race results. Not that losing, falling, or screwing up in any way makes me happy. I think deeply about where things ate shit, and consider how I might have done them differently. But it's not a bother. In fact, I enjoy the introspective side of racing. That's why I do it. That, and the inhuman speed.

I admit I've considered that if I'd won the Flachau races, I'd have also won the 2004 World Cup overall. The thought has wandered through my mind more than once. There were a couple other close ones that season, too. I didn't finish eleven out of forty races, but so what? Think about it, but don't ruminate.

I don't dwell on losses. That's dopey. If I don't worry about the next race, why would I worry about the last one? The World Cup overall, like any superlative, means something, but what? You can't really reduce ski racing to a number; there are too many variables for that.

I speak for myself and no one else. I'm laid-back about medals and awards, but the U.S. Ski Team is definitely not. Its front office is interested in medals, and you can understand why. In contests where the winners and losers are separated by hundredths of a second, there's virtually never a dispute over who won. Medals are a nice, solid, objective standard that they can measure their business model by. Napoleon invented medals; he found you could pay people with them instead of money. It still works.

The size of the win is all but immaterial. Race results are measured in units of time humans can't perceive. A huge one- or two-second victory is interesting and exhilarating and weirds out everyone's FIS points (the International Skiing Federation is a French organization, which is why the letters in the acronym don't line up), but it's worth 100 World Cup points, no more or less than a squeaker. If I win a race by a couple hundredths of a second, it may have been because I was reaching over the finish line, grasping at it. I win for having longer arms than the other guy? What's that got to do with skiing? Medals, and even finishes, when the times are so proximate, don't measure much. I've seen it so unimaginably close that they ought to give out all golds. Or all bronzes.

The day after the 2002 Olympics ended I did an interview on MSNBC with some yakker who had the temerity to ask me on national cable television—with literally dozens of people watching—

"Hey, Bode, you did a great job for America in Salt Lake City, two silver medals, but your teammates . . . not a medal among them. What happened there?"

I'm paraphrasing here; he might have been more gracious, but not in my memory. It was like saying, "Hey, Bode, the dam broke and drowned all your neighbors, but you survived. What's up with those dopes—couldn't they swim?"

I explained to him that we ski-race six months of the year, every year, on the World Cup. Forty races plus four more at the National Championships at the end of the season. When it's summer in the Northern Hemisphere, we train in New Zealand and Chile, where it's winter. That's a lot of skiing. Consequently, you have on days and off days, and sometimes the Olympics fall on an off day. It's the law of averages.

America's stated medal goal going into Salt Lake was twenty. That may have been low—everyone plays expectation games—but the final count was thirty-four, an average of two a day: ten gold, thirteen silver, and eleven bronze. The first thing the media did was point out that it was one fewer than the Germans. So much for the struggle outweighing the triumph.

On the other hand, there were seventy-seven countries competing for three spots on the podium in each event. The Olympic Oath appeals to that silent, seventy-four-nation majority, acknowledging that there are always far more also-rans than winners, and that laying down your best run is all that's important. Imagine if people didn't take this attitude—picture hundreds of grumpy, dejected, pissed-off athletes mau-mauing for the TV cameras at the closing ceremonies, cringing at the thought of returning home to jeering hometown crowds. Sounds like bad television, unless there's a riot, which I suppose is possible.

As it was in Salt Lake City. Because of some sketchy ice-skating outcomes, the Russians were defensive; the Canadians were totally irate—the Canadians, mind you: these are people who excuse themselves when they bump into furniture. As it turned out, there were international bookies involved and a fur-dragging, Gauloises-smoking judge on the take. I don't even want to think about the death-threateningly disappointed Koreans over in the speed-skating venues. They scared me.

To make matters worse, on the last day of competition—just as we were proving to the local oppressive authorities that we could hold our non-3.2 beer—twenty drunks got busted in Bud World for hooliganism. Nice going, boys.

The Salt Lake City officials already had their issues. Planned Parenthood love-bombed the Olympic Village with 250,000 condoms "for the athletes." Hey, I like a good time, but that's 166 rubbers apiece for two weeks. That would cut into my game.

This was all against the backdrop of a cash-and-gifts scandal over how the 2002 Olympic Games came to Salt Lake in the first place—a scandal that went right to the top of the International Olympic Committee and then . . . uhh. What did happen there? Anybody know?

And where was the spirit of the Olympic Oath that year? I had it, such as it exists with anyone, but I always do. That's my whole deal: fun-win-fun. Screw everything else. I don't make as much money when I don't win, and people don't say nice things about me when I don't win, but I still have a good time. And fun is the source of all joy. Write that down; you read it here first.

Some of the Olympic suits, judges, and sponsors wouldn't know a hard-fought ski race from a lopsided scissors fight in the school yard. It's the athletes, the people who have their entire lives wrapped up in a single run down the mountain or a routine on the ice, who are expected to be selfless about the outcomes. And we are.

It's easy for me. I don't respond to praise or insults; I don't pay attention to them. I never read what's written about me or look at photo spreads. It's not that I don't appreciate the work that went into them, but reading about myself seems like a waste of time. I'm not even going to read this book.

However, during the Olympics I began to worry about the television "news" coverage of my family, which was hard to miss since I lived in a hotel room and had conversations with the television. I was portrayed as unsophisticated, raised in a shack, unschooled, a lost savage in a modern world. That's not nice, and not true. But try to tell that to someone on deadline.

Besides, if journalists are going to write about outhouses, they might devote some time to their uses and advantages. For instance, animals that normally wouldn't approach you, such as a weasel or a fisher, will come right up and check you out when you're on the crapper. They know you're indisposed; they're aware.

In the wintertime, bring the toilet seat into the house with you and put it on a hook by the door. This keeps it nice and warm and makes for an attractive wall hanging. Everyone knows the outhouse is a good place to read, and also where you should put the ashes from your woodstove—after they've cooled down, of course; you don't want a methane explosion. If you think nuclear winter sounds bad, try a shitstorm.

Growing up, we were never embarrassed by what we didn't have. Just the opposite. I was raised in Shangri-la, not a refugee camp. If I was shoeless, it's because I didn't want to wear shoes and, more important, nobody made me. When I was a little kid, there were times in the winter when all I wore was a pair of snow boots and, on my head, a toaster cozy that I had a particular fondness for. I'd be headed to the outhouse bollicky-bare-ass, and on my way back something would catch my interest. Could be anything: a swarm of snow fleas, a pile of deer shit, new bear scratchings on a tree. I spent a lot of time hacking holes in the ice in the brook, watching the waters rage beneath. I'd be out there puttering at any one or more of my many pursuits, naked in the elements, and a half hour later my mother would stick her head out the door and ask, "You want some pants?" Jo didn't question my right to do as I pleased. I never got frostbitten anywhere essential. Most important, I didn't just feel free; I was free.

In the middle of the 2002 Olympics my mother got a call from a producer at *The Tonight Show*. He wanted her to overnight a photo album. I had a week off between races; she was in New Hampshire and was coming out the next week for the giant slalom and slalom. The day before, I'd won silver in the combined, the first American ever to medal in the event, and suddenly I was a much-sought-after talk-show guest.

"Why do you need it?" my mother asked the producer, never one to do anything without an explanation. That's when she found out I'd be on Jay Leno's show Thursday night. She took the guy's address and hung up, then immediately called me on my cell phone.

"Bode," she said. "You're going to L.A.?" Her tone said the rest. I assured her it was okay, it was cool with the coaches, and I'd only be gone a short time because they were sending a private jet for me.

"La-di-da," she said, unconvinced. "What about the GS and slalom?" I told her I had it covered.

"Bode," she said, her tone now a warning for me to consider the situation more seriously than she assumed I had. "What's important here: doing your best at the Olympics or being on television?" And that was the end of it. She never sweats me too much about anything. Never has. And, of course, as far as she's concerned, anything is more important than being on television.

The next night I was sitting on the couch with Denzel Washington, cracking wise with Jay Leno about sex and skiing. It was surreal. Of course, I'd seldom seen television when I was a kid, so *The Tonight Show*'s iconic place in the culture was a little lost on me, but not entirely. I mean, I'd been around some since I'd left home. Ten years earlier, I was a shrimpy kid whose chances of making the team were only slightly better than my chances of giving birth. At that moment, wearing makeup, with those intense TV lights in my eyes and an Olympic medal bulging in the front pocket of my jeans, I got a flash of how far I'd come.

Jay asked me precisely about that: home, my humble, hippie beginnings. We lived in the woods, three-quarters of a mile from the nearest road, no electricity, no running water, and a frickin' *outhouse*! As Jay enumerated these small tragedies in my short life, his voice trilled higher and higher, more incredulous with each item. And then he was congratulatory, as if to say, Good going, bud; after making in the woods all those years, you went out and won an Olympic medal.

We were having essentially the same thought, but reading from completely different teleprompters. I'm not a hard-luck case. Anything I've ever done is because of my upbringing, not in spite of it. I wanted to explain that to Jay, and I started to, but it always sounds like whining, and I didn't want to bring the room down. If I did that, I'd be the Harvey Pekar of *The Tonight Show*. Not that there's anything wrong with that. But I let it drop. I'm never comfortable explaining. I gave it up a long time ago. I mean, what the hell is there to explain?

A few days later I silvered in the GS. So going to Los Angeles didn't affect my game at all. A couple of days after that, I boned the slalom big-time. This was for an Olympic medal in my best event, and that made it more poignant, maybe a little more disappointing, but I don't get caught up in the drama of racing; it has nothing to do with the race itself. Some days I'm on the right side of the clock, and other days I'm off the course. I don't beat myself up over it. I owe that nonchalance to the same calm acceptance my mother had for my naked snow walking when I was a little boy.

In the woods, you invent, grow, or carry in everything you need. We lived off the grid before off the grid meant anything. We were without money, but not without means; vast natural resources were within easy reach. Back then, Easton Valley was undisturbed by development, an old-growth forest full of deer runs and moose hollows. Our gardens were terraced along the hillsides; fresh water flowed ten feet from our back door; we had the sun, clean air, and the mountains. What more can you ask for?

This isn't exactly the picture painted in the press. The reportage has had a distinctly Dogpatch flavor, which makes my mother Mammy Yokum, and I can't have that. I'm not denying a certain white-trash chic around here—come to my house on any given night and you'll likely find a half dozen or more guys standing around shirtless, drinking beer from the can, rap music playing so loud that it chases the mice out of the house. As I write this they're all out front with a pair of my old K2s, road-skiing. This means getting dragged up and down Route 116 behind a motorcycle, and if you go down it's a nasty road rash. But we see progress. This was a dirt road when my mother was a kid. A state dirt highway. She used to set up her lemonade stand smack in the middle and force passersby to stop and pony up for some refreshment. Road-skiing would have been impossible back then.

There are two types of journalists who irk me: those who haven't been to Franconia, New Hampshire, but find it easy to poke fun at—they're just this side of Jayson Blair; and those who've actually been to Tamarack and Turtle Ridge and still, somehow, can't see it for what it is—they are plainly hopeless. This memoir isn't a rant about the press, but the need for it had its genesis in media coverage that consistently missed the mark. In fairness to the reporters, my story, like everybody else's, is too complicated to tell in a thousand words, or in ninety seconds. I hope I fix that here.

Franconia, New Hampshire
April 2004

BODE:
   GO FAST, BE GOOD,
         HAVE FUN

1

Tamarack

November 10, 1946

> Won $22 on the horses last night (my first win since
> 1938). Good thing, too. Peg and I were down to $14.
> Won $3 playing cards. Not bad for an hour's work.

> *—from my grandfather's journal*

My grandparents met on skis, which in itself isn't so strange. But I often think about the bit of luck that paired Jack Kenney with Peg Taylor for his first ski lesson on the slopes at Sugar Bowl, California, in the late fall of 1944, and then for life.

She was his instructor, and a lesson was what he needed. He was a naval officer on leave from the war in the Pacific; she'd just graduated from UC Berkeley and was the fastest member of the women's U.S. Ski Team. When she could stay up, that is. She knew going fast had serious consequences, such as falling and crashing, and she could live with that.

He'd traveled up from Hunters Point, where his ship, the USS *Belleau Wood,* had put into port. Peg was a ski racer enjoying life as much as anyone could in the midst of a world war. She wasn't looking for anything or anyone in particular; she was just taking it slow, planning on nothing but skiing, and finding what little fun she could otherwise.

Jack, on the other hand, was desperate for a ski lesson. He had to learn to ski, because after the war, should he survive, he was going back to New England to open a ski lodge. In his mind, there was no greater calling than running a ski lodge—although he'd barely ever been to one and couldn't ski to save his life. Nonetheless, this was the course he'd charted.

It's hard to say what put this precise vision in Jack's mind—one too many Bing Crosby movies aboard ship, maybe. But when it was over over there, Jack Kenney would be a ski lodge innkeeper, and there was no talking him out of it.

Jack was in a hurry that day on the sunny slopes of Sugar Bowl because his shore leave would be short-lived, lasting only until his air wing was reassigned to another flattop and sent back to the Pacific to fight the Imperial Japanese Navy.

A few weeks earlier, the *Belleau Wood* had been on patrol with the USS *Franklin* in the Visayan Sea, a small body of water that loops in and around the Philippine Islands. They were doing their jobs, searching the skies for Betties and Zekes, and splashing as many as they could. The world was at war, and Jack was a warrior. If you knew him, that fact alone would underscore the seriousness of those times.

On the morning of October 30, 1944, off the coast of Cebu, three Japanese bombers broke through the cloud cover in pursuit of the *Franklin*. From the flight deck of his ship, Jack watched the *Franklin*'s antiaircraft guns pop the first bomber out of the sky; it went down off the starboard side. The second came fast out of the sun and crashed onto the deck, killing fifty-six and wounding sixty. The third plane dropped a bomb on the *Franklin*, caught a shell from the *Belleau Wood*, and then dived, suicide style, onto the flight deck of my grandfather's ship. It exploded into a rolling fireball, sliding into rows of planes on the deck, exploding their bombs and fuel, and sending black smoke and billowing red flames high into the air; it burned through the night.

Ninety-two of Jack's shipmates died that day: burned alive, drowned, or both. Many were never found. The survivors worked day and night in enemy waters to extinguish the fires and keep the ship afloat. Its major systems—electricity, navigation, everything— were damaged by the attack. Charred corpses lined what was left of the deck. Jack had to have been deeply affected by this, as anyone would be; his emotions always rode close to the surface, right there where you could see them. He was never good at false faces, or hiding his discontent. On the upside, he was equally incapable of masking his joy or admiration. These must have been horrible days for Jack.

The abruptness of war itself probably set him off badly—the way a calm, sunny day in the South Pacific could quickly become a ship on fire and sinking, 20 percent of the crew dead. Jack always liked a challenge, but rolling with that had to be tough.

Weeks later, when the *Belleau Wood* limped into San Francisco for repairs, Jack was eager for that ski lesson. He wasn't one to ruminate, unless he was depressed. If he was feeling well, he met a problem and immediately set out to solve it. So in his berth, there in the belly of the blackened and wounded *Belleau Wood,* my grandfather planned the rest of his life.

The day he told me about his war experience he was sprawled in his chair. We were watching some war movie on television, and suddenly he spilled the beans. Alzheimer's had all but taken him by then, and he told the story with such passion that I never doubted him. His journals and the stories he's told others bear it out, as do scraps of paper noting bombing runs and times, the names of the men he served with. War was the ultimate team sport for those guys, with the added dimension of good and evil. They were on the side of good, and they would prevail. Of that they had no doubt. That sense of power and survival encouraged Jack to create for himself the life of his wildest dreams.

His decision-making process was invested almost entirely in planning, so he tended to make the decision itself early on, sometimes within minutes; then came the how-to phase, which was more involved and required lots of writing and sharing of ideas, often with people who weren't all that interested. When the plan was prepared, written, rewritten, and discussed at length, he knew that the first thing he needed to carry it off was a ski lesson.

But not long after his first ski lesson, Jack's air group was reassigned to the USS *Monterey*, where they served with Lieutenant Commander Gerry Ford, the ship's physical fitness instructor. They were all headed back to the Pacific to fight for, among other things, the right of every phys ed teacher to grow up to be president.

Jack was a full lieutenant, serving in naval intelligence and attached to a bomber group. He briefed the pilots on their missions, told them where to bomb, how to get there, how to get back, and how much fuel they'd use, given the weather and the wind. It was complicated, especially in the day of the slide rule. Jack was a numbers man for the war effort, all said and done, and that was a little odd because math had never been his game.

When Jack graduated high school in 1933, the Great Depression was the new big thing (we got the Internet, they got mass unemployment). So life was one big suck for Jack, and like everyone on the planet (except the filthy rich), Jack had much trepidation about the future. What would he do with himself? He was a smart kid, a talented writer with an inquisitive mind, a great athlete in tennis and golf, and good at anything he'd ever tried. But his family was broke, and college was expensive.

Along came the invisible hand that Jack would believe guided him through life. He was a spiritual person—not religious, but definitely in touch with God on a regular basis. A friend of his family's, a woman who spent her life in a wheelchair, admired Jack's sense of humor and his athleticism, especially his tennis, and offered to pay his way through college. This windfall was like hitting the jackpot, but Jack still had a problem.

Those were pre-SAT days, of course, and students had to have their grades certified as satisfactory in order to apply to most colleges. Jack's math grades sucked out loud and, consequently, were uncertified. But so what? Jack could be very persuasive, and he had far more luck with teachers than I ever did. His math teacher agreed to sign off on his grades under one condition: that Jack never take another math course as long as he lived, so as not to "disgrace" his teacher. Seemed like a deal. Jack didn't like math anyway.

I imagine the conversation like this:

JACK: Sir, I need your opinion on something mathematical.

TEACHER: Little late for that; the grades are in.

JACK: It's a statistical question—

TEACHER: Statistics! You can barely say it, never mind understand it.

JACK: My question is this: If I miss my opportunity to attend college, which is my only opportunity to do anything at all with my life except sell apples on the street corner, what's the probability that I'll call you on the phone every day for the rest of your life to remind you of the part you played in mine?

So Jack Kenney, the mathematical illiterate, went to Dartmouth College in Hanover, New Hampshire, graduating four years later, second among the eighty economics students in his class. And that should tell you something about economists.

He had a quiet graduation dinner with his parents at the Hanover Inn; they were both proud of him, and impressed by his accomplishments. That's about all we really know about them. It was tough for Jack to discuss his folks. They'd be gone within a year of his college graduation—his father from cancer, his mother suicide. It was a classical tragedy: the king died, so the queen died of grief. Jack was laid very low by the loss, sparking perhaps the first of many depressions.

Luckily, a family friend and physician from Jack's hometown of Reading, Massachusetts, Swede Oberlander, had just accepted a new job as the campus doctor at the University of New Hampshire. Jack went with him, partly so that Dr. O could keep an eye on him, and partly because Jack had nothing else to do.

It was a good respite for Jack, and he got a master of education degree during his two years there. After that, he moved to the North Country and taught history at Berlin High School for a couple years. Berlin was a happy little mill town then. It still is happy, I suppose, but not as happy as when the mills were in business.

Jack coached tennis at Berlin High and dreamed of being a writer. All his cognizant life (which ended a decade or so before his physical life), he kept voluminous journals, which he wrote in while taking a bath every night. Life and the universe were discussed most in those pages; otherwise, he filled his journals with sketches and directions for everything from rope tows to artificial ponds to robots that could help disabled athletes practice their tennis. Jack had a busy mind.

When Pearl Harbor happened, Jack signed up, and since he had such a certifiable way with numbers, they made him an intelligence officer in charge of calculating how far and fast a bomber should fly from an aircraft carrier before it dropped its payload where and when it was supposed to. And this should tell you something about war.

Jack got Peg's address that day at Sugar Bowl, and wrote her often for the duration of the war. She was interested, maybe infatuated with Jack's enthusiasm, which was a force of nature. It should also be noted that Jack's situation was more than mildly seductive for Peg, who wasn't only a ski bum being courted by an aspiring ski lodge proprietor but also an army brat being romanced by a naval officer off in the Pacific, keeping the world safe for democracy.

Jack's ship was the first to Tokyo Harbor, his captain the first American ashore after the surrender. It was a great day for everyone, except maybe the Japanese. He often said that his military service, his personal battle to survive, was the most affecting and solemn time in his life—but it was the most fun he ever had, too. Every day during the war, just being aboard ship instead of wrapped in a flag at the bottom of the sea was an accomplishment. And foremost in his mind by then were Peg and his ski lodge.

Peg and Jack were very different. She was less emotional, less volatile, a solid presence even when she wasn't there. And she was tough. Very tough. If something bothered her, Peg dealt with it. And she had a reputation for brooding at times—oh yeah, that whole still-waters-run-deep deal. I'm told that back in the ski lodge days, when there was no snow, no guests, no income, and a household full of "help" to feed, Peg could be hard to be around.

They were a funny match, Jack and Peg, but perfect as these things go. They were purely a case of opposites glomming on to each other, filling in the gaps in each other's lives. Jack livened up every room he entered, a funny guy with a kind word for everyone, probably wearing a bad hat. Peg played her cards so close that she couldn't read them. She was conservative in that way, and bottled her energy for when she needed it, which was often.

She was a ski racer for most of the 1940s, won some national races, and missed the Olympic team by two places in 1948. She was reckless, especially for a young woman then. She drove like a bank robber, drank whiskey from the bottle, loved to gamble, and was a kick-ass competitor. No wonder Jack loved her so much.

When my mother and uncles were kids, the family took a lot of road trips. All her life Peg thought nothing of climbing into a car and speeding all the way across America for some warm days on the slopes. Once, in a particularly gnarly pass through the Rockies, Jack grew increasingly uncomfortable behind the wheel and, as the landscape grew larger and more distant, he began hyperventilating.

He herky-jerked the Vista Cruiser to the shoulder of the road and, after braking, sat frozen to the wheel. He couldn't go on; it was too high, too unprotected, too narrow. Peg pried him away and slid into the driver's seat. To the delight of everyone in the backseat, she did a Dukes of Hazzard through the rest of the pass. Kids didn't have video games back then; they actually needed to drive fast in a car to experience it. That was Peg's attitude: How are you going to know unless you try? This is not to say that Jack shied away from work and adventure, just that Peg had an extra gene for a challenge. In fact, it was Jack himself who was the biggest challenge of Peg's life. And she was up to it.

Given what we know about Peg, it's hard to imagine what Jack said to her to convince her to leave California in 1946 and come east to the Easton Valley of New Hampshire. He looked for land in Conway, but it was too expensive. Go over to Franconia, they told him. Land's still cheap around there on the stonier side of the Presidential Range. Franconia is on the northern end of Franconia Notch, and Easton is a few miles west of there.

Jack and his navy pal Bob Allard bought 450 acres with a house and a barn on it for $10,000. They were building a ski lodge, and they made a very slick offer to my grandmother and her friend Mimi to come east to work as maids and cooks at this as yet unbuilt, unnamed ski lodge that had no guests. Who knows why they did it?

Jo, Billy, Davy, Bub, and Mike, 1960

Maybe because at the end of the war there was a man shortage in America, or maybe everyone's biological imperative to pair off and reproduce had been heightened by their brush with extinction. Whatever it was, east Peg and Mimi came.

It was a lean existence at Tamarack Ski Lodge, in the shadow of Mount Kinsman, that first frozen winter. In Franconia it's not uncommon to get a solid month of twenty-below-zero weather. It's too cold to snow, and even if it weren't, it's forty below on the mountain with the wind, and thus too cold to ski. When that season mercifully ended, it seemed clear that it would be a long time, if ever, before Tamarack attracted enough business to support two families.

Jack bought Bob out after that first season. But by then, after the long winter, the whole bunch of them had gotten engaged. Winter does that to people. So after spending the winter together in the same cozy lodge, the four of them became two couples, hopped into the woody for a road trip back to California, and got hitched.

This was when Route 66 was the way to go, and you drove cars with mechanical brakes and no heat or air-conditioning across the

Aerial shot of Tamarack, 1973

Great Plains, over the mountains, and through the desert. They did it like it was nothing. They'd survived the Depression, been to war and won, and now fancied themselves entrepreneurs who could do anything.

For the first few years, in the summer Jack would go off to teach at some fancy tennis club in Newport, Rhode Island, or North Carolina, staying for two or three months at a time. He also went to New York to do voice-overs for ski movies and newsreels, which played at movie theaters across the country. And since he was a well-known, well-respected ski writer by this time, he was often off covering a race or researching a story on skiers like Dick Barrymore and Bill Beck.

Jack would have preferred to be right by Peg's side 24-7, he had such true-blue love for her. But they needed the money, and short of farming or logging or working in a sawmill, there was little chance to make any in the North Country. None of those options appealed to Jack. He was a tennis pro, a raconteur, and a word-smith—the hell with heavy lifting.

My mother was born in 1949, and she was, by all accounts, a major pain in the ass. Jack decided early on that he needed to keep

Peg, SoCal beach babe, 1942

closer to home if he and Peg were to breed any more. And breed they did. Five kids in eight years. After Jo came four boys in quick succession: Billy, Davy, Bubba, and Mike.

Jack was never at a loss for ideas on how to make a buck or improve life, but with that many hungry mouths to feed, avoiding heavy lifting became a luxury. So Jack did what he knew, and started a tennis-court building-and-maintenance company. He called it New England Tennis Company, or NetCo. His hard work and big smile grew it into a great business. My uncle Mike runs NetCo today, and he's a lucky guy. My dad worked there when he was young, I worked there forever, and virtually all my cousins and friends have worked for NetCo; some still do.

It left its mark on me. Building tennis courts taught me to look at a piece of land and see the lay of it, every dip and mound. That's useful in skiing, but it's a secret weapon on the putting green. And here's another legacy from my days at NetCo, something that happens all the time. I'll be out cruising in some small, back-of-the-balls town in Massachusetts or Vermont or Maine that I could swear I'd never been in before and then I'll have a déjà vu flash: Hey, right around the corner there's a big yellow house with pillars out front and two clay courts out back. And it'll be there. There are NetCo customers all over New England. Jack built that business.

In the winter of 1958 there was so little snow, and so few customers at the lodge, that Jack and Peg lost their minds momentarily. They invited all the other innkeepers, who also had nothing to do, along with some other friends, none of whom ever had anything to do, to a dinner party. They were big partyers; this was before cell phones and e-mail and cable TV, and, like anyone, after a week they were starved for conversation, news, and gossip. Jack held court and made fun of Vice President Nixon; Peg smoked little cigars.

When dinner was done, Peg skulked over to the piano and slid a custard pie from its hiding place. She turned and fired it at Jack's head, catching him square in the mush. Within a few moments, everybody in the place was throwing pies like it was a Three Stooges movie. They were slopping and smacking each other; people were screaming and laughing. This was paintball without the pain, and you can't buy fun like that these days.

When there was no more ammunition, six inches of custard and whipped cream lay on the floor. Everybody went home that night smelling like an eggy Popsicle. It was quite a monumental mess, the nastiest cleanup job anyone can ever remember. But it gave the help something to do the next day, and the day after, and the day after that, and seeing them busy made Peg feel better. People still find crusts in cracks when they clean the lodge.

Jack liked the ski business—he once said there was no higher calling—but it took a lot of time and didn't make much money. Jack needed to use the Tamarack facilities in the off-season to generate some cash, and when that realization hit him, he immediately envisioned a tennis camp there. He was an idea man, and he got this idea one night in the tub; that's where his best inspirations came to him. By the next day, he had it all planned. It was the most excited he'd been in a long time, and true to form, he got on the phone to promote it.

Jack and Peg were committed to making sports and recreation affordable to families with children. They ran the ski lodge that way; naturally they'd do the same with the camp. As always, afford-ability seriously cut into the profit. Still, they preferred to be thrifty or to work harder than let their life's work drift out of the reach of regular people.

Jo, Bill, Bub, Peg, Mike, Davy, and Jack—a tough crew on the courts. This was a 1961 promotional photo for the camp.

Jack couldn't believe the idea for the camp hadn't occurred to him sooner. There's not a whole lot of skiing in New Hampshire in June and July, and they had to do something to stave off the bill collectors. He once wrote, in *Hospitality* magazine:

> A shopping trip to town is an adventure. You walk across Main Street dodging creditors like a halfback dodging tacklers. A quick dash across the road to avoid the insurance man, a dart down the alley to avoid the oil man. The inevitable happens and you bump headlong into one of them and he opens up with, "Now about that—" But you interrupt him with the rosy story that Old Farmer's Almanac predicts a big winter, and so very shortly he'll have his due.

To test the waters, Jack used the ski lodge customers' roster as a marketing list for the new camp. He got on the phone—he lived on the phone, loved talking to friends and strangers—and gave them the tennis camp pitch. It was 1952, the infancy of the sports industry, and Jack was a pioneer. (Jack, apparently, was also a telemarketing pioneer, but nobody's perfect.) Jack went on the road to interview every prospective camper. Actually, it was to market to them directly, but it was also to weed out the ones whose parents seemed like they might be pains in the ass. Lots of people jumped on the idea. These days there are camps for everything: chess, Web design, water polo, curling; back then, specialized camps were virtually nonexistent.

When it looked like Tamarack Tennis Camp might actually happen, Peg had to build it: the additions, the plumbing, the chimney, the cabins. Jack was an inventor, but without Peg he couldn't start a lawn mower.

So there was a strong, unmet desire for sports-specific camps, and Jack and Peg stepped in to fill the gap. Nobody has ever gotten to the U.S. Open, or even made the college tennis team, without some individual instruction. Everyone needs to be taught the basics. After that you can forget it all and do what works for you. That's what I tell kids. Don't take instruction as a set of principles; lessons are guidelines to help you find your way.

For instance, I don't like the oompa-loompa service motion people make, as if they're conducting the Boston Pops with their racket; I say pop the ball up in the air with as little movement as possible, and whack it hard in the direction you want it to go. There's a proper technique for everything, but it's very personal— how fast, how hard, how junky. Within reason, variations are always encouraged. I'm not a taskmaster on this, or anything else. My best advice is to do whatever it is you want to accomplish over and over again, until you get it right.

Jack was more rigid. His journals are full of logorrheic instructions for how players should stand, address the ball, and look at their partner and opponent, plus detailed descriptions of how they should exercise and train. He had an idea about everything when it came to teaching tennis. He prescribed the first isometric exercises I'm aware of. Jack pretty much had an idea about everything—politics, God, golf, sex, skiing, farming, construction, you name it. But tennis he actually knew.

So Jack and Peg built a couple of courts and some bunk-houses, got a partner named Glenn Sargent who could teach, and hit the clay running. That first season they had ten kids; by their fifth season they had two sessions, with fifty kids in each. It's now twice that size. After all these years, Tamarack remains a thriving camp where thousands of people have learned the great sport of tennis. My mother and Uncle Mike are the big cheeses now; my father, Woody, is the director; and my sister Wren and I are co–head counselors. My uncle Mike built a money soccer pitch, which added a soccer season to the summer. Jack and Peg's hard work and genius live on.

Raising a family in the middle of so many going enterprises was complicated, but they tried to maintain a normal family life. Not too successfully, but the effort was there. It didn't really work out all the time. On top of all his business ventures, Jack remained a writer. Here's an excerpt from a piece he wrote in 1952 for the magazine *Tourist Trade:*

> The late fall months are what we innkeepers laughingly call "the off season"—that period when we can relax and re-paint the rooms, sand the floor, re-paper the walls, put on the storm windows, cut and split firewood, write promotional letters, put in that new improvement and, in general, take it easy.
>
> It's the no-income season which itself presents some stimulating challenges. Bills begin to pile up, and though you let children play with them, the pile doesn't seem to get any thinner.

This is the life my mom and her brothers were raised in. It was nearly fifty years ago, and getting to the North Country was no small task for people. After a long, cold car ride up from Connecticut or Massachusetts or New York, guests usually arrived after midnight expecting coffee and sandwiches. Everybody in the house had to get up to greet them. Well, the kids didn't have to get up, but what kid would stay in bed with strangers in the kitchen and people laughing and eating?

If the guests decided to stay up the next night and sing college fight songs or Scottish mating chants, everybody in the lodge had to listen to it. Jack and Peg were accommodating to a point; Jack was known to cut off the hot water to a bad guest's room, just to get rid of him or her. "Nope, can't be fixed. Sorry about that. Let me help you with your bags. . . ."

Jack wrote:

> The night before the season opens, the lodge looks like a cross between a saw mill and a rummage sale. Naturally, all the cleaning is left to the last minute, and now that the moment comes, you don't see how it's possible to be ready for opening day. Sawhorses, tools, and wood shavings litter the floors. The family's clothes are spread all over the house in closets and dressers—and the midnight safari begins to move. The lush days are over and the Okies are on the go.

In other words, they were displaced from their own beds, seasonal refugees planted in other places around the property, places not suitable for guests. It was hectic and financially unrewarding, and it spread my grandparents so thin that Jack once wrote that his kids "were raised in a business, not a family."

Of course, another perspective says that they were raised in a huge extended family and met some weird, nice, and boring people they'd have never known otherwise; plus they had a lot more towels and dishware than most people. Not to mention tennis balls.

My mom and Jack were close when she was young; she was daddy's girl. But that didn't last. Whether it was puberty or teenage angst, nobody knows, but something changed. Jo became a little soured on her childhood. It took another ten years for her to articulate how and why to Jack. In the meantime, she did it in other ways.

Jo's immediate problem, the one that had surfaced, wasn't the temporary nature of inn life, but jealousy. She was jealous of the guests for all the time they took with her folks, and jealous of their lives when they skipped out on the North Country and went back to civilization, jealous of the apparent normalcy of their lives.

Jack with Tamarack staff, 1973

All summer long, she'd spend her days and nights with interesting kids from all over. It was a life filled with things and ideas that one seldom encountered up here at the time. Then, at the end of the season, when they'd all gone home, she went back to Littleton High School, where she was Joanne Kenney from way out in Easton. Or she went to St. Mary's School, which was an earlier, private, all-girls Episcopalian incarnation of the White Mountain School, where she learned how to steal Jack and Peg's car to drive down to the Holderness School and hang out with boys. But no matter which subset of friends she was with, she didn't exactly fit in; she was always trying to pass. It's the same identity crisis that's haunted teenagers for five millennia and counting. Me included. So cry me a river.

Years later, when my older sister, Kyla, was the same age, she demanded that Jo give her a curfew, because all her friends had to be home at a particular time and Ky yearned for the same sort of restriction. Jo agreed, but insisted that Kyla set the time herself. It was a tongue-in-cheek indulgence, Kabuki parenting, a sword fight with dull blades. But that only goes so far. When Kyla stole Peg's minivan to go partying when she was fourteen years old, Jo was authentically pissed, much more pissed than I've ever seen her. Then someone mercifully reminded her that she used to steal Peg's car, too. So she chilled.

But Jo got no similar indulgences from Jack and Peg. So she made trouble instead, even took to the road once or twice, which was intentional mischief. Then she got a horse, which was unintentional mischief.

Peg loved the idea of a horse, despite being allergic to it. Jack didn't like the horse. It was nothing but trouble, as far as he was concerned—it consumed without producing anything but shit, which he was obliged to pick up around the camp, because no one else would. The horse also ate the grass in the front yard, which at the time was fenced in by a row of elm trees, before they all died off, and it left deep hoofprints in the sod. Its name was Revante.

Jo was fourteen years old, and she chose a particularly bad time to test Jack's mercurial nature. Glenn Sargent, his friend and partner, had committed suicide earlier that season. Glenn was gay, this was 1963, and attitudes were fucked. Because Jack's mother had taken her life, any suicide at all was a touchy subject with him. But Glenn's cut his heart out.

Not long after Glenn's death, on a cold gray November day, Jack found Revante snacking on the final few blades of his front lawn. Jack says that he just touched the horse's hindquarter to shoo him, but it is possible, he being a tennis pro and this being a tennis camp, that he had a tennis racket in his hand and that he applied said racket to Revante's ass. And Jack could really whack the ball. We don't know exactly what happened. What we do know is that Revante kicked Jack a good solid stick to the right upper arm and shattered his humerus. Not funny. And an especially bad break for a tennis pro. Reports are that it was quite painful and that Jack lobbied hard into the night for the glue factory.

A day later, he lay in bed in Littleton Hospital, his arm trussed up to keep it stationary, as it would be for months to come, watching on TV the breaking news that President Kennedy had been shot.

Over the years, Jack had developed a fond admiration for Kennedy, beginning in 1946, when he first ran for Congress. It was the navy careers they shared, both Irish American Ivy Leaguers from Massachusetts, both Democrats, liberals, athletes, and so on—plus, there was the obvious similarity of their names: Jack Kennedy/Jack Kenney. Suffice it to say that though he didn't know him beyond his public persona, Jack felt simpatico with John F. Kennedy. And now he was dead. Murdered.

As soon as Jo heard that the president had been shot, she hurried from school to the hospital, knowing Jack would be upset. When she got there, he wouldn't talk to her, he ignored her, and then he lit into her as if everything had been her fault—as if she had kicked him in the arm, then shot Kennedy and Glenn, too. It had all been a bit much for Jack, whose mental health could be a fragile vessel, and easily upset.

So she didn't speak to him for a few months after that, not even at Christmas. This was Jack's first indication that Jo had issues with him and Peg, that the whole Tamarack in-the-shadow-of-the-customer life was a bad deal in many ways. They all had their own gripes and bad memories. The truth was that Jo, like everyone else, was ambivalent about the way she'd been raised. Her response to this ambivalence, in stellar Kenney fashion, was the ever-popular rash and extreme mode of juvenile behavior. Not that it's any consolation to Jack and Peg, but we all did Jo more than proud at one time or another, and drove her even crazier than she drove them.

Jo and Peg had the same relationship that Peg had with most people: a little distant, perhaps, a little closed. I understand that quietude, and I know that it isn't necessarily what it seems. It's only occasionally a deep thought, or a hair across your ass; usually, it's simple musing, mostly about what's happening at the moment and how ridiculous it all is. I imagine this is what Peg was thinking a lot of the time.

Peg was always the picture of cool under pressure. More than once, for instance, Jo would yell into the kitchen window, "Mommy, Billy or Davy is floating in the pond. . . ."

And Peg would drop everything and storm out the door, rush down to the little pond that Jack had built, and fish out whoever was facedown in the water. She'd shake him upside down, bang his

Peg, 1974

back, and press his belly until he coughed up a sunfish and staggered away. Peg would thank Jo for the heads-up, shake her head wearily, and go back inside the lodge to continue folding or ironing or cleaning.

Peg was tough. She ran the Tamarack show, and she treated Jack as a junior partner at times. She was the final word on all things Tamarack. One time, my dad, Woody, decided to take down two giant pines up at our house in the woods—partly because they obscured our view, but primarily because he wanted to expand the house to accommodate us all better. So he needed the lumber.

With a friend, Woody topped the two giants, then felled and limbed them and cut them into eight-foot logs. All of which is extremely hard work.

Then he borrowed my uncle Davy's skidder and moved the eight-foot logs down the mountain. He made lots of trips trucking them to the sawmill in Littleton, where they were—for a price—sliced into boards. Then he trucked the new lumber back to Tamarack. Peg had been watching this long operation, and when Woody finally pulled up to the lodge with the last load, she claimed all the wood for the camp. They needed it for projects, she told him, and there wasn't much Woody would or could say.

When Jack retired, the ski lodge part of the business had been long closed, and both sessions of the tennis camp were always full, with waiting lists, and no marketing effort at all. So nine months out of the year he was at a loss to fill his days. He tinkered and wrote, and contemplated tennis the way Stephen Hawking noodles the universe. Beyond that, he was open to anything.

Jack came to think of himself as a mechanical magician. His specialty was building machines for handicapped tennis players to practice with—"Charlie," for instance, which was basically a Shop-Vac with its suction reversed to blow exhaust, so that a tennis ball floated on the poof of air above it. People could work alone, whacking away at the ball all day until they hit it. True, Charlie was a little noisy, and this was way back when electricity was cheap (before Seabrook went online), but Jack was a genius.

In 1972, Jack visited the Crotched Mountain Rehabilitation Center to see if his teaching methods could be used by developmentally disabled and physically handicapped kids. That visit, at the age of fifty-six, opened up a whole new box of ideas for Jack. From then on, when he wasn't involved with Tamarack, he was developing his approach to play for the handicapped, called "game therapy." In addition to Charlie, he had tennis balls attached to strings and a hoop to swing them through. Jack designed an inclined tube filled with tennis balls that could release them one at a time, slowly and gently, for a child in a chair—for children who may have never before gotten to play with a ball.

Peg was busy with other things. She was a surrogate mom to a lot of people over those years; it was her avocation. Elizabeth Buxton, an errant Harvard Law student–ski bum–Tamarack nanny and maid, said from the start that Jack and Peg had created a world that proper southern girls like her had never seen. It was open and funny and free in a time when Eisenhower was president, Joe McCarthy was running loose, and Elvis was the devil. But at Tamarack, Jack and Peg were the gurus of fun and life's potential—not beatniks, but upbeatniks. Jack and Peg's time was split among a small army of Tamarack alums, staff members, guests, and campers, who had come to rely upon my grandparents for their Zen.

And the connections were never broken, not in life, anyway. Elizabeth, for instance, got married and bought a house down the road from Tamarack in the 1960s, and despite having worked everywhere from Los Angeles to Moscow, she still lives there today.

Although Jo sort of resented it about her own mom, she was everyone's mom when we were growing up, too. People relied on her to be cool about things, to listen and not judge, to offer advice about problems they couldn't discuss with their own folks. We all shared moms when I was a kid, but my mom got spread way too thin. She knew everyone and everything in our lives.

A loose family structure worked out pretty well for Jo and her brothers, and if nothing else it left them with a sense of steward-ship over Tamarack and the surrounding property. It's the largest piece of land around now; nearly everything else has been carved up into ticky-tacky homesites. My uncle Bill farms it; my uncle Davy logs it; my uncle Mike runs NetCo out of Tamarack; and we all live there, to this day. All except Uncle Bubba of course. Bub died.

Bubba (né Peter) drowned, and I know the date: April 4, 1981, my sister Wren's first birthday. It was a bright clear spring day, T-shirt warm, mud up over your shoes. We were at the lodge. I was three, riding my Big Wheel along the porch railing back and forth, frontward and back. I couldn't fall off if I tried.

It was that first great spring morning, the kind that makes you realize how antsy you are to do something different now that win-ter is momentarily gone. So Bubba announced he was taking his kayak for a spin around Echo Lake. This is among my earliest mem-ories: my sister Kyla and I are telling Bub to wear a life preserver, harping about it. It's so clear in my mind: the sun on my face, the glint on Bub's eyeglasses, him hoisting his red kayak out of cold storage, hefting it onto his shoulder. He said he didn't need a life preserver, because he was only going for a quick paddle. He was all smiles. We insisted; he demurred, hugged us, and off he went.

Bubba was fearless, and could be reckless. He'd jump right off a bridge without bothering to see how deep the water was. But he was smart and usually levelheaded. He had Peg's stability and tran-quillity and Jack's enthusiasm and creativity, all rolled into one magnificent person. He was a nationally ranked skier and fast—an all-around athlete, a genuinely good guy, and the most admired real person I've ever known. The earliest home movie I'm in is Bubba teaching me to ski down my grandparents' driveway. My last memory of him is him strapping a plastic kayak on the roof of his white Toyota. Kyla and I both told him to wear a life jacket one more time. I think we must have learned about life jackets from my Vermont grandparents, Woody's folks. I can't imagine my folks putting them on us.

A little later that morning, the sky got dark, and it got cold way too early. It was winter again, suddenly. Then the weather started in with big cold drops of freezing rain and pounding winds. As the storm raged, the head counselor at Tamarack came back from town to say a kayak had been found on the shore of Echo Lake. Could it be Bubba's?

Jo, Woody, Jack, and Peg rushed down and found a tempest inside the little glacial lake at the base of Cannon Mountain. The trees on the shore were bent in the wind, the water was a mass of whitecaps; it was the kind of weather that frightened primitives like us. But nothing supernatural had happened to Bub. The ungodly wind had flipped him over, and the cold had taken him quickly. Maybe he'd gone as easily as one could, given the circumstances; the divers found him in the water still wearing his glasses. When Woody and Jo and Peg went to the morgue to identify his body the next day, he still had them on. My parents were crushed. Bubba wasn't just a brother; he'd been the best man at their wedding, the go-to guy for everything, the peacemaker, the prince of the family; gone, he left a huge void. People were as scared as they were shocked and saddened.

My uncles are all interesting and great guys in their own ways, very talented skiers, builders, and thinkers. But it was Bubba everyone noticed. He was bigger than life, the most talented athlete you can imagine, sincerely modest and unassuming, helpful, friendly, and never acted like he was special. At the time of his death, he was racing the Peugeot Grand Prix pro tour, and they named a good sportsmanship award in his honor. He was, as best as I can tell, the good citizen, the better angel. The Force took a major hit the day Bubba died. And so did Jack.

It's sad to read Jack's journals from the years before Bub drowned. You knew what was coming, and it was hard to sit still for. Bub had gone to Middlebury College, ski-bummed, and done some Europa Cup racing, then finally took over NetCo from Jack. No one

Bubba (left), the best man at Woody and Jo's wedding, 1974

else was interested, and Jack had tired of the day-to-day grind. He'd worked all his life; he was looking to lie low and invent a few things.

Bub's grasp of the reins was a godsend for Jack. It saved the company and gave uninterrupted service to the clients Jack had accumulated over the years. He felt his legacy was in good hands. Jack, who'd always loved Bubba just as everyone who ever met him had, now revered him. He couldn't have been prouder. From this time on, the journals were filled with "Couldn't be happier with Bub. He's turned into such an admirable young man. This morning he came down and cooked me breakfast, gave me $10, and told me it was my allowance for the day. What a guy."

A year after Bubba's death, Jack was diagnosed with Alzheimer's (he called it Anheuser's—ironically or not, I don't know); he stopped writing in his journal a few years later. Much of what he wrote during that time was about Bubba. Bubba worship, really. Then one day he scribbled a little less legibly than usual: "Having some trouble with my immediate memory, but it doesn't seem to be a problem." It was the last thing he wrote.

I prefer to think of the Jack who one wintry Saturday afternoon erupted when *ABC Wide World of Sports* cut away from World

Cup skiing coverage to show figure skating. It was usually a month of skiing packed into a twenty-two-minute segment, but this was an actual race, and they cut it off. Sometimes there are more than seventy racers in the first run of a World Cup race, and you seldom got to watch even the top thirty.

Jack sputtered at first, said some extremely unkind things about network executives, and maybe even Jim McKay personally. But then his mind went to work until he saw how to solve it. He turned to his beloved telephone.

Jack had a way with the phone; he played it like a tenor sax: smooth, very sweet. All the operators were women back then, and it was a sanitary way to flirt. He was a charmer when he wanted to be. But honorable, which was a good thing too, because he could get people to do things over the phone. He'd just talk and talk to operators as they looked up numbers for him so that he could market one of his businesses. People pay huge sums to marketing companies today; back then, Jack had the phone company doing his research for him. He got to know individual operators by name over the years. Knew their voices, maybe even knew when they worked. If he had only half a name, they'd go through the Farm-

Jack at his beloved typewriter, 1974

ington, Connecticut, or Rochester, New York, phone directory Smith by Smith until something sounded right to him. Then they'd try Farmington, New York, or Rochester, Connecticut.

Many years later, he and Peg had a house built on the property by an "avant-garde" architect. I think this means an architect who's never designed a house before, because it looks like a miniature high-rise office building in the middle of the woods. It's cool, but you expect to find a tiny parking garage next to it and a bunch of raccoons out by the back door smoking cigarettes in the cold.

One of the custom details Jack insisted upon was a phone jack in the bathroom. He didn't care about much else. Jack enjoyed talking on the phone almost as much as he liked to write. Wearing a wool sweater and skullcap like 50 Cent's, he'd slip into the tub with about six inches of water in it, lay a wide board across the top as his desk, and hold court. There, he'd write, yak on the phone, and write some more. Part office, part warm, moist nirvana.

Jack loved connecting with people. He was glib and witty and liked that spark that comes from making someone happy. With Jack, the smallest transaction became a conversation, and a con-

Jack and Peg's house, 1972

versation could go on forever. By the time he got all his phone numbers, he'd know more about the operator than her neighbors did, maybe even her husband.

Elizabeth Buxton had originally been too late for a job at Tamarack and had made the rounds from Franconia to Stowe, Vermont, looking for work close to skiing. Not long after she left, somebody Jack had hired dropped out, and he needed another maid-nanny after all. He knew where he'd sent Elizabeth looking for work, so he called there, and found out that that place had sent her somewhere else. This went on for several ski lodges, until he lost her trail and had to refer to a map to figure where she might have gone next. Many hours after he began his phone search, he called the pay phone at the Stowe Inn. Elizabeth was standing there, waiting to see the manager about a job, and perhaps in an effort to look industrious, she picked up the phone and said, "Hello, Stowe Inn." It was Jack; he asked for Elizabeth Buxton. "Speaking," she said, and he offered her the job at Tamarack.

But the day ABC interrupted the great sport of ski racing—in the middle of a race, no less—for figure skating, Jack got on the phone with a subversive purpose in mind. He charmed and cajoled every operator and receptionist he encountered until he actually got some suit at ABC in New York on the other end of the line. Granted, this was the schlub who worked Saturdays, but he had a "Mr." in front of his name, and that was good enough for Jack.

I said Jack was honest, and that was true, but he knew that this television guy wouldn't be easily swayed by some crank call from the mountains of New Hampshire. So Jack told him he was the owner of WMUR, Channel 9, down in Manchester, and that he spent plenty of goddamn money with them, and had chosen ABC because of its ski-racing coverage, so what was he supposed to do now? Then he threatened to become an NBC affiliate if they didn't put the ski races back on immediately, that moment. The guy claimed it was out of his hands, apologized profusely, and promised that someone from a higher pay grade would call Jack first thing Monday morning.

"Uhhh, okay," Jack said, "I look forward to it," and hung up. So nobody got to see any more ski racing that day, but Jack was pretty amusing, and that's what life was all about for him.

2

The Feral Life

My mom and dad—Jo and Woody—got hitched on September 7, 1974. Don't ask me why; it was very unhippie of them, if you ask me. I do know why they chose the date: Woody figured out that it fell directly between his birthday on August 4 and Jo's on October 11. He likes things to have some significance, and if they don't, he assigns them one.

Getting married may have been the last vestige of Woody's conservative upbringing, or it may have been the legal status he needed to never have to return to medical school, which was torture for him.

His father, Don, had decided early on that Woody should be, as he was, a doctor. Preferably a surgeon. Maybe even a cardiac surgeon. So Woody was pre-med at Middlebury College in Vermont and hated it. Then he went to medical school at the University of Vermont, and hated it more.

It wasn't just medical school, or the profession, but the expectations placed upon him. Woody's grandfather was the president of the American Medical Association; his dad was a pioneer in performing open-heart surgery. So no matter how well Woody did, he didn't feel like he could measure up. To Woody's great credit, he never passed that penchant for unrealistic expectations along to us. He was happy when we were happy. No superhuman feats required.

In his first year of medical school, he decided that the best way to prepare for finals was to burn all his notes and books two weeks before exams. This must have been a brilliant plan, because he passed. So he took a year off and worked at Tamarack. This is how uncomfortable he was in medical school: working for no pay was a better deal.

His first trip to Tamarack was when he was fifteen years old, to play in a tournament. (This was way back before eight-track tapes.) He and his partner won the doubles competition, but Woody lost his singles match. By the next summer, he'd logged five thousand miles and played in a dozen more tournaments.

After high school, when he was looking for a job, he called Jack and got a spot as a Tamarack instructor. This went on for a few summers. He considered it, as many do, a sanctuary from the real world of trouble and obligation. Or from any real world you can name.

He and my mother took up with each other that winter after Woody's first year of medical school. The cold will do that. She'd just finished at Boston University and was hanging around, looking for things not to do. The next year the two of them went back to Burlington and lived in a trailer, while Woody went to med school and hated it all over again.

Woody's older brothers, my uncles Don and Dick, had gone to medical school and happily had become doctors. So everyone just assumed that Woody would too. This was his first object lesson in the consequences of strong-arming other people's lives, especially your children's.

Woody's final ploy to escape from medical school was to flunk pediatrics. You can get away with boning a lot of things in the medical profession, but not baby doctoring. Even the AMA frowns on that. He got the news from his mother, because his professor was a close family friend and felt it would be easier for everyone if Woody got the boot by proxy. Woody was elated—not at his failure, but at having the weight of the world lifted from him, and for the potential the future now held.

He and Jo went back to Tamarack and built our house in the woods, three-quarters of a mile from the road up a steep dirt path, and left the world behind. They carried almost everything in on their heads and built the first part of the house without electric tools; they tilled the soil behind a workhorse, and then defended the harvest against four-legged vegetarian predators. They cut wood, split wood, and burned wood. Life itself was a job, but a good job, and satisfying. My father always said that if Tamarack hadn't been there to tempt him, he would probably be a doctor today, and hating it.

The house my folks built

He even tried attending the Santa Fe College of Natural Medicine years later. He actually started classes on his and Jo's seventh wedding anniversary. They moved us all out to New Mexico and bought a house in the Santa Fe barrio, in sight of the highway. It had a small backyard full of snakes and nasty little cacti.

When we first moved out there we stayed in a campground. New Mexico state law said you could only stay in a camping space for a week, so we'd move to the space next door every few days; we

*My Santa Fe
cowboy period*

stayed in every space in that campground, I think. We were the only ones there.

Jo and Woody tried hard to make the house in Santa Fe a home. One day, not long after we moved in, Jo was in the house fixing something, and Woody was out back trying to get something to grow. We were all so spoiled by our lives on Turtle Ridge at Tama-

The backyard in Santa Fe, 1981: cozy for the desert

rack that they both felt pressured to work on the Santa Fe place, to make it livable. Wren, one and a half years old at the time, decided a walkabout was in order, and when no one was looking, she booked it out the front door to explore the neighborhood.

She'd been gone about fifteen minutes before anyone realized she was missing. When my folks did, they both ran around their new Mexican neighborhood yelling, "Gennie Wren, Gennie Wren," like the whacked-out gringos they were.

On Jo's third circumnavigation of the neighborhood, our new next-door neighbor, whom we didn't know yet, came trundling out of her house with Wren in her arms. She'd found her in the street wearing only a diaper, and a dirty one at that, so she'd taken her inside to clean her up. When Jo came across her, she was outside waiting for the police, whom she'd called to report the abandoned child. The cops in turn put all this in their report to the state child welfare office. And from then on we had regular visits from a state social worker, to make sure that Jo and Woody weren't abusing us. Not exactly the Welcome Wagon.

Woody studied hard at herbology, and everything else they threw at him, and as much as he loved the idea of it all, in practice he hated it. At the end of the academic year we were all back at Tamarack again. Try as they might to escape, it wasn't happening.

Woody likes trying new things; he has an open mind and heart. When I was born, in 1977, he was, among other things, a food entrepreneur. He invented, produced, marketed, and delivered the Futz Bar: possibly the first all-natural, organic power snack made of nuts, dried fruit, and maple syrup—and guaranteed to give you gas.

He lived in fear of the Food and Drug Administration, paranoid that they'd swoop down on him while he was baking, impound the bars, his stove, and the house, and put us all in foster care. But that never happened. The only thing that he did was one night, while he was cutting a cooled batch of bars and watching *The Importance of Being Earnest* on the generator-powered television, a rat snuck up and stole some Futz. (This, by the way, is exactly what the FDA was talking about.) Woody lunged at the big fucker, hacking at him and completely missing, cutting the TV cord instead, burning the knife, and destroying the television. He knows the importance of being earnest anyway. Futz Bars were a going enterprise for six years or so; Woody hoped to someday be a "full-time Futzer." That never happened—too much of the rest of life got in the way.

Woody was a man of many pursuits and obligations. Just before my first birthday, he got busted at an antinuke demonstration in Seabrook, New Hampshire. He was with a couple thousand nonviolent pacifists taking their frustration out on a chain-link fence. Woody didn't think direct confrontation was a smart tactic, because it had no educational value for the cops or the public; but hotter heads prevailed that fall day on the beach in Seabrook.

Woody and me, 1984

When the pitchblende hit critical mass, the state police ran him and scores of others down, cuffed them, booked them, and tossed them in the can. He woke up the next morning with four other guys in a five-by-seven-foot cell, sore all over, with one eye swollen shut. Not from a beating, though. When he was making his unsuccessful escape, he'd skedaddled into a big poison ivy patch, hoping not to get snagged in the dragnet. No luck.

Since he wouldn't give them his name, they wouldn't give him any calamine lotion to spread on the rash, never mind oatmeal (which is what we would have used). He was finally released on my mom's birthday, the day before mine, and came home to a pretty good party.

I accompanied him to later Seabrook demonstrations—less violent ones, and a good thing, too, because he made me wear a papier-mâché turtle shell. Hard to run in.

Eventually, Woody and Jo wanted to invite others to live communally with them on Tamarack's 450 acres, to create a community of farmers, Enlightenment philosophers, naturalists, and the occasional nudist up on Turtle Ridge. Jack and Peg said, Not bloody likely—you let people move onto your property and you can never get rid of them. This may have been a Great Depression memory of theirs; it has the ring of truth.

They neither saw the point of nor shared my folks' excitement for communitarianism. So the four of us left Tamarack when I was a year old and Kyla was three, and we headed down east to live on Vinalhaven Island, Maine. It's off the coast of Owls Head in Penobscot Bay, and not much goes on there outside the Memorial–to–Labor Day window.

We went there to join a geographically closed community; there were some hippies living communally in a beautiful little house with a farmer's porch and a small patch of land. If my folks couldn't organize people to live communally, they'd go to where it

Alternative child-care methods, 1984

went on as a matter of course. They believed that living on an is-land would force the sense of shared responsibility they craved. Well, actually Woody craved it. Jo just enjoyed it.

But all they found was a long winter and a gray, flat, skiless boredom. Well, that's what Woody found. There was too little for him to do there (he likes to keep busy), and he was more of a back-to-nature purist than the people we partnered up with were. So he left at Christmas; Jo and Kyla and I stayed on the island until spring. Within a year, we were all back, once again, at Tamarack.

By example, my parents and grandparents offered me alternative notions about everyday life, and in these small everyday subver-sions, they made me who I am. Being at odds with conformity doesn't mean there was unanimity among us. Just the opposite. It wasn't just a new set of rules they taught us, but a genuinely inquis-itive way to look at the world, challenging the conventional view of everything—including theirs, and why not? They were serious. This catholicity didn't come in with Kennedy and go out with Nixon; there was nothing faddist about it.

For instance, the same women who delivered me also deliv-ered my sister's two kids, just within the past couple of years, up in the same house my mom and dad built in the woods. We still get our groceries from the food co-op my mother helped found; we even had solstice parties before political correctness forced them on people.

Once at a solstice party, when I was seven years old and my friend Noah was eight, he and I got it in our heads to piss on the stove in the sauna. Boy, that was funny. It seemed like a real hoot at the time, anyway. The adults discovered what we'd done when they found themselves in the sauna gasping for air, looking for a way to dissipate the urine stench. They weren't getting nearly the chuckle out of it we'd imagined when Noah and I found their beer—three cases of it—out behind the house. We could have drunk it, and a few years later we probably would have, but on that day we had other plans.

I picked up an emerald green Molson Golden, hefted it in my hand, and was suddenly struck by the brilliant idea to hurl it at the big rock in the middle of the stream. So I did. It made such a cool, wet explosion—a boom and a swoosh all at once—that Noah had to try it too. He loved the sound as much as I did, and by the time some adult wandered away from the pee-warfare carnage and got wise to what we were doing, we'd blown up two six-packs of beer.

The glass in the water could be dealt with, but the lost beer, the waste, was a high crime that far from civilization. Everyone gathered around, and I heard a *crack!* behind me. Uh-oh, I thought: Noah got smacked on the ass by his father. Our parents weren't hitters, so this was a shocking development. Noah's dad was a psychotherapist and pretty much let his kids do whatever; I'd have thought Noah could have exploded a thermonuclear device and gotten away with it.

Then the crowd looked at Woody, and Woody looked at me. He grimaced slightly, probably at the mental image of him whipping my ass. Then he rolled up his pants, and I rolled up mine, and we waded into the water to clean up the mess. Luckily, I cut my hand on a piece of glass early on, so I didn't have to pick up much of it. Woody and Noah did most of the work cleaning out the shards, while I hung out on a rock cheering them on, scoping out the pieces they were missing.

Earlier that year, up on Cannon Mountain, I'd told Noah I was going to win the World Cup one day, and he hadn't laughed at me. Instead, he'd nodded knowingly, as if it made perfect sense to him. He was always a smart, stand-up guy who took me seriously, and he also took a whack in the ass for both of us that day, and then cleaned up the glass. Friendship.

I don't know why we were so destructive. We once cut up my mother's all-time favorite hammock just to hear the strings go *boing!* All boys are brutal little apes, but most of us outgrow it long before we're men. Those who don't, run the world.

It's not just Woody and Jo who were drawn to Tamarack. The whole family still lives there—my brother and one sister, my uncles, aunts, and cousins. Often, a homeless family my father can't find shelter for will live up at the lodge.

That's the way it is here, and it's not just Tamarack; it's also Franconia and Easton. For instance, in 1998, the people of my hometown donated money, pooled their frequent-flier miles, and contributed in any way they could to help send my whole family to the Winter Olympics in Nagano, Japan. This is a town of nine hundred working people.

When I was a kid, if people heard or saw that I needed a piece of equipment, the problem was soon solved by Mickey and Marge Libby, or somebody. There was always somebody—it wasn't even necessarily clear who. Nobody around here worries about getting credit for being a good human being. We watch out for one another, and we help when we can, and sometimes even when we can't.

Mickey Libby helped me out all those years because he loved my grandparents and he was impressed that I had goals that were larger than myself. Plus, he knew we had very little money. Around here, if somebody's house burns down, we have a benefit for them; if a kid racks himself up on a motorcycle and has no medical insurance, people pitch in; businesses and artists donate products and services. Then we hold an auction, and a concert afterward, all to raise money for a neighbor in need. If that sounds like it's corny or small-town, then so am I. You can't dream up a place like this, though you might like to.

At a young age, I mean five or six, I knew I'd be an athlete in the same way other people decide to be artists or doctors or pilots when they're in college. Actually, I might have been a little unfocused at five, but by the time I was seven years old, in my mind I was a World Cup ski racer in training. Of course, I was completely on my own in this, and I might not have trained smart all the time. But I was out there. I logged serious hours on the mountain. A few years running, I skied every day Cannon Mountain was open. Nobody squeezed more out of a weekday pass than yours truly.

Actually, it was at this age that I developed my Unified Theory of Training and Fun, which means that I can golf and kick soccer balls, or play tennis all day long, and get myself into reasonable skiing shape. Actual weight training and running nowhere for no good reason can be minimized—I figure thirty-seven days for me—if I play as hard as I would have worked otherwise.

But that's me. When I was a kid, I timed myself in everything I did, always trying to go faster than the trip before. I ran up to the house from the road and down again, measuring the moments, how many times a day I couldn't tell you; I climbed trees and rocks with a clock ticking in my head, always trying to beat myself.

I was an ordinary kid. My lofty goals weren't so much unnoticed as expected, and so everyone was a little blasé around the Kenney household. I came from a family of skiers, two generations of nationally ranked racers, and I was going to be one too. My uncle Bubba had a sticker on his truck from racing a Europa Cup in Austria, and when I was five I told Kyla that I was going to run that race someday.

I realize single-mindedness of purpose isn't uncommon, whatever the sport; very few players stumble to the top of the heap. They get there by doing whatever it is that they do well, over and over and over again, until they do it perfectly.

That means a lot of kinetic energy with some kids. Those with insufficient outlets for all the spunk are often penalized, discouraged, held back, or, sometimes, drugged.

I worry how many great minds and ideas are dulled by Ritalin, or just plain boredom. I had hard-core ants in the pants, and I imagine more than one teacher would have liked to sedate me in some way. Even today, I like to be doing something, always. If I party until three A.M., I'm still up at six-thirty cooking an omelet and planning the day. I fill every day; I always have.

Any success I enjoy is largely the result of the boneheaded perseverance I inherited from my grandfather, the skiing genes I got from my grandmother, my mother's fearlessness, and my father's ninja-like calm on the field of play. Other than that, I did a lot of skiing. I mean a lot. And that was because of my mom's approach to homeschooling. Some people call it no-schooling. It allows the student to do whatever he or she wants, and the teacher weaves an education into that, somehow. It served us well.

I was born on October 12, the day after my mother's birthday and a few hours after a total solar eclipse. My grandmother's tradition was to cook a special birthday meal to order—anything you wanted. One moment Mom was eating her annual lobster; the next she was huffing and puffing and pushing. I was early, a little quicker than anyone had expected.

A few days before I was born, Woody had started thinking about expanding the house to accommodate me, and now that

Jo and me celebrating our birthdays, 1989

they would have two kids, he was eyeing a $325 Vega station wagon down at Hunt's junkyard. But he eventually ended up buying a $300 Datsun with no heat.

My mom wanted me to be born in the house in the woods, but as Jack described his apprehension in his journal: "Woody isn't exactly a ball of fire in an emergency," and so I was born in the Tamarack Lodge, as Kyla had been before me.

Actually, Woody is pretty good in an emergency. He's cool enough to defuse bombs. And he was a more than competent midwife; besides, the rest of the baby-birthing contingent was present. But this was a long time ago, and their track record wasn't nearly as long and impressive as it is today. Jack was concerned, and he was placated. But not Peg; she didn't care one way or the other. She would have given birth on skis if she could.

Wren and Chelone, my younger sister and brother, were born in our cabin in the woods: no electricity, no running water, no doctor, no trouble at all. Well, actually Wren had the umbilical cord wrapped twice around her neck, and was born not breathing. But Woody, despite having flunked pediatrics in med school, wisely objected to cutting the cord until they had her breathing on her own. This took a while as Woody blew little birdlike breaths into her mouth until her lungs finally took over. It must have

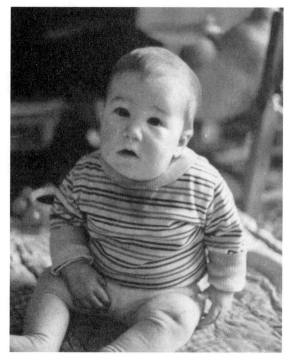

My big head, 1978

My big unhappy head, 1978

worked; she's an incredible athlete and the smartest of the four of us. Ask her.

Because of the way she came into the world, she and Woody have always had a special relationship. Naturally we were jealous, so we tormented her, telling her she wasn't really our sister, that we'd found her in the woods, and that her real parents were coming to take her away someday. No wonder she went to college in Montana.

Anyway, we were all delivered in this way. In fact, all my mom's friends delivered one another's babies. Most of my friends and cousins were delivered by my mom, and I was delivered by their moms. It makes for a tight community.

Chelone came last, and got the longest name. Ky's name is Kyla Miller; she doesn't even have a middle name. That's almost lazy. Then came me, Samuel Bode Miller; I got a middle name, and its diminutive form stuck. Bode, by the way, means to indicate by signs, but it was the sound of it that my mother liked. Then came Genesis Wren Bungo Windrushing Turtleheart Miller, whose naming was a family effort. Jo gave her the "Genesis Wren"; I called her "Bungo," after the Bungay Jar, the local wind, because it was so breezy the day she was born. Kyla gave her "Windrushing" for the same reason, and "Turtleheart" was the ever-present and recurring Woody-inspired turtle meme in our lives up on Turtle Ridge. The turtle may be Woody's totem. It wouldn't surprise me.

And then, last but not least, came Nathaniel Kinsman Ever Chelone Skan Miller. We call him Chelone. My folks hiked Mount Moosilauke when my mother was good and pregnant with him and found a flower on top they liked so much that they brought it home. When they looked it up and found that it was an herbaceous perennial called chelone, also known as turtlehead, they considered it a nice omen and planted it outside the door.

Three days after he was born, my mother was headed into town with the new baby, named Thane at the time. She was going to the laundromat when she came across a turtle in the road. It was big and blocked their way, so she had to stop. As she watched the shell waddle across the Easton Road, it occurred to Jo how little she liked the name Thane, and how much she liked the name Chelone.

Woody and me, 1978

So Thane became "Nathaniel," and "Kinsman" is the name of the mountain we look out on, which is way better than being called Moosilauke. "Ever" is exactly what it sounds like, as in: I want to be the best skier in the history of ever. "Chelone" we've discussed. And "Skan" in Lakota legend is the spirit of Great Blue Sky and the giver of all energy. After a week, that's the name he finally got, but by that time Peg had taken to calling him Chuckie, and always did. I'm sure they were planning to homeschool us all the way through, because some of those names are hell on standardized tests—shading in all the little bubbles with a number two pencil.

By virtue of being the youngest, Chelone became something of a barbarian. Of course, I mean that in the nicest possible way. He always kept up with us no matter what we did, despite being

Ky sneaking up on me. That's a toaster cozy on my head.

half our size. He's uncommonly intelligent and a great athlete, so we let him tag along. As if we had anything to say about it. And as a result, he grew up fast.

Chelone kills on a snowboard, and he'll basically try anything. When he was eleven years old he went over the back of Cannon Mountain on his board, looking to shred some backcountry with our friend Cam. When they hadn't returned by dark, we called out the fish cops, and they went hunting for the boys in the cold and dark. But they couldn't find them either.

A few days earlier, Cam's big brother Adam, who was and still is into the sickest stuff on skis, had shown him on a map how he could tip off the back of Cannon and ski-hike the Cannon Balls all the way to our house. The Cannon Balls are three smallish humps in a row running almost parallel to the Easton Road. If Cannon was called Bear Mountain these would be the cubs. The notion that you could traverse them by board and bushwhack the rest in the middle of winter is ambitious. Adam skis through chest-deep

Wren, me, and baby Chelone, 1983

powder regularly now, and he's always had a good grasp of hard-core fun, but I don't ever remember hearing about him tackling the Cannon Balls himself. Big brothers can be cruel.

But Chelone and Cam bit, and it was way more than they could chew. Up the tramway to the top of Cannon they went, like respectable snow-sport enthusiasts, instead of the snowboard terrors we now know them to be. They chose a spot in the direction that they wanted to head and set out. They boarded through some extra-sketchy glades at first, which encouraged them greatly and drew them deeper into the bad idea of it all. Then, abruptly, the riding stopped. House-sized outcroppings of granite got in the way, and blowdown fields where giant tree after giant tree lay on their bellies across one another for as far as the eye could see. It made for tough snowboarding.

Eventually, the snow got so deep that when they post-holed through it they dropped into pits way over their heads. To get out of the holes, they devised a technique of popping their snowboards up, out, and over the snow hole; then they leaped and chinned up onto the boards and slithered out. At lunch they snacked on crunchy uncooked noodles and ramen-flavored snow cones. Yum.

Chellie wasn't scared that night, even as it got dark, because we were always allowed to roam in the woods at will. Mom had told us if we ever got lost, all we had to do was find the stream and follow it down. We'd either come to the house or, if we were already below it, we'd eventually come to the road. In the end, Mom's advice came in handy that night, sort of. They found a stream and followed it, but it was dark and moonless, and they couldn't see where they were going.

When they arrived at Bridal Veil Falls, they realized where they were too late, and slipped and slid and got washed over the twenty-foot drop-off into the icy pool beneath; it was a chilling end to an exciting day of snowboarding. They came stumbling off the mountain by themselves an hour later, boardless and nearly beaten. But it could have been worse—Fish and Game charges for those searches now.

We got lost, or at least turned around, in the woods a lot, but the only time it was ever any fun to get lost was when Woody was in charge. Not that Woody didn't know where he was going, but he was very adventurous. He loves the woods. I mean, his middle name is Wood.

We all went up Mount Adams one day, in the Presidential Range of the White Mountains. It was us and another family; there must have been twelve of us. Our group, led by Woody with Wren on his shoulders, went up and down the mountain, and then waited so long for the other group that we headed back up the mountain to find them. That was our mistake. Somehow we missed them coming down, and passed them in the woods as if we were all ghosts.

We were on the losing side of dark before we realized we should turn around. So we took a shortcut through the woods. "Shortcut" generally denotes a *shorter* route than the conventional, more traveled one. Woody likes the unconventional and less traveled part, but shorter? I don't think so. As we dropped deeper and deeper into a ravine, and got turned around by the absolute lack of recognizable landmarks, we were screwed.

You have to bushwhack into an ancient forest to truly appreciate how otherworldly it is. And I don't necessarily mean in the *Lord of the Rings* sense. There are places where the moose like to shit, tidy beasts that they are, and if you find yourself in the middle of a field of moose droppings, then you're also likely to be covered in big black buzzing flies.

But you can also come across secret fields of pink and white lady's slippers, or a stash of fiddleheads to be harvested next year at a nice profit. In the deep shadows there's moss so thick you can bounce on it like it's a trampoline. Or fields of sharp granite rocks as big as tall ships, plowed up by the glacier that came through here a hundred thousand years ago. You don't see any of this on the Appalachian Mountain Club–approved trail.

In fact, according to the flatlanders and forest fascists of the AMC, you're not supposed to get off the trail at all. The forest the public gets to see isn't much more interesting than a hilly airport terminal, or the woods in a New Jersey subdivision. North Country people are proudly provincial, and they consider anything south of the notches as greater Massachusetts. This land is our land.

Woody's orienteering finally brought us out of the woods and upon a road. We found a motel attached to a gas station, a funky little place that's still there today, and Woody called Jo from the pay phone, but he didn't get her because they were still looking for us.

Woody knocked on the manager's door, getting the poor old codger out of bed, and he rented us a room for the night. The next morning, when we finally got Jo on the phone, she asked, "Where've you guys been?" as if we were forty-five minutes late for dinner instead of stranded in the national forest overnight. But Woody was with us, so she'd known there was nothing to worry about.

The next time Woody led us into the vast beyond was up Mount Kinsman late one afternoon, in search of a secret pond where Venus flytraps reportedly grew. I was probably six at the time, Wren was four, and Chelone a toddler. This time we took sleeping bags in case it became an overnight expedition, and we probably had some ramen and a piece of fruit apiece to eat, too.

We walked and we walked and we walked, with no luck. No flytraps, no pond. We'd go in one direction and then another. We weren't lost; we were searching. But it was hard work. And as it turned out, the pond wasn't secret; it was mythical. Or at least it may as well have been. We'd have had better luck finding D. B. Cooper out in those woods. When it started getting dark, Wren objected loudly, but Woody was sure he knew where we were going. When it started to rain, I joined Wren, and together we outvoted Woody to head back home.

It quickly became clear that the house was now as elusive as the bug-eating plants, and we wandered in the cold, wet darkness until we found a big boulder with a little bunker carved into its base. We climbed under and got out of the whipping rain. We spent the night there, cozier than you'd think, but not exactly comfortable. It was a where-the-wild-things-are trip. Woody kept it light by singing camp songs and explaining what relatively little chance there was for us to be torn apart by coyotes as we slept. Which turned out not to be an issue, because we didn't sleep.

When we came down off the mountain the next morning, no one had been worried about us up there in the wicked weather. It was summer, after all—how much could go wrong? To this day Woody swears we were within steps of finding the Venus flytrap, but I haven't seen any.

Chelone was shaped by these experiences. He was as much of a wood troll as I was. In the middle of winter, loggers would find him wandering the woods far from home and give him their gloves. If he heard a noise, he'd check it out; he could be gone all day and nobody worried. He hunts now, and he's as good at it as he is at everything else. He'll never go hungry, anyway. Chances are if he's not snowboarding somewhere, he's out in the woods killing whatever is in season.

You can't really live in the woods if you're going to sweat what your kids are doing outside. You have to trust them and their judgment, at a very young age; you have to empower them to go where they want to and find their way back. Otherwise, Jo would have had to tie us all up like bad dogs. Not that there weren't people around who would have appreciated that.

Last Easter, Kyla's daughters and her friends were hunting for eggs when somebody realized that my three-year-old niece, Izzy, was gone. Most mothers and grandmothers would have popped a cork, but Jo and Ky just shrugged and said she'd be back. And she was. She'd snuck down to my father's place to gorge herself on her chocolate stash in private.

Woody put their philosophy best in a written interview for the website Bodelicious.net:

> Bode's mother and I tried to do what we could to avoid the need to earn money—see *Living the Good Life* by Scott and Helen Nearing, whom we had met and admired. Although our income was small we felt rich in our ability to spend the bulk of our time with our growing family. I think Bode got a very pragmatic understanding of the world around him and what was going on. We were not particularly protective even from an early age but we were alert and ready to come to their rescue as they explored the world around them, which included a constantly changing mountain brook. Living in a house that was often not much above freezing helped develop a stoic element, as well as an understanding of the need to develop and maintain a supply of firewood. In other words, a work ethic. It was a very interesting, peaceful and demanding place to grow up, I think.

We all turned out well. Chelone, despite not being homeschooled, is an upstanding citizen, in a snowboarder sort of way. But he could never abide public school. For him, it was like chewing aluminum foil while listening to ABBA. He went as long as he had to and then, by mutual consent with the school district, he stopped. For Chel, school was a detention center. He was smart and disruptive, like a small Jack Nicholson in the classroom—hence, the mutual parting of the ways. Chelone's much calmer and quieter now. Sure, he's had a few minor scrapes with the law—but, as I said, he's a snowboarder.

So, yes, we lived deep in the woods by some accounts, not deep enough by others. My folks built a house on a stream in the midst of 450 sylvan acres, the parcel Jack bought in 1946. They homeschooled us, grew organic vegetables, cut firewood, and tapped sugar maples for syrup. We lived as people did a hundred years before us, and I don't ever remember hearing anyone complain. Not about our bucolic lives, anyway.

Waiting for the school bus—another good reason to homeschool.

This is from the preface of my mother's 1984 homeschooling proposal:

> Early this morning I picked a quart of raspberries to share for breakfast while Kyla watched Chelone, Bode and Wren slept, and Woody split firewood. We use 15 to 20 cords per year for heat, cooking, and maple sugaring. After breakfast, everyone worked on firewood until it started to rain. I then went to Tamarack to do office work while Woody schooled the children. . . . It was 7 P.M. before I got home with Kyla and Chelone. Bode and Genny Wren stayed with their grandparents for the night. Woody had dinner cooking and a nice hot sauna ready.

Did the superintendent of schools care much about raspberries or saunas? I doubt it. Mom continued in this vein:

> We live ¾ of a mile up a four-wheel-drive logging road in a house we built ten years ago and have added on to a few times since. We usually walk the road unless we have big loads. We use sleds, cross-country skis, and snowshoes in the winter—we can get in and out with our four-wheel drive with chains, if

need be. We have no phone. We cook with wood and use an outhouse, which is located across the stream and up the hill. The stream provides water, refrigeration, education, and comfort. We have a small TV, a radio, a cassette player, and one electric light hooked up to a 12-volt system, which we recharge with our generator.

There is a young apple orchard, a bunch of small gardens, half-hidden amid the mountainous terrain (our main garden is in the valley below). We have a frog pond, a seesaw, slide, sandbox, playhouse, and the clothesline. This is where we live. We love it, and we love learning from it.

I'm not exactly sure what we were supposed to be doing with the clothesline—hanging from it I guess, or high-jumping over it into the stream.

She used the proposal as an opportunity to plead her case. This was the early 1980s, when most homeschoolers were fundamentalist Christians, and that was definitely not us. Jo and Woody used the Oak Meadow homeschooling curriculum, to the extent that they used any at all. Jo felt she needed to distinguish us from whatever preconceived ideas the school department might have about homeschooling.

I believe public school assignment would be anxiety-inducing for Bode. . . . Our children don't want to go off to school every day and spend most of their time confined to a desk. They need to feel free to explore the world in their own way.

Not exactly a conservative approach to education. My parents are spiritual people, which means they like the idea of God, but not religion. As far as I knew, the only god around our house was Mother Earth.

For good measure, Mom implied that Kyla had been chased by coyotes one morning on her way to the bus. Kyla had voluntarily gone to third grade at the Lafayette School in Franconia, a few years before, as a means of rebellion. She thought she was missing something, and when she found what it was—boredom, rote memory exercises, catty school-yard bullshit—she wanted back into the

homeschool fold. She was in trouble a lot in school, anyway—
always in the shit for something, just like Jo.

Homeschooling was more than uncommon back then; it was
radical. And it added to some locals' ongoing consternation about
exactly what in hell was going on out there in Easton. There'd
been some incidents—one of my uncles got caught growing pot
on the property, and the hippies who made it to town always
seemed to find their way out to Tamarack.

In the 1960s, the counterculture had arrived in Franconia, and
its influence informed much of my parents' lives and, by association, mine and those of my sibs. The town was, and still is, a
Carhartt town, where everybody has a pickup and virtually every
pickup has a snowplow on it half the year. It's a tolerant place, with
happy people, and the ones who aren't naturally happy enhance
their moods with everything from skiing to hunting to drinking to
whatever. And those who aren't tolerant get told to fuck off a lot.

For most of the 1960s and '70s, Franconia was home to Franconia College. It's gone now, as extinct as the SDS, the Black Pan-
thers, and Richard Nixon. It started out as a shirt-and-tie school in
an old grand hotel overlooking Mount Lafayette and Cannon
Mountain. It was conservative and forthright, a liberal arts institution with a little skiing and hiking thrown in. Local folks served on
the board of directors. People thought the college was a good
thing. And it was.

Eventually, it grew into a counterculture way station with self-
designed majors in fly-fishing and blues music, with no grades, or
sometimes even no classes to attend. These things only served to
confuse the educational process. When it went bankrupt in 1970,
the famous overachiever Leon Botstein, now president of Bard
College, was brought in to run it. He was twenty-three years old at
the time, the youngest college president in the country, probably
the world. He'd just finished grad school at Harvard, and he figured if he knew anything at all, it was how to run a college. He
stayed five years—an honest effort.

Franconia College was alternative in its approach to education, not to mention an alternative to serving in Southeast Asia; it
attracted a lot of interesting people—hippies, commies, misfits—
and that was just the faculty. Botstein himself had left school be-

cause his academic deferment had expired, and he'd done alternative service in the Boston mayor's office. A nasty, rough-and-tumble place, no doubt. Perhaps he was sympathetic to the idea of a higher-education draft haven, but Franconia's reputation as one preceded his tenure there.

The civil rights and antiwar movements came to town via the college—as did different ideas about spirituality, a tribe of genuine hippies (as opposed to kids from the burbs who snuck out of the house with holes in their jeans), and anarchists, drug dealers, and flat-out kooks. Conceptual artists with a code of "Do what you like," came face-to-face with Yankee republicanism, whose code is "Just leave me the hell out of it." If it sounds like a Christopher Guest movie, it was. Still is.

When the Vietnam War started, and the draft meant more than spending a couple of years in Kansas or Germany, suddenly going to college in the White Mountains, where they didn't have grades, got very popular. After matriculating at other institutions of higher learning for the better part of a decade, people got their academic deferments denied, which meant they'd have to find some other scam to stay out of the Marine Corps. So they went to Franconia College. There was a time there, long before I was born, when it was definitely an institution of higher learning. Those who graduated and hadn't gotten into medical school or gone to a monastery were draft bait. Fortunately for them, there was a psychiatrist a few towns away who would write you a crazy letter. Back then, being crazy excused you from going someplace and killing people you didn't know. The shrink's compensation for a get-out-of-'Nam card was either $250 or a roll in the hay. I know a few guys who allegedly got out with crazy letters, but I've never asked them how they put their hands on 250 bucks way back then. That was about two months' rent, or a bus ticket to Vancouver, B.C.

In the fall of 1967, caravans of young people regularly sailed into town looking for the college; some of them were even students. Soon, large boxes from Nepal started arriving at the post office; cows sometimes roamed freely inside the administration building; Hells Angels from Montreal crashed the frat parties. Eventually, the ROTC was pushed so far off campus you'd have thought it was the KKK. It was never necessary for Franconia College students to take over the administration building because the administration was never really in control.

In 1969, Middle America's paranoia about drugs got my grandparents busted for growing pot on the Tamarack property. They both liked a pop or two now and then, especially when they were dancing to Duke Ellington music up at the Pioneer Club in Sugar Hill, but Jack was fifty-three years old, Peg was in her mid-forties, and not only weren't they guerrilla pot farmers, as alleged by the state, they weren't even pot smokers.

It turned out the pot patch was owned by four Franconia College students who, thankfully, confessed, exonerating Jack and Peg. This was when people began to realize that having hippies around was like having raccoons.

When the war and then the draft ended, the college had trouble staying in business. In its final grasp at life, it conferred an honorary doctorate on Muhammad Ali in 1978, hoping that he'd rip them a life-support check. No dice. Ali, who was so big that he tore the shoulders out of the robe they gave him to wear, took his sheepskin and boarded his bus, never to be seen again.

As with all places except, perhaps, the South Pole and Atlanta, Georgia, there are natives in Franconia. These are the locals who've been here for longer than guys named George have been running the country. They've seen the coldest winters with the most or least snow, the driest and buggiest summers, the year when it snowed every month, the spring the bears came to town to steal cars and tag all the storefronts like an L.A. street gang.

Then there are the immigrants—those who came and stayed. They include the hippie ring-around-the-tub left when Franconia College went down the drain. They often originated in cities and suburbs. They stayed because this place is so beautiful that it's hard to leave. Jack and Peg were both émigrés from other states. Peg was a vagabond, her last known residence before Tamarack being Berkeley, California; Jack was a flatlander from Reading, Massachusetts, which was a suburb of Boston before Boston even needed suburbs.

Eventually, the folks who stay here for the long haul do it for the flintiness of it all. Jack and Peg fell into this category. You constantly have to figure out how you're going to survive in the North

Country—it's less developed, less commercial, and less crowded for good reasons. Every time I hear a politician yapping about improving economic conditions in the North Country, I think of all the people I know who moved here precisely because there are no jobs.

That's not true for everyone, of course. Some people see the North Country as an easy mark, so they move here to get rich and usually go broke in the process. Others come to ski, or hike, or rock climb and decide that playing is what they really want to do in life. So they give up their jobs in pharmaceutical sales or commercial insurance and move to Franconia to work in a pizza shop, or they call themselves artists and get their real-estate license. They do whatever they have to do to make it. A lot of entrepreneurs around here are in partnership with eBay these days.

It's a three-season wonderland, as in: I wonder when the hell all the tourists are leaving. There are a fair number of weekenders in Franconia, and more every year. Trophy houses—the spoils of tax cuts and the real-estate bubble—abound. One day last year Kyla took her kids for a drive up on the ridge that overlooks our land from the north. They were tired and fussy and crying, and all she wanted was to get them to sleep. She nearly ended up in tears herself. Up there, amid the hardwood forest and overgrown logging roads, she found that a sprawling McMansion village had somehow popped up when we weren't looking.

Now hordes of flatlanders in L.L. Bean old-fart duds look down on us; they're the people you see at Cannon in hot pink racing suits *schussing,* and the folks you see in the bars enthusiastically après-skiing, and then weaving their SUVs slalom-style up and down the back roads, sliding sideways through stop signs while they yak on the cell phone. We love them.

When we were kids, people often asked my parents if we were sufficiently "socialized" through homeschooling, as if we were feral, or recluses, just monkeys up in a tree picking nits off one another. We didn't go to town much; that was true. Well, I didn't, because I didn't like it. But I had plenty of friends—we all did—and our friends wanted to come to Tamarack to hang out. When we were young kids it was the coolest playground imaginable. As we got older, our friends still came out here to the valley to play. Our household was always warm and inviting, especially for kids. My mom was cool, so you could get away with more. Way more.

That may be why nobody wanted their kids spending the night at our house. They said it was because of the outhouse, or because we lived so far in the woods that a witch might lure their children into a cage, fatten them up, and make soup out of them—which some of us deserved. I don't doubt they disliked the outhouse, but I'm pretty sure the real problem was because we had the smell of freedom about us, and that's funky as shit to some people.

We were socialized all right, but we weren't institutionalized. Nobody taught us to sit at a desk and be bored thoughtless for seven hours every day. Nobody instilled the so-called virtues of un-fettered capitalism in us, or fed us rat-turd-laden hot dogs for lunch. We never believed the tissue of lies, the love-it-or-leave-it bullshit that passed for a free society. We're free citizens, and we got that way by being free. As a result, none of us were cut out for corporate America, or any other kind of workaday job; our folks trained us for happiness, to seek it out and maximize it. So we do.

Nearly everyone in my extended family is self-employed. I'm technically an employee of the U.S. Ski Team, so I come closest to working for the Man. My father is the tricounty homeless advocate, which he does because someone has to and there are no lines forming for the job. Other than that, we're all loggers and farmers and businesspeople; my mother co-owns an antiques shop with Eleana, who is Noah's mom, and one of the women who helped deliver me.

Where the fundamentalists have God at the center of their homeschooling curriculum, Jo and Woody put happiness. Woody, especially, was on a constant happy-hunt; he'd been so unhappy at times in his life, he felt he was at the mercy of his disabling emo-tions if he didn't actively look for the good in things. As a result of this philosophy, life for me is one long seek-and-enjoy mission. I re-member being shocked to learn that there are people—religious leaders, philosophers, bankers—who regard suffering and strife as the natural human condition. For us, happiness was the overriding lesson in all things, including school. If you're not fundamentally happy, something's wrong.

This isn't to say it was all peaches and cream, or that every chore was a joy to perform. Hardly. My father left home when I was six. (He wasn't happy, so what can you say?) Actually, he and Jo put an ad in the *Mother Earth News,* looking for people to share a communal living arrangement. They were still high on the concept— and it's a great idea—of farming together and cooking, eating, and caring for children communally. They had some takers, people came halfway across the country to join, and it went well for a while. Unfortunately, Woody and one of the women took the whole sharing thing a little too far. Anyway, it was hurtful and sad for the adults involved. And things weren't going to be the same after that. This we could all see.

"Dark times I've dragged us into," Woody wrote in his journal at the time. Maybe my grandparents were right—it's hard to get rid of people once you invite them to stay. Woody decided it would be best to put some distance between himself and my mother. So he went to Nashville.

Once he returned, it took him and Jo very little time to get along again. At first, being civil was mostly for us kids, but they're both such nice people that the idea of them staying angry at each other for long would be like the Hare and the Tortoise locked in a cage match to the death. It's just too far outside nature.

But that doesn't mean it got better right away—I had to go to public school beginning in fourth grade. I wrote Woody a postcard not long after: "I hope i can come and visit you soon. I am doing good in school. I have cot up." Right.

Woody came back for the first time about a year later, and when my mother carried Chelone up to him and said, This is your father, Chellie was genuinely happy to see him. Later, however, during subsequent visits, Chelone put Woody through the wringer—punched him in the nose, and chased him around my grandparents' house with a knife when he was about four. It was a challenging relationship, but they worked it out eventually, over the years. Turtlewise.

But before all that upheaval, I was a little kid and everything was good. I looked around and never saw anyone sweat a thing, and so I got hardwired for the same outlook. I got that crucial, life-changing mother's milk of happiness and freedom, and I never lost it.

I also skied nearly every day of the winter, no matter how cold it was, and I jacked into that, too, in a big way. One day I walked to Cannon Mountain in my ski boots, just because I could. Took me all morning, but I didn't care. My friends were all tied up in school, that medium-security prison with the chain-link fence and the monkey bars down in Franconia, and I was free to do as I pleased.

That may be a bit of an overstatement. When you live off the land, there's always something you should be doing, and when that's all done, there's always next year's firewood to deal with. But I spent most of my time running the woods, looking for animals, building ineffectual traps. I knew a kid who thought "frostbite" was an actual critter that lived in the snow. I never saw a frostbite, but there were plenty of voles, moose, fisher cats, bobcats, deer, fish, albino frogs, two-headed snakes, larcenous raccoons, and overly industrious beavers; they were all around, watching us, so I decided to watch them.

I learned the art of solitude in those woods; I came to appreciate my company, the comfort of my own thoughts. To this day, no matter how much I love hanging out with my friends, I'm perfectly happy alone, too. I ski by myself, I golf alone, I can go to the movies or out to dinner as my own date and have a perfectly good time.

There's a certain solitary flintiness to being from northern New Hampshire. So much so that our state symbol is a great stone head: the Old Man of the Mountain, a granite outcropping Daniel Webster once used in a speech:

> Men hang out their signs indicative of their respective trades. Shoemakers hang out a gigantic shoe; jewelers, a monster watch; even a dentist hangs out a gold tooth; but up in the Franconia Mountains God Almighty has hung out a sign to show that in New England He makes men.

Big-time bloviating, if you ask me. He even got the name of the mountains wrong—just another politician.

A couple of years ago, the Old Man finally broke off and crashed into the ravine below. He'd been there ten thousand years and had seen the entire evolution of human society around here. But nature hates outcroppings, and this one would have been swept off the mountainside fifty years ago if he hadn't been trussed up tighter than the Gimp. Had he decayed naturally, if entropy—the universal force that's slowly eroding everything, including you and me—had been allowed to reshape the Old Man, who knows what he might have looked like?

There was a time when the Old Man enthralled America's literary biggies. Hawthorne, Webster, Longfellow, Frost, and Thoreau all waxed away about the Old Man. But you didn't need to be a poet. Nobody could go by him without looking, which wasn't an issue in the nineteenth century. But there's a lot more traffic now. Even when he was there, the Old Man wasn't easy to see from the road unless you knew where and when to look. The combination of location and timing was crucial.

Still, motorists watched out for him, swerving and slowing, usually while flossing or feeding the DVD player. The Old Man's been gone for a couple of years, so now the rubberneckers look for where he was, as if it were a crime scene or a battlefield. They crane their necks and zigzag, sometimes bouncing off the double-sided steel divider between the north- and southbound lanes. The guardrail is a working memorial in itself, put there for those who drifted into the oncoming lane while catching a glimpse of the Old Man and nearly killed somebody coming the other way; it literally curbs the uncontrollable urge to look up.

My mother used to talk to the Old Man as she passed. It was like an Easter Island head to some people, a granite totem, and there was no shortage of people under the spell of this giant silhouette of ourselves. But that, I'm afraid, is all it was.

Dig the giant face, the tourists seemed to say. Or they'd stop by the busload and take photos. Of what? It was five overlapping cliffs—five exposed ends of the layered rock in the long-ago formation of Cannon Mountain; it's all that remained after the stone and soil had shaken loose in an earthquake, a flood, or maybe a sneeze. People transform oddities like the Old Man into miracles of nature, and many of these same people think Mount Rushmore is a natural formation. I don't believe the Old Man fell at all; I think he jumped.

Deep thinking, a natural by-product of solitude, is an essential part of living in the woods. Read Thoreau, read Defoe. Every major religion has a prophet who came to special knowledge in the wilderness. I bet I spent as much time outside as the average Native American did three hundred years ago, and I related to the world on that level. The seasons were more important to me than the actual date; the sun's position in the sky is how I kept time. I wasn't afraid of the boogeyman, but I was afraid of bumping into mama bear and her cubs.

With the notable exception of a few choice Transformers and some Hot Wheels, toys were of little use to me. I tried playing with them, but I learned if I needed to keep my hands busy, I'd rather split firewood or pound nails into a stump than play with some stupid thingamajig. When I was five years old I tried building a model airplane out of balsa wood and glue—tedious, messy, sticky, frustrating "fun." It was so deadly that after working on it every day for a year, I just threw it away. I tried long enough to know it wasn't for me.

Not much happens in the woods that you can't deduce with some effort. Calm determination accomplishes most things. My father won the John Lennon Peace Prize in 1982 for inventing the Turtle Party, which stood for The United Resolution To Love Earth. The platform advocated thoughtfulness, inclusion, hard work, and patience—the virtues of the turtle, a long-term view of life. And anyone who knows Woody will tell you that he's rather turtlelike at times himself. His kindergarten report card from 1955 has comments like: "Soft voice, sometimes hard to hear when reading," and "Natural and flexible." His final evaluation from prep school in 1966 says, among many things, "Woody is a delightful paradox. A bright lad who can mosey along, turn on the heat, and shine when he wants to. Without some of us 'old crocks' to goad and prod him along at college next year, he might easily come a cropper." Whatever the hell that means, but it doesn't sound good. Another report card states in terse tones, "Woody's failing the term exam is inexcusable. Passing him is a reward for his sonnets. He needs to be more conscientious about academic pursuits. Tennis and running shouldn't absorb quite so much of his time."

Woody liked what he liked, and while he may not always have

known what he liked, he followed his heart like a loyal servant. In his Turtle Party essay he defines love as "a feeling of strong personal attachment induced by that which delights or commands admiration."

The Turtle Party piece was really a sort of Jules-Verne-meets-Noam-Chomsky visionary tale. It began: "By the year 2006, the people of the Earth were celebrating, with one heart, the completion of global disarmament." But right or wrong, Woody is the real deal. He might not have managed global disarmament, but he's lived his life according to the ideals he laid out. Rather than cut wide trails through the forest to harvest firewood, for instance, he rigged a Chutes and Ladders steel cable network that used only gravity to haul tons of logs every year. I've ridden down out of the mountains on it, and it rips.

I started skiing when I was two years old. If I wasn't skiing, I was wading through waist-deep snow. My calves were dried and gnarled like a Hobbit's, my hands were red-raw, my ears glowed translucent pink. Yet I remained in the great outdoors, where endless possibilities lay. The solitary nature of the woods appealed to me, the absence of people and machines and noise. Out there, I was on my own, and that was how I liked it.

I could never understand my older sister's imaginary friends. I reveled in the aloneness of it all. From the beating ice storms of February to the perfect calm of August, I loved it all. I still do. It's family and friends that anchor me to this place, not the skiing. There are plenty better places to ski.

Anyway, for me skiing was always just a means of going fast. And that was how I got into racing—I could go fast without the ski patrol kicking me off the mountain for doing what came natural. I don't mean to slight the ski patrol; we have more in common than not. Their attitude was "If you ain't fallin', you ain't haulin'."

That's for them, of course. They got around the speed limit by becoming the law, which made us speed demons the bad guys. In the end, they had their job to do (chasing me), and I had mine (giving them someone to chase).

I was a skinny kid whose mother dropped him at the mountain most mornings in the winter, and I stayed all day. There were times when I was up there alone that I'd have to find someone to open the bathroom door for me because I couldn't reach it; sometimes I had to find my own way home at night. But Kyla was usually with me, and Lars, Roland's son, and Wren, and then Chelone, eventually. Ky didn't ski as much as I did, especially when it was cold. Wren was an early adapter to the snowboard, as were Lars and Chellie. But Kyla would hang around the cafeteria, the gift shop, the ski shop, wherever it was warm, and make a nuisance of herself. Not really. Everybody knew us, and most people who worked at the mountain liked us, I think. They never chased us off with sticks, anyway.

I skied with older guys because everybody else was in school. White Mountain School kids were there in the afternoons, and I skied with Roland and Mac, Pete Stagpole and Dick Newby. I skied with a guy named Marc Benoli who ran the ski shop and fed me gummy worms when I had no money for lunch. He died on Cannon Mountain, ran into an immovable object right where the Rocket run hitches up with the work road, where we used to cut over to the tram. He was cookin', as he always was, and a prerelease of his binding sent him into the woods on one ski, into a tree. I was seven years old, and this was an early object lesson in the realities of ski racing. I'd been at the top with him; he went one way, and I jumped on Avalanche and sped to the bottom. Then I heard all this crazy shit on the radio—the ski patrol was freaked at something that had happened. I jumped on the tram and headed up there. The ski patrol was fast; they'd gotten his body into a sled and rushed down the mountain by the time I arrived. But they said his face was already blue. I remember the bloodstained snow, the red footprints traipsing around the scene, the culprit maple tree in the center of it all. It was tragic and frightening then, and remains a somber memory today.

Still, I skied fast, and when it wasn't icy cold, Ky skied too. We took our regular route—all the way up top, and a total tuck and roar down the mountain, as if we were racing a downhill. Now that I think of it, we were.

My mother was well aware of how fast those trails were, because she'd skied them herself when she was our age. She tried to make it a little simpler for us by, for example, giving us some gorp or noodles to take with us. When she was a kid up at Cannon her lunch was usually a few saltines that she'd snitch from the cafeteria; her favorite combinations were relish and crackers or crackers, ketchup, and sugar. Chelone was a mayonnaise-and-crackers guy. If Kyla saw someone who knew Jack and Peg, she'd cadge a dime for hot chocolate. Otherwise, we'd get a glass of water.

So Jo worried about us skiing sixty-five miles per hour at six years old, but she never dreamed of stopping us, because she'd done the same thing when she was our age. The terrible truth is that to this day poor Mom worries about me all season long. Racers crash and get hurt, or worse. She loves that I'm a racer, because I'm happy, but she's ambivalent about the risk. There's a big part of her that will be happier when my World Cup days are done. I won't mention speed skiing (165 mph plus!) on the pro circuit to her. Maybe I could just tell her I'm playing golf.

When Jo sped into the Cannon Mountain parking lot and offloaded us in front of the lodge many, many mornings, then zipped off to work, I never felt abandoned up there. It seemed the most natural thing in the world. It's actually a very European attitude. Nearly every little town in the Alps has a sports center that's full of

Cannon Mountain racing, 1987—always a short, sharp shock

kids most of the time, sometimes located within walking distance of the base of the mountain. People leave their kids there and go do whatever they have to. It's healthy. Cannon Mountain is a state-owned resort, so maybe my mom figured she was getting a little bump from her tax dollars. The people who work there today are essentially the same crew as when I was a little kid. They still talk about how they'd leave us at Kelley's Supermarket in Franconia, at the bottom of Three-Mile Hill, at the end of the day, and then somebody else would deliver us out to Tamarack from there.

My mom picked us up at Cannon when she could, and her boyfriend, Roland, was always there when you needed him. It was nothing for him to ferry five kids around in his Toyota pickup truck, all of us jammed up front, music blasting, everybody laugh-ing—except Genny Wren, of course. She was watching the speedometer.

Roland had a way of keeping things interesting. Once, he spun his rig into a 1,080 (three consecutive 360-degree turns) on a snowy back road. We spiraled out of control and out of sight, like the Red Baron in a tight barrel roll, all of us kids screaming bloody murder, the countryside going by a little too fast. When we finally plowed into a snowbank (and thankfully not a tree), Roland told us he'd done it as an example of how not to drive. Even though I wasn't in school, my education never stopped.

That type of risk taking was encouraged in a way. Even when my mother took us sledding, we were expected to pull out all the stops, and she told us that in no uncertain terms. It taught me fear-lessness, and to love to go fast, because nothing bad ever hap-pened to me.

Ten years to the day after Bubba's death, my luck very nearly changed, but instead the "Go fast, have fun" ethos was bright-lined in my life. It was Wren's eleventh birthday, and Mom and Roland decided that that was as good a reason as any to skip school and go skiing up at Tuckerman's Ravine on Mount Washington.

Mount Washington is the highest mountain (6,288 feet) in the Northeast and bills itself as having the "Worst Weather in the World." This is one hell of a claim to fame. It's like a person brag-ging on their "Worst Bad Breath on the East Coast" or a restaurant advertising "Filthiest Kitchen in the Northern Hemisphere."

Mount Washington came by its motto in 1931 when instruments there clocked the fastest ground wind speed on record: 231 mph. Hold on to your hat.

There are a number of ways to get up Mount Washington, including an auto road, which I'd like to jet up and down in my Porsche without anyone else around, because otherwise I'd get stuck behind a minivan from Rhode Island and burn out my clutch. There's also an old cog railway that went into service in 1869 and still runs. Its trestles are marvels of nineteenth-century North Country technology. Of course, there are many hiking trails up Mount Wash. We took the Tuckerman Ravine Trail that day; I was intent on skiing Tuck's for the first time. I was thirteen years old.

Carrying all my equipment on my back, I hiked up ahead of everyone else with Roland, while he explained the ins and outs of skiing the ravine. It's not for the faint of heart, but I'd been skiing Roland's ass off for years up at Cannon, so if he figured I could handle Tuckerman's, so did I.

The most prominent feature of Tuckerman's Ravine is the headwall, carved out of Mount Washington by the Worst Weather in the World. It sits just below the summit, and at its base, over many years, avalanche debris has grown into talus piles arranged across the bottom like the strewn ruins of an abandoned castle. When you're finished skiing the steepest and fastest run that gravity will allow—its forty- to fifty-five-degree pitch straddles that fine line between skiing and free-falling—you then have to negotiate a granite barricade and a hard-slab minefield at the bottom. Dozens of people have died up there.

After about three hours of good hiking you've arrived. Once you're above the tree line, Tuckerman's rises up ahead of you like a giant drive-in movie theater screen showing a Warren Miller film. The closer I got, the faster I hiked, and I soon realized that I'd left Roland behind.

He and Jo and the rest of them stayed below on Lunch Rocks, while I and a couple of young guys attacked the headwall. It was a tough climb, especially in ski boots, with the rest of my gear in a backpack. I was out in front when, twenty or thirty feet from the lip of the bowl, one of the guys slipped and fell, sliding out of sight.

The two of us who were left climbed higher, and then the second guy went down, sliding on his back, but managed to grab a pine sapling and keep himself from plunging down the slope.

I had nowhere to go but up. When I reached the top and put on my skis, I wasn't sure what to do next. The lip hangs over a rocky face, and I couldn't see a route down. There are ten, but I'd been counting on these goobs I'd hiked up with to point one out to me from up there. That wasn't happening.

I shouted to the guy clinging to the tree, asking him what the hell to do next. The only advice anyone ever takes is the advice they ask for—but that doesn't mean it's good advice. He told me to traverse the length of the lip and tip off from the other side. I looked for Jo and Roland, to get their attention and let them know I was coming down, but the people at the bottom looked like fleas from up there. I couldn't make anyone out.

It was a beautiful clear day—blue-blue sky, the warm sun on my face—and I gingerly sidestepped along the lip and took a line down. Almost immediately I felt it fracture ever so slightly beneath my skis and drop away. I imagined myself hanging there for just a moment, like Wile E. Coyote, before I looked down and saw that doozy of a first step everyone talks about.

The entire headwall fell away. It dropped and poofed like one of those old buildings they implode instead of knocking down; it just fell, and there was no stopping it once it started. Soon, hundreds of tons of snow and rock were barreling down the basin, bearing down on a thousand people. It was a cold white wall, threatening like a lava flow about to smother Pompeii. I'd have been more worried about them, but I was trapped inside the avalanche, completely disoriented between up and down, and dropping precipitously. I felt like I was going over Niagara Falls in a paper bag. And this is a fine example of why I seldom listen to advice.

Suddenly, my foot hit a stationary rock; I reoriented myself, and momentarily popped up out of the tempest. Up and down was no longer the problem; I could see where I was, but keeping my head above the snow wasn't easy. I started swimming to the top, literally, as if I were coming up from the bottom of a lake. I knew I had to get my head out of the snow while it was still in motion, because when it came to rest at the bottom, it would be hardpack, compressed by its own weight and impossible to move in. If I didn't break the surface of this snowslide, I'd end up like Bubba, ten years later to the day.

That's what was going on in my mom's mind as she sat on the rocks and watched the tidal wave of snow rumble by. When it finally stopped and settled, my head and one arm poked up out of the snow. Everyone who could get near me helped dig me out. I was packed into cold concrete, my body twisted a little unnaturally, my hat missing, my gear long gone.

I wasn't shocked at all; I wasn't even scared. Looking back on it, I felt incredibly calm. I'd never been up there before, and I figured the mountain shook the snow off like that all the time. It was only when I saw how shook up Jo was that I began to understand the seriousness of it. This was the same Jo who, when I was a year old, regularly skied down from our house with me on her back, and one day caught a tip, catapulting me out of her backpack. I landed headfirst in a snow pile. According to her, I laughed my ass off. And she laughed too. But nothing was funny this time; it was too close, too weird, and she just wanted to go home.

There are two types of avalanches: naturally occurring and human triggered. Notice that nature simply occurs, while humans trigger. This ties causality and responsibility firmly around our necks. Therefore, if you lost your equipment or your lunch that day under a cruise ship–sized snowslide on Tuckerman's Ravine, I apologize.

3

The End of the Beginning

The Feral Life ended a few years after Woody left. Living in the woods became unmanageable: too much work, too far to go in the morning to the bus stop, lions and tigers and bears, oh yeah.

My father left home, and that's a familiar story that could end right there. But as with most things in my family, it wasn't that simple. In my own six-year-old way I supported his decision. Not that I had any choice, but he was unhappy, and around our house that was considered a terminal illness if not treated. He didn't want to leave, but he wasn't in love with my mother anymore and had been distressed about it for a long time.

I don't pretend to have understood much of this at the time; it wasn't exactly explained to us. But I was highly aware. Maybe more aware than the average adult, because kids don't have all those noise filters installed between their brains and their ears yet. Eventually, I had a partial comprehension of why, but why wasn't all that important to me. Woody was going to Tennessee—that much I knew for sure; and I knew there was nothing I could do about it.

Woody believed that if he stayed around town, inevitably there would be anger and resentment between him and Jo. In order to spare us that ugliness, he took a job in Nashville. He worked in the trees, and the season was longer there; plus, it was a big city and the pay was better. He'd make enough to live on and to send money home. You couldn't bring in that kind of cash in the North Country back then. Especially if you worked in the trees.

Despite my father's best intentions, a lasting shift occurred when he left. We relied on friends and family in ways we never had before. Woody's peripatetic nature changed all our lives, but as far as I can tell, it wasn't for the worse. It made things different. I'd had the freedom of a wild animal, and before long it would be off to the zoo with me. So that sucked. Still, adversity can underscore the importance of happiness, and so, if used in limited quantities, it has its place. And like all those other things, too much unhappiness begins to feel like a curse, or a penance of some sort, and people slowly accept it; unhappiness becomes a way of life. At a bare minimum, he wanted to keep the fun in "dysfunctional." That's why Woody left.

Terminal unhappiness didn't happen to us. Peg stepped in and helped us survive financially and logistically, despite the increasing demands of Jack's Alzheimer's. She became another parent to us—she always had been, for that matter. Jack and Peg had always been more than grandparents; they were like überparents—the people even Jo and Woody listened to. We all lived nearly within shouting distance of one another, though very little shouting went on, and I spent many nights at their house, cuddled up on a mat on the floor by the woodstove. Up at the house in the woods, all of us kids pretty much slept in one big room upstairs, with me on the floor under some shelving. Later in life, I moved up into the attic, which I accessed by a Tarzan rope. But staying down at Jack and Peg's was like going to a spa—with a hot bath and TV.

So we weren't entirely abandoned when Jo went off to work as a seamstress. I think about that now—my mother working in what some might consider a sweatshop. It was much better than that: the people were nice, the hours flexible, and the wage nearly livable. Two out of three. And besides, where I'm from, it has to be July to sweat at all, for any reason.

We spent a lot of time up in the woods, left to our own low-tech devices. Peg tried to keep an eye on us, but as I've said, she had

Woody decked out for tree climbing

Jack to care for. Truth be told, when I didn't feel like going to school, I didn't. I couldn't get away with it often because Kyla would have ratted me out to Jo—and if not her, then Wren would definitely have given me up. But when I could manage to skip out on school, I rode my bike, I swam, I skied, I ran through the woods like a troll. Anything was better than the hard plastic seat of the classroom, the smell of chalk, the yellow wax on the floors, the pasty food—I hated it all.

By this time, danger, speed, and the outdoors were essential parts of my life, and it's tough to find that inside an elementary school. Even the glue isn't poisonous. Of course, all little boys feel like this; they believe they're knights, or superheroes, and they throw some serious bullshit around. I once swore up and down that I'd seen a six-mile-long shark on a television documentary at my grandparents' house. Actually, when pressed hard enough, I still claim this is true. The difference between me and other ten-year-olds was that I had the opportunity to act out all my craziness, to patrol the boundaries between fantasy and reality, and to hop the fence quite a bit. That's probably the difference between me and most adults, too.

So Woody was gone a few years, but it's not as if we never saw him again. Far from it. We spent summers with him in Nashville, where he worked as an arborist. He trimmed trees and bushes for Grand Ole Opry rich folks (music executives and guys with big hats who sang through their noses), while we swam in their banjo-shaped pools.

Eventually Woody returned to Tamarack, as he'd been known to do. This time, he brought his new wife, Holly, whom he'd met in Nashville, and his three stepchildren. So that was a little different, but definitely not a problem. The ethos around Tamarack was welcoming, the family structure tribal; there was always room for more people. We're a laid-back bunch. My mother still gets freaked when somebody knocks on her door before they come in; she says it sounds like bad news.

Anyway, it was great to have Woody back because he was our dad, and also because he was a great tennis pro, and a patient, mindful teacher. So of course he and his new family belonged at Tamarack, with us.

I realize it sounds like a sitcom: ex-husband lives on land with ex-wife, and they run a rural sports camp together while a rat pack of stepsiblings runs wild. In truth, it was all pretty uneventful. My stepbrother Aaron punched me pretty hard once, I do remember that, and I didn't like it a bit. We were on a trip with Woody and our accommodations were tight, and people got uptight. For the most part we got along well on that trip. Seven kids on a mattress in the back of a Chevy Luv truck, roaming around the South, going to a Rainbow People gathering in North Carolina (tie-dye, dread-locks, drums), or hanging at the beach on the Gulf Coast, sleeping on the side of the road. That was how I spent my summer vacations. Woody was Ken Kesey and we were the Merry Pranksters.

It was the good life, and I sort of emulate it now with an RV in Europe on the World Cup tour. I admit the new version is a tad more luxurious. And Aaron and I got along fine after he willfully assaulted me, but I think I still owe him one. I did knock a beer out of his hand with a tennis ball last summer—that probably counts.

In Nashville, Woody lived with a guy he knew from Franconia, who had moved down to Nashville a year or two earlier and started the arborist operation. Woody had gone down there to work for him, so the two bachelors shared a house, and it worked out okay for a while.

Then there was the dog, a German shepherd whose name I forget, and don't care to remember. One day, as we were returning from work with Woody, Wren got out of the car first, and for some still unknown reason, this nameless mutt chomped Wren right in the face. I can't picture her provoking him in any way; there wasn't time, in any case. I think it was because she was five years old and just the right height to bite. He took a piece out of her face, nearly tore her left eye out of her head; I beat the shit out of that dog to get him off her. I kicked him in the balls, I punched him in the face, and like all bullies, he was a pussy and ran off. But had she been alone with him, he might have mauled her to death. (This wasn't the first time I'd saved Wren's life, by the way; I'd fished her out of a lake in New Mexico once, when she was about two. She'd already gone under and was unconscious when I got to her. I was four years old at the time.)

That Wren still likes dogs at all is testament to her good character. Or maybe she was so traumatized by the attack that she can't remember it. Woody swears to this day that the dog was okay, that something must have spooked him. But Woody's pretty forgiving. Wren doesn't talk about it. Freaked me more than a little, though. I take no shit from dogs, but a good rule is not to get too close in the first place.

The rest of the year, back in Franconia, Jo continued homeschooling us. But it got to be too much for her after a three-year valiant effort. It was inevitable: working, educating, cooking and cleaning, chopping wood, and keeping a garden deep, deep in the woods is a three-person job. We helped, but we were kids. Kyla was the oldest and got hung with a lot of chores; and once we started going to school, she was the prime motivator to get us up and out the door in time for the bus.

Anyway, when I was in fourth grade my mother reluctantly sent us to public school. Robert Frost's dark and lovely woods were now a nasty, icy walk to the bus stop before the sun came up. While once I'd spent my days slogging through fields and streams, exploring and investigating, I now stood on a hot-topped playground with hordes of different-sized kids, most of them running and screaming, and some plotting in the corners, pointing us out. Many were way bigger than me and seemed to know things I didn't know, such as what all those bells meant, and why we had to stay inside most of the day, and how to talk to a teacher without getting your ass chewed out.

Fortunately, I didn't have much academic catch-up to do. Mom's curriculum and the school district's didn't exactly jibe—skiing versus penmanship, for instance, or baking bread versus science class. My reading skills were behind most of my classmates', but my math was adequate. I liked numbers, so no worries. In fact, our skill levels were surprisingly high, given the casual nature of our formal educations. We all read a lot, and thought a lot, and discussed issues openly at meals, such as sex, and the government, and why it's not okay for twelve-year-olds to drive cars after everybody else has gone to bed at night. So I considered myself pretty well informed.

But Kyla was sweating it. I was afraid she might take to the road with a rucksack on her back or go into the witless protection program, rather than face the music down at the school, where she was sure she'd be exposed as an uneducated wood nymph. My attitude was: Who cares? What are they going to do?

As it turned out for both of us, the kids who had been inside that building all that time, listening, not listening, becoming socialized, whatever—not one of them knew any more than we did. Poor bastards; what a waste of their precious childhoods.

The truth is, if I'd been sitting in the classroom from first grade on and had been behind in all my subjects, that's just the way it would have been. If that's the kind of kid they decide you are, then that's that. It's a tough climb out of that hole. Not that they want to code or brand people, but thirty kids is a lot of individuality for one teacher to absorb. They're stuck with a one-size-fits-none program.

But, like anything, it wasn't all bad. Every Friday afternoon, the public school brought us up to Cannon Mountain, a former World Cup venue. (My uncle Bill was a forerunner for the World Cup slalom Jean-Claude Killy won at Cannon.) Its narrow pitches are north-facing, and often locked in conditions the ski areas call "hardpack," what we call "boilerplate," and what the rest of the world knows as blue ice.

Even by European alpine standards, Cannon is steep. When Ky and I were sent to public school, we had to take ski lessons up at the mountain. They were taught by an Austrian woman, who is still there and is very nice, but she used an old-school method that involved skiing in lines, like in the Ice Capades, and never doing anything that didn't involve everyone else doing it at the same time. I could already ski, so I didn't need any french fry–pizza pie instruction. I skipped ski lessons and just skied. It made so much more sense.

When they finally let us all go up the mountain, we ran our chaperones ragged down the steepest, iciest slopes, through the most treacherous glades in the world, over moguls like ski jumps. The chaperones were our teachers, mostly, or somebody's dad taking his lunch hour up on the mountain. Most left with sore shoulders, wet asses, and bruised egos. I don't think many of them ever really looked forward to it.

When we'd finally lost them, the ski patrol would put an APB out and hunt us down like the dogs that we were—outlaws of the mountain, the kids all the other skiers wanted to boot in the ass, if only they could catch us. I was going fast and having fun. But was I good? It was on my mind, it guided my thoughts if not my deeds, but there were other priorities.

And all this was not without consequence. We skied this way for many years, and I still do. But I've known several people who died on Cannon Mountain—Ian van Houten, one of my oldest and best friends among them. It happens with regularity. So we were aware—young and invincible, but aware.

After the 2002 Olympics, where I'd won a couple silver medals, the Cannon Mountain Ski Patrol asked me to sign a poster for them. I wrote, "You'll never catch me now," and they hung it in the lodge where everyone can see it, as if I were Jesse James.

As we got a little older, the outlaw tag might have been more accurate. Weekday season passes necessitated a certain amount of skipping school, which inevitably led to a fair amount of dope smoking and early-onset sex.

Back then, there was literally no police presence in Easton. And not unrelated to this fact, a lot of people chose the Easton Valley to grow their pot in. Not that people weren't growing it everywhere back then. But all I can swear to is where my boys and I were the lords of the forest; we saw it all and took what we wanted. Which was a fair haul, I guess. It was a long time ago, and it's hard to put in perspective. How do I feel about it now? By the time I was a teenager I'd already done pretty much everything I wasn't supposed to do and had put it behind me.

My opinion is that if you're an addict—drugs, alcohol, tobacco, whatever—you've got a problem. On the other hand, if you've reached adulthood without ever trying something off the menu, something forbidden, like drag racing on a public street or a little illicit hooch of some sort, then you've got a bigger problem: you're scared of life. And you can't fix that in twenty-eight days of rehab. Act from conviction, never from fear, and know the difference in yourself. That's basic.

If any of us grew up with a monkey on our backs, it was the righteous sugar jones we all acquired from harvesting the elixir of the North, the treat inside the trees: maple sap. On just the right days in March, when it's cold at night and everything melts during the day, that's sugar weather. The sap flows from the maple trees like beer from a tap.

All winter long a tree stores starch in its roots, and then in the early spring it converts it to sucrose. There are no leaves yet, so no transpiration occurs. This puts all that sap literally under pressure inside the tree. If you drill a hole three inches deep in the trunk of a sugar maple, drive a metal spout into it, and hang a bucket on that, it'll fill with a sweetish water. Each hole gives about ten gallons of sap over the month or so that it runs.

Legend has it that a Native American discovered this one day when hunting in the sugar bush; his arrow hit a maple tree instead of a deer, and when he worked it loose, he found a sticky, vaguely sweet water on the end of the arrowhead. Having nothing else to do, he gave it a lot of thought, and invented maple sugar snow cones, pancakes, and those crumbly little brown candies that make your teeth hurt.

The Indians tapped plenty of trees. There's proof of that everywhere; the huge ancients show the scars where the Abenaki flayed them open with hatchets and let the sap pour. This was way back before acid rain and urban sprawl; the sugar maples were as big around as VW Bugs and taller than cell-phone towers.

When you've collected thirty to fifty buckets of sap, you haul it all down to your draw tub, which for us was a big galvanized bucket on a big old wooden wagon, pulled by our workhorse, Coco. When it was nearly full, we brought it to the sugar shack, which looks like any other shack except the walls only go three-quarters of the way up to the roof; this allows the steam to escape during the boil.

Woody eventually installed a tube system, which is like putting the whole maple orchard on a giant IV. In our minds, the bucket system was far superior because we drank the dregs from the buckets; it was blood fresh from the xylem of the sugar maple, and we didn't want to waste it. We hoisted each cold, galvie snifter to our moist lips and, if we didn't freeze to it, drank the last half mouthful of semisweetness. I think Chelone lived on that shit. He'd just pick the snow fleas out of it if he had to.

The maple-sugaring process is dictated largely by the weather. The trees don't get much say in it. It's not uncommon for it to get really cold for a few days right in the middle of sugaring, and shut all the trees down without further notice. When the sap flows, you've got to be on the balls of your feet, and it usually requires a lot of late-night boiling in the sugarhouse, accompanied by a fair amount of Pickwick Ale for warmth, and a pitcher of cream to squelch an overboil.

When it boils to just under 222 degrees Fahrenheit, it's soup. I mention the exact temperature because it's important. Sap starts out only 2 percent sugar and 98 percent water, but by the time it drools down the side of your short stack at breakfast, it's 67 percent sugar and 33 percent water. That's a delicate balance. If you mess up the boiling phase, you get maple snot. So this is no amateur undertaking. Woody is a serious maple farmer. I learned all I know from him. My sister Wren teaches at the Farm School, and she coordinates the maple-sugaring operation in the spring. She apprenticed at the evaporator of the master.

But back then, very little of this other stuff interested me. I was ski-racing regularly all winter long by fifth grade, and winning some by seventh. That was the year of my first big payday, when I won the Roland Peabody Race (a newspaper clipping of Katie Bishop and me still hangs in the Village Store in Franconia) and got a free season pass to Cannon. Peg didn't have to buy it for me that year; I was pulling my weight—skiing was paying off. And didn't that put an idea in my head.

It wasn't until high school that I showed serious promise on the piste. I'd always assumed I'd be a professional tennis or soccer player. I'd grown up at a tennis and soccer camp, so naturally these were the sports I excelled at. I was the state tennis champ in high school, made the varsity as a freshman. I barely made the ski team that year. But, being a kid, I figured that if I liked sports and did them well, that should be my job.

Every summer for the past ten years I've taught tennis to kids at Tamarack, and the most important thing I do for each student is get to know them. People are different, and I relate to them on that level. It's called rapport, and everything else flows from it.

I don't mean to criticize the public schools or their teachers, but I do object to the system they're caught up in—the one that puts control and discipline ahead of learning and life. Freedom wasn't invented in the 1960s, and living a wild, adventurous life wasn't created by reality television. They're elements the natural man can't happily live without. Don't take my word for it. Read Rousseau, read *Don Quixote*, go take a white-water canoe ride.

When I have children, they'll be homeschooled. Even if I have to do it myself. Outside of love and the essentials (food, water, shelter, and skis), it's the greatest gift you can give your kids. Besides, they have police in most schools now, and what kind of parent would I be if I packed my kids off to a place so treacherous that they need a cop on duty all the time? Sounds unsafe.

I'm on that ball!: 1978

*I'm on that one too:
1995*

Without homeschooling, I might not be the outdoorsman that I am, and I certainly wouldn't have been the Tasmanian devil on skis that I'd already become at age nine, when I started doing time. After the 2002 Olympics, the principal asked me to come to the school and speak to the kids, which I was happy to do.

It was a nice time, and the kids were great, but I left there with a hollow feeling in my belly. The same one that school had always given me. I wanted to tell the principal that the school had never met my needs when I was a kid, and that it could be worse now for all I knew; that my lasting impression of the public school I'd attended was how institutionalized and controlling it was, as if freedom were a pure abstraction that they taught in civics class, never expecting any of it to stick. I didn't tell him that, but wish I had, because maybe he's the kind of guy who'd do something about it.

When I was kid, I had little, if anything, to worry about. When I got to be eleven years old or so, I'd hang around downtown with my buddies who lived there in apartment buildings on the river, and when their parents got sick of feeding me, I'd call Jo to come get me.

All that was well and good, and life seemed pretty simple until 1992, when Peg died of brain cancer. I was sort of prepared. It's not like I hadn't known she was sick. It was a protracted illness, and hard to watch its progression. She was the toughest, bravest woman I've ever known. My mother, the other toughest, bravest woman I've ever known, cared for Peg right up to the end. She was surrounded by her family, and visited by scores of people whose lives she'd helped shape over the years. Typically unsentimental, Peg said that all the sympathy and emotion made it seem like a death march. She was glad to be with friends, and reminded in small ways of the full life she'd led, but when your imminent death is the elephant in the room that no one wants to mention, it's not exactly a tea party.

I didn't go to her funeral. I got as far as the church, but I couldn't go in. Luckily, I had my skateboard with me, so I just fooled around out in the parking lot of the United Church of Christ, while my family and friends went inside. I'd already said good-bye to Peg. I didn't need to do it again.

Jack had gone to live in the veterans' home in Tilton a few

years before that. When Peg got sick, she couldn't handle him any longer. Jack was a handful, a wanderer. He'd regressed to a very young age and liked to walk around looking at things. Following him could be tiring. At the VA home, they solved that problem by strapping him into a chair.

Woody's father, my grandfather Don, also had Alzheimer's. Woody's family lived on Lake Champlain in Burlington, Vermont, so we got to see quite a bit of them when I was a kid. My dad's folks, Don and Em, were different from Jack and Peg—more conventional, maybe a little conservative. It was good for us to get that balance in our lives from people we loved. It made us tolerant, and taught us a few manners. For instance, who knew that after being in the lake all day, you should wash your feet before you went into the house? Made no sense to me, but I did it.

Woody and his dad had issues. The medical school debacle, living in the woods, and most of the rest of Woody's adult life was a source of hard feelings and contention. But Alzheimer's mellowed Don, made him less judgmental in Woody's eyes, and gave him the ability to live in the moment.

Beefcake on the lake, 1983

When Don got sick he went down to Tennessee, where Woody and he put their relationship back together. After a while, Woody decided that my grandfather would be happier at Tamarack. There was room to roam, and a small town was a better place to cope with the logistics. As with Jack, Alzheimer's had made Don a wanderer; Nashville was a tad too urban for that kind of activity.

Once, before he'd moved down to Nashville with Woody, my grandparents had come over to Tamarack for a cookout, and Don had decided to borrow one of the other guests' cars. Everybody leaves their keys in the car around here, so he had his pick. He drove it all the way to Woodsville and stopped for an ice cream. When he got back in the car to leave, it was the wrong car, and he drove off again. Jo and her friend Irene, the car's owner, reported him missing, and the state police finally caught up with him in East Haverhill. So they drove over to pick him up, and then Jo dropped Irene off at the ice-cream stand to get her car.

It was clear that the responsibility of keeping my grandfather safe and out of trouble was too big a job for my grandmother; and that was when Woody decided to pitch in. Eventually, because no one was living in the cabin in the woods at the time, Woody and Holly moved my grandfather in and cared for him there.

To keep him clean, Woody and his friends built a beautiful stone-and-tile room with a tub in it, like a backwoods spa decontamination unit.

Then they just cut Don loose in the woods, as he and Jo had done with us. My grandfather wandered the forest, stuffed leaves and rocks down his pants, fell into the stream, and cried like a baby. He was like a little boy, and for the most part he enjoyed the latter days of his life. Woody got his closure somewhere in all that. He also got the undying respect of his own children, who watched it happen.

4

The Anti-Preppie

I attended Carrabassett Valley Academy, a northern Maine prep school that educates and develops nationally ranked skiers. From 1992 to 1995, CVA gave me a great education; in 2003 they gave me my diploma. There's a story to that.

This was my grand awakening to real competition—my first glimpse of how good I'd have to be just to get into the race. Before CVA, if I made it down the mountain without falling, I won. Generally, what you saw next to my name in the standings was either the number 1 or DNF, for Did Not Finish. Now I was training with some of the best young skiers in America, and I was having trouble.

So CVA was a great opportunity for me. It taught me to fake patience with rigid systems, and it quickly matured me enough to know that until I had a winning record, and therefore some power, I had to project the appearance of conformity, or at least camp in the vicinity of conventionalism. I had no intention of putting down roots in the land of do-as-I-say, but I needed to be an apt pupil of the old line and the pious if I expected to survive. Needless to say, my matriculation at CVA was not without incident.

I ended up there in the second semester of my freshman year in high school—not by chance, and not without a helping hand

from John Ritzo, the headmaster. John is married to one of my
mother's oldest friends, Patty Lawrence Ritzo. He taught at the
White Mountain School in Bethlehem, one town over from Franconia, for seven years when I was a kid. He also ran the ski program
there, and has known me since I was a baby. We ran into each
other quite a bit up at Cannon Mountain. I'd often tag along with
the WMS kids, skiing as fast as them when I was only seven years
old. John noticed this.

Patty Ritzo, me, and John at the 2002 Winter Games

One day when I was five years old and up at Cannon by myself,
I lost a mitten. It was cold, and my nose was snotty—I might have
been crying. I had a way of making my needs known. John led me
down to the lost and found, where we rescued an old mitten from
the box and my right hand from severe frostbite. I was appreciative
in a five-year-old's way. I said thanks, stopped sniffling, and headed
back outside to chase down the WMS guys and show them how to
ski.

John's interest in me didn't end there. When I began racing a
few years later, I saw him a lot—sometimes as a spectator, some-

times as a scout, sometimes as a judge. He was always supportive, and suitably impressed by my velocity. By the time I got to CVA, we hadn't seen each other in a while, but we were more than casually acquainted.

This was around the time I'd been jettisoned from the Franconia ski team. A friend of mine, Katie Bishop, was attending CVA, and John asked her one day what had happened to me. He hadn't seen my name in recent race results.

John pictured me languishing without direction, but by that time I was plenty busy, and back on the ski team. Still, John had it in his mind that to be noticed by the right people, I needed to hook up with something sanctioned and quantified. He also remembered that I could ski like a house on fire before I was old enough to tie my shoes.

He asked Patty to call my mother and suggest that I come over to CVA for an interview. Jo was dismissive at first, telling John that there was no way she could swing the tuition. John reassured her that if I was accepted, he would find a way to help pay the freight. For my part, I was excited at the prospect of getting out of town, going to a new place where I'd have a clean slate, and training with some full-time coaches. My racing buddy Patch Connors had gone to Burke Academy, over in Vermont, the year before. When he left, we were evenly matched—any given race was either of ours to win. But when he returned from Burke, he smoked me time after time. Damn, man, you got good, I told him. I wanted to be that good.

If Franconia is remote, then CVA is Brigadoon. It's located in the town of Carrabassett Valley, Maine, at the bottom of the access road to Sugarloaf/USA. The school is actually closer to the mountain than my house was to Cannon. Sugarloaf is similar to Cannon in that it's a short, sharp mountain covered in boilerplate, with wind some days that'll blow you back up the slope.

It's also a fancier operation than Cannon, with a hotel, condos, and even a brewpub. Cannon has more of an if-Stalin-had-skied feel to it. It's a state-owned operation, and none dare speak of change because it might cost something, and this being New Hampshire, that something is seldom in the bare-bones budget.

Sugarloaf has a quad lift and more ski space than Cannon, as well as a dedicated competition run for CVA students, including a downhill and super-G course named the Tote Road. My roommate, Worm, and I liked to make a Tote Road tuck run first thing in the morning—we called it a TR^2.

"Tote Road," by the way, refers to the oversized path loggers cut into the forest to haul the big logs out. All the slopes are named for logging there. Quaint, huh? Of course, the average logger can't afford a lift ticket these days, much less equipment, or even a day off from work to go skiing.

Worm almost bought it on one TR^2. It was a freaky morning, after a night of howling bad weather. Everything was so frozen over that Chip Cochrane, our coach, wasn't setting the downhill course and told us to bring only our slalom skis to the mountain. Worm had other ideas. He was sure a TR^2 would be fast and fun, and he was right.

The TR^2 was a warm-up for us, a way to set the tone for the day—fast and reckless. So we took our bullet right off the chair and charged down this course. It was icy conditions all around, and we were on our long boards traversing the slope in opposite directions, carving figure eights like the Blue Angels on snow. We knew the next pitch meant big air—we'd done this a hundred times before—so I hit it left, Worm went right, and all would have been great, except the grooming machine hadn't gotten to Worm's side of the course yet. Out of the corner of my eye I saw moguls the size of VWs, a minefield that Worm landed in at about sixty miles per hour. Unable to stop, I kept going.

I got to the bottom and waited, but it didn't take long for me to figure out that something was up. He should have been right behind me, and he wasn't anywhere in sight. I took off my skis and started hiking back up the mountain in my ski boots. Eventually I saw him all yard-saled and unconscious on the slope. He was coming back down when I reached him. Luckily there was somebody as crazy as us out on the Tote Road that day, and he was helping Worm down. Worm definitely had his bell rung. He was all glazy-eyed and uncoordinated; it was all we could do to get him off the mountain.

Worm and I remain close friends. He came to watch me race in Park City last November and showed up without a coat. It was twenty degrees out. Plus, he works in the energy industry now—

coal, nuclear, and petrochemicals—so I can't help but wonder about the long-term effects of that TR^2 bop on the noggin he took that day. Could account for a lot.

I can't say I liked CVA right off. It was a bit of a boot camp. It amused me to be off my home turf and out in the world among new people, and I felt for the first time that I was doing something purposeful with my skiing, that I'd elevated it from avocation to vocation. It was a quantum step up to the next order of performance, especially for a raggy-assed fourteen-year-old kid like me. That was the upside. The downside was the structure, the schedules, the be-here-and-there rush all the time. On bad days I felt like a tied-up dog; on good days I felt like a dog on a leash, out for a walk.

My first semester at CVA, in the winter of 1991, I couldn't swing the room, board, and tuition, so John Ritzo got creative. There was a day student named Sam Andersen; he and his brother, Woody, and mother, Paula, lived in a cabin a mile into the woods. That's a Formula One drag strip deeper into the forest than we were bivouacked back in Franconia. Paula had told John that if ever there was a deserving student who needed a place to live, she'd be happy to take him in. Since the Andersons' homestead was rustic like Turtle Ridge, John put the problem and solution together quickly, hooked me up, and I moved in. And there was the synchronicity of names: his brother had the same name as my dad, Woody, and my real first name is Samuel. So it seemed meant to be.

Paula didn't charge me anything—she's a generous person, a former teacher who cares deeply about kids, and she wanted to help. She also worked me harder than Jo ever managed to.

In the woods with the Andersens, I lived the same bucolic life I was accustomed to, and I knew the drill well. Getting to school meant snowmobiling the mile into Kingfield every morning in the winter (mountain biking in the warmer months), then catching a ride the rest of the way to school. The Ritzos lived in town, so John often gave us a lift. Some days we'd just hitchhike.

At the end of the day—after classes, after training, and after any additional academic work we had to do at the school, such as in the computer lab—we did the same thing in reverse. Catch a lift to John's, hop on a snowmobile, and head home through the forest.

We always had a lot of homework to do, at least a couple hours' worth a night—CVA is, after all, a college preparatory school. After CVA, Sam went to Bates College in Lewiston, Maine; he's now a stockbroker on Wall Street. I understand that the school has ramped up its academics even more since I left, which is a good thing, because there are only a handful of new spots on the U.S. Ski Team every year.

So it's smart to have a Plan B. I didn't. Even though things worked out better than anyone except me might have imagined, my best fallback positions were in professional soccer and tennis. Or, if it came to that, race-car driving. Sometimes you have to make sacrifices.

Once we were home at night—and home was every bit as beautiful as Tamarack—before we could hit the books, we had to hit the woodpile (some things never change), then help with dinner, and then help clean up (there are no automatic dishwashers a mile deep in the woods, not to mention plumbing or electricity). At about eight-thirty in the evening, we started our homework, reading and writing by kerosene lamps.

I'd never been what you'd call a homework fanatic, and I also might not have had the best study skills. But academics were never difficult for me. At CVA, however, the homework was copious, given the amount of time I had to do it, so I began to fall behind, a little further every day. That's "fall behind" given their objective standards—which, of course, they needed and I didn't. I was reading, writing, learning, skiing, sitting and thinking, and then thinking more, all the time. I spent a lot of time sitting in John and Patty Ritzo's living room, waiting for a ride, holding forth to anyone who'd listen on my newest idea about how to squeeze more speed out of my skis. I also ate all the kids' chocolate turtles, even though they tried hiding them.

I was learning and maturing. That's what's supposed to happen at this age. Unfortunately, my theories on education weren't of primary concern to anyone but me. Teachers seem to believe that maturation is a by-product of learning, and I think the opposite is true. They wanted me doing math, history, English, and geography, which was fine, but I was there to ski, and there are only so many hours in a day. You have to sleep during some of them.

Eventually, my grades slipped, my racing style was frowned

upon, and it wasn't long before I found myself in the headmaster's office, planted in a chair in the center of a circle. There, the headmaster, my teachers, and one or two others, including Paula, surrounded me and unloaded their displeasure with me, on me.

It took me by surprise. I was doing my best under the circumstances. And they all knew exactly what those circumstances were. It's not that CVA was less structured than the public school I'd been attending; actually, it was more so. The major difference, as I saw it, was that I couldn't skip school at CVA. Ever. I was there, they knew I was there, and if I wasn't in class somebody came looking for me. This was a new concept, and it took some getting used to. But it wasn't the real problem, and they knew it.

In the end, they told me to smarten up or I'd be out on my ear. It was some sort of academic intervention, I suppose. What was interesting was that not one of them asked me if there was anything I needed to succeed—such as a room on campus. My problem at the school was academics, but not because I lacked the gray matter to keep up; I needed more time. I needed a thirty-hour day.

One of their main complaints was my aloofness. I was a fourteen-year-old kid who'd grown up in the woods; I liked to ski and read fantasy novels. When I didn't know something, or care what the answer was, I'd shrug. It's a fairly universal gesture among boys. And that makes me aloof? According to some, I had such an attitude that they didn't know if they could help me at all. It was pretty harsh for a kid.

Paula had called my mother the week before and asked her what to do with me. She wanted to know what kind of direction I responded best to. "Directness," my mother told her. "If he's screwing up, let him know." This wasn't always a winning strategy to take with me, especially back then, but my mother didn't feel that Paula should have to coddle me.

Criticism generally beads up on my back and evaporates, but I didn't know where all the vitriol came from that day in the headmaster's office. I was the same person I'd always been, and they acted as if I were some academic terrorist, an agent provocateur sent to Sugarloaf/USA to put all their shorts in a knot. So I didn't take them too seriously. I thought, Screw 'em; I've got this figured out.

Educators sometimes miss the point that students, and not they, are at the center of the process. A teacher with no students can't function, has nothing to do, no purpose in life. But anyone who truly wants to learn something can do it without a teacher. The world is full of autodidacts, and I'm one. Too many teachers mistake themselves for pirate captains or drill sergeants when they should be simplifiers and expediters for the gathering of knowledge. It isn't about how they want to teach; it's about how I need to learn.

My first emotion when I left the room was anger—I'd wanted to cry while I was sitting there, but I'd held it in. I never back down, and I wasn't about to roll over for this crew. I quickly regained my composure and was tranquil again. I refocused to maintain custody of what was truly important to me. I knew that if I was to ever get anywhere, it'd be on my own. That was clear. Other people are entitled to their agendas, and I might or might not be included, so I'd come to expect nothing from them. All my short life I'd weighed how badly I wanted something against how hard I was willing to work for it. I'd simply continue on.

The lesson they taught me that day in their gotcha circle jerk was that it's important to at least appear to do what's expected of you. And sometimes that entails actually doing it. You can't fake everything. I know this now and I didn't know it before CVA: people in authority will not be ignored or seriously challenged without consequences. This is what high school taught me. This is why when a traffic cop pulls you over, you kiss his ass to avoid getting a ticket. So it was a useful lesson—not pleasant, but useful.

I must have been more shaken by the gauntlet incident than I remember. Paula was there, and appalled. Her presence in the room may have been what stopped me from telling them to all go fuck themselves. She agreed with them in some ways, but disliked their methods; she wanted to do something, but not that. The next day she returned to CVA and body-slammed John Ritzo for orchestrating such a crude Cultural Revolution–type lynching. It might have seemed like a good idea at the time, but it had everything to do with their frustration with me, and nothing to do with my difficulties.

I'm sure the Inquisition sat me down that day with my better interests in mind, and that they were convinced that it would put me on the straight and narrow. And maybe in the end it did help me out. But in my mind, educators need to chill and not take shit personally—especially from prepubescent boys. I mean, honestly: count to ten, take a breath, try to remember what it was like to be a kid, and relax. Despite what it feels like sometimes, you're a teacher, not a prison guard.

A few years later, during an Olympic slalom race, I skied backward and uphill. A bad case of misdirection. I could have won that race, maybe should have won that race, but instead I totally boned it in front of maybe two billion people watching on television. But it didn't bother me nearly as much as the tongue-lashing I took that morning at CVA.

In fairness to everyone else, the school was close quarters—living, eating, training, teaching—and my nonconformity, or maybe my low heart rate, got on some people's nerves. The school is a former ski lodge, so it's not exactly spacious. (Plans for a new campus are, as they say, under way.) Downstairs there are classrooms, some offices, a couple of couches in the lobby that everyone jockeys for, and the cafeteria. Upstairs there are a few more offices and the boys' and girls' dorms. I was used to intimate living space, and comfortable with people in the house. So I was cool with it.

It wasn't only the academic side of the CVA equation that found my performance lacking. The coaches were underwhelmed by my results, my style, my attitude, and even the sport I'd chosen. One told me I'd never do squat in a real race, that I'd already maxed out on any gains I'd ever make with my backseat driving and hokey-pokey dance down the mountain. So that was all a real confidence booster and well worth the price of admission.

Then they hit me with the biggest truckload of bullshit I'd ever heard . . . they wanted me to become a snowboarder. A snowboarder! Hey, why not a frickin' sex change while I'm at it? They tempted me with equipment deals (at the time, my best equipment hookup was a two-for-one deal with K2), but I wasn't buying it. I was a ski racer.

I'm not saying I'd never been on a snowboard; in fact, I was pretty hot. That's why they were on me to switch. At the end of the season I decided to enter a snowboard race against the best specialists in the Northeast, and I came in second. But despite the fact that Karl Schranz has called me a snowboarder on skis, boarding just didn't appeal to me.

Not that I regret my brief fling with snowboards—they showed me the beauty of the parabolic cut and gave me the idea for the shaped racing ski. Way back when we were kids, Noah and I tried to figure out how to ski on two snowboards. It wasn't until I pressed George Tormey, a K2 rep, for a shaped-ski prototype that I actually skied on two skinny snowboards. It was a revelation, like the difference between a $99 Kmart bike and an $8,000 handmade mountain rocket.

George once said I skied "like a cat thrown across an icy driveway." This was not a compliment, but he came to realize that mine was an equipment problem. I ski straight, even when I'm going around a gate, because that's where all my speed derives from. Back in the day, conventional skis had no side cuts, which meant rolling from one edge to the other was nearly impossible. So to make it roll, I'd bow the ski by leaning back on it and rip into the turn. That's what the coaches called "backseat driving," a bad habit they tried their hardest to break me of. To them, I was a puppy peeing on the rug, while in my mind, I was an innovator.

That next summer, between my freshman and sophomore years at CVA, my uncle Mike gave me more hours on the job at NetCo so I'd have more money for school, plus a dollar bonus for every hour I worked that summer. It still wasn't enough, so he lent me the difference. And along with gifts from Peg, Mickey and Marge Libby, and others, I got there with gear and five bucks in my pocket. CVA managed to find me a room in the dorm in the spring of tenth grade, and life was sweet. The sun was out, the crocuses were up, and I was number one on the tennis team. Then I won the state tennis championships, which was sort of like being the best breakfast cook at a supper club, but it made them feel partially compensated for all the falling I'd done racing that winter.

My sophomore year was smoother, less of a shock to the system than the year before. I decided that CVA was where I wanted to be, and that I was going to do whatever was necessary to stay there. But my skiing was iffy as shit. Despite growing four inches that year, I was still skinny and small, no match for most of CVA's skiers. Some excellent racers were there then: Forest Carey, Josh Silver, and Josh Pike, to name a few—guys who were good.

Never mind stacking up against them; I wasn't even good for my age group. In terms of results, the skiers at CVA were way above my level. These were serious kids who'd listened to their coaches and done what they were told for years. As a result, they were technically excellent skiers, exemplars of a certain classical style. I, on the other hand, was blazing my own trail and hadn't gotten far yet.

I'd bulked up a bit over the summer before my junior year, and I'd gotten much stronger. I was heavy into leg presses in those days. But I was still under six feet, and only about 165 pounds. Six years later, I was six foot two, 215 pounds, which means my body mass increased by 30 percent during that time. Those were my Wonder Bread years.

My gear was coming together then, too; I was starting to get better equipment from K2, my ski sponsor, and it showed in my results. A guy I'd known from childhood, Todd Simones, and I skied some Eastern Cup races that year. He trained down in Waterville Valley. I got a first and second that day at Loon, and Todd got a first and second too. I'd never been so evenly matched with anyone in my life. He made the Junior Olympics; I got screwed by a whack-job coach, which I'll explain in detail in another chapter. Anyway, I went home and smoked some pot and felt bad for myself for a day or two. Then I shook it off and got back in the race. Years later, Todd showed up as a student at CVA. He and his brother Tyler were hot racers, big strong kids, good guys with nice gear.

That winter, I won the 1994 Maine Alpine Racing Association (MARA) slalom championship, which wasn't like bagging an FIS race in Europe, but it wasn't bad.

The same year, Paul Fremont-Smith, who's a great benefactor to American ski racing in general and to me in particular, gave me some money to go to Europe for some FIS races. Talk about an eye-opener. I'd gone to Mexico once when I was twelve, to the beach in Tulum. This was different.

I'd never been anyplace where ski racing was an A-list event. When I was a kid, as far as I could tell, ski racing in the United States was a bit more popular than three-dimensional chess, but way behind bingo and lawn bowling. Now here I was in Europe, where World Cup skiing was a reason to get up in the morning for a lot of people. This was culture shock.

And those races that winter were sick. I'd typically start around 80th position, sometimes in the 90s. Hogan, one of the guys with us, started 105th in one race. I barely made it down the mountain some of the time; usually the course had been destroyed by the time we tipped off, and the g-force I was pulling, skiing on what amounted to broken frozen asphalt, had my arms and legs going in opposite directions. I don't think they'd seen too many skiers like me. I got a lot of sideways looks and disapproving head shakes; I saw old people bless themselves when I walked by them after a race. But my mom and everyone back home were fairly impressed by my European vacation. It wasn't like I cured cancer or stupidity or anything. They were all just happy I was enjoying life.

I didn't know it at the time, but guys who race European FIS races might also be running the World Cup, and winning. Now, if there is an FIS race on a mountain I'm unfamiliar with but know I'll be racing World Cup on sometime, I might jump in it. FIS races in Europe are a trial by fire; I highly recommend the experience.

So the FIS crew was a tough one and we got paddled on very badly most of the time. But I took sixth in a slalom in Anzere, Switzerland, which was a nice boost for the home team. I was encouraged to do it the way I wanted to; in my mind, concrete results verified my instincts, made me feel like a prophet of skiing. I kept those thoughts to myself, of course. But my first European vacation cracked the world open for me.

In general, we got smoked so bad in Europe that it sent us back to school with a renewed vigor to train and win. It never occurred to us to say, Hey, these guys are killing us, maybe we ought to start studying for the SATs. We were stoked by seeing how good you can get. We wanted to be the best.

I played soccer at CVA, too. We had a coach, but I was the de facto; out on the field, I ran the show. I don't want to sound like an asshole, but soccer is a fast sport and needs somebody on the pitch calling the shots. I'd been apprenticing at Mike's soccer camp since I was ten years old, and playing in the men's North Country league since I was a kid, too. I know plenty about how to get the ball down the field.

That was a damn good soccer team. We also played hockey—serious hockey, not to mention world-class wally-ball. Naturally, I continued to play tennis. And intramural basketball. I bet CVA was the only ski academy in the world with four guys who could stuff the ball.

I grew pretty attached to the people around me. It was a tight group of good friends. I'd known Worm since we'd skied PeeWees against each other—me for Cannon, him for Waterville Valley. The rest of us, including Kirsten Clark, were like a ski posse in the Great White North, but we left competition on the mountain, and never let it be a wedge between us personally. To lord your talent or success over anyone, especially a friend, is as lame as it gets. We had respect for one another. We also had an underground social life that rivaled *Hogan's Heroes*.

Worm had reached puberty at about nine years old, so with cash money to spend, he could always procure what we needed—which was usually big plastic half gallons of Black Velvet and some cheap beer.

The living arrangements at school were sort of mini–town houses; three or four people shared a big living room downstairs and a loft sleeping space upstairs. It was nice. Dirty most of the time, slovenly even, but a pleasant arrangement. We'd usually host the parties in our room, and they were numerous. It didn't need to be a weekend, or somebody's birthday, or even a rainy day. We were all just so damn happy that we'd break out the party hats for absolutely nothing.

Each loft had a skylight or, as we came to think of them, a party door. People would wait until lights-out, then hoist themselves up through their party door, silently straddle along the ridge of the three-story building, and drop down through our party door. Somebody might score a big box of chips, or some other munchies or mixers, and we'd have adult beverages. Boys, girls, intoxicating snacks—all the ingredients for major fun except one: noise.

There were dorm parents, after all, and they'd get wise to fifteen or twenty people in our room kicking it. So we had "silent parties." We'd play cards, quietly belch our Black Velvet mixed with Dr Pepper, click on the strobe light, and dance in the stone-cold quiet. It was like watching television with no volume or a music video for the deaf. I dug it a lot. It was a different experience for my friends, but I'd grown up without electricity. I could party on the down-low-tech, no problem.

The nightly mime-rave anti-raged on for a good long time, and nobody was the wiser. Not until, that is, we transgressed the first principle of a charmed life: never, ever break more than one law at a time. But we couldn't help it. We were emboldened by our nearly effortless hoodwinking of the adults around us, and then tempted by riches well beyond our abilities to resist.

It started one day at lunch, down at the brewpub at Sugarloaf. We watched as a forklift shuttled boxes back and forth from a cleared area in the woods out behind the brewery. What could that be all about? I asked Worm. He shrugged and suggested we find out.

That night, after lights-out, we got our flashlights, snuck out of the dorm, and bushwhacked through the woods to the rear of the brewpub. In a small, stumpy clearing were two tractor trailers side by side, like giant silver fish beached from the Great Flood. Okay, we thought, what's in here?

I unlatched the door of one—it wasn't locked—and swung it open wide to look inside. Worm held the flashlight, illuminating a wall of unmarked boxes of a familiar size and shape. They towered over us from floor to ceiling. Freeze-dried pub fries? I wondered. Or a whole lot of individual ketchup servings?

I stepped up onto the trailer's bumper, slid a brown box off the top of the pile, and pried it open. My eyes lit up, my mind reeled. Holy shit, I whispered. Look at all the cases—full cases of bottles. I looked again into the truck and then at the other truck and realized that between them they contained thousands and thousands of bottles. I felt like Indiana Jones in the Temple of Beer.

I carried a couple of cases on my head; Worm carried four. We ferried case after case over to the rear of the school; other people filled their knapsacks, cargo-pants pockets, and tams with bottles and smuggled them up to our room. Soon we were dancing in the dark; the small whooshes of caps popping and empty bottles tinkling together made the silent party just a little noisier. This went on nightly for about a month.

We thought we were pretty clever pilferers. When we liberated beer from the trucks, we cleared a tunnel to the back, and took it from there. And that covered our tracks for a while. Eventually, however, we'd taken enough beer so that it became obvious to the people at the brewpub that something was up. Of course, it could have been anyone swiping the stuff, but it didn't take Hercule Poirot to investigate the possibility that the hundred or so teenagers who lived less than a quarter mile through the woods were somehow involved. Plus, the tracks in the snow that led from the beer trucks to the back door of the dorm were a clue they couldn't ignore.

I first learned the jig was up when Worm dragged me out of bed one afternoon. I was napping; he was frantic, near panic. "We've got five minutes to get down to the kitchen," he said. This didn't make a whole lot of sense to me, or to the girl I was napping with. "Five minutes!" he said again, this time holding up five fingers, as if that would make me understand. "They're searching the rooms and everybody has to be in the kitchen in five minutes." This time he said it slowly, and it began to sink in.

Nonetheless, I said, "Dude, I'm naked, get out of here." But then I looked hard at the thirty cases of empties stacked up against the wall, and the problem became clearer to me. We considered putting them up on the roof, through the party door, but we were down to three minutes of working time and would have needed an hour to pull that off.

My mind was foggy, which meant a brainstorm was rolling in. We were running out of time, so I concocted a bold and imperfect solution. I pulled my dresser away from the wall, picked up a ski pole and smashed the plaster, dug it out with my fingers, and smashed it again. Worm quickly got hip and joined in, beating on it with his fists. We lay waste to that wall right down to the studs. Then we filled the dresser drawers with the demolition debris and threw clothes on top of it. Worm handed me bottles and I stacked and stuffed them into the hole in the wall. It was beginning to seem like a good idea. Finally, we slid the dresser back, and it looked as good as new.

Impressed as hell with our ingenuity, we surrendered to the kitchen just in time for formation. We all waited there until it was time for our room to be ransacked. Finally, we went up with our interrogator, expecting to stand around and shrug and shake our heads and say, See, we told you there was nothing in here. We were ready.

But it didn't go like that. He didn't even poke around the living room; he just stormed up the stairs, walked across the room directly to the dresser, and pulled it away from the wall. Therein lay the telltale beer bottles, and we were busted. How he figured it out, I'll never know. Was there a homing device in one of the bottles? Was it the plaster dust all over Worm's shoes? Maybe it just wasn't as clever a trick as I'd thought.

They had the goods on us, and the shit soon hit the fan. You'd have thought we were making pipe bombs or sacrificing virgins instead of having some good old-fashioned fun. They sat me down and asked for the truth, unvarnished and complete. Okay, I thought. In my experience, people often ask for it straight, but they seldom really want it that way. So, as an experiment, that's exactly how I gave it to them—what we did, how much, and how often. And also that we did it all until two A.M. They nearly died.

Somebody said, "But you're at the six o'clock run every morning . . ." They couldn't conceive of our stamina. We were sizzling, hyperenergized eighteen-year-old athletes; too bad there were only twenty-four hours in a day, because we could have easily packed in more fun and games.

They knew damn well how boring it could be up there near the Arctic Circle. What did they think we were doing—going to bed at nine o'clock every night? Maybe they did. But they never assumed anything ever again.

I don't know—maybe they felt that if it had been that easy for us, then they were our unwitting partners in the silent parties and the Great Beer Heist. For whatever reason, we never got any double-secret probation or anything. Not that I knew about. Given the circumstances, they treated us rather humanely. Worm and I had to replaster the wall and stack a bunch of cordwood, but that was it. Even today I can do that in my sleep. So it was all definitely worth it. And if we'd just fessed up in the first place, we could have saved ourselves a plastering job. Live and learn.

Things have changed at CVA since then. I suppose it's because everyone likes to believe that the world has changed, that it's more

*Skiing onto the
U.S. Ski Team,
1996*

dangerous and less predictable. I'm not sure that's entirely true; the world is as it has been for my entire life. For obvious reasons, Americans are more aware of it now. So among other things, they're on their kids about every little thing. Kids these days don't have the time to get into trouble—which, if you ask me, is a huge hole in their educations when you consider how much you can learn from a fully formed fuckup.

Plus, at CVA, the essential elements of our high crimes are gone—the beer trucks are locked, razor-wired, and patrolled by mercenaries, and the girls live in a completely different building, a half mile away. It's like the Taliban came to town.

Despite being a reprobate and a corrupter of youth, I was becoming a golden boy on the piste. On March 12, 1995, I had more than an inkling that I was going to do well that day. I could smell it, feel it on my skin. It was the National Junior Championships—I'd finished eighth the day before in the downhill, and ninth a few days before that in the super-G. But this was slalom, and I was wearing my new hourglass skis. I told my coach, Chip, that I thought I could win it. Never one to discourage a confident attitude, he smiled and nodded encouragingly. But I'm not sure he believed me. There may have been better skiers there that day, but I was the fastest racer.

A year later, I took three golds and a silver at the Junior Nationals. And on March 26, 1996, at the National Championships at Sugarloaf—which is sort of the *Star Search* for ski racers, and the

Loving the podium at the Junior Champs, 1996

quickest route to the U.S. Ski Team—I skied third in the slalom and nailed my audition with the national team.

I didn't own a speed suit, so I wore a cheap cross-country deal that I'd bought wholesale from the ski shop in Franconia. It really wasn't much more than a Halloween costume. It looked like red long underwear, and by that point in the season, the crotch was duct-taped together. During that race, on a particularly wide gate, I blew it out completely. Talk about a wardrobe malfunction. I'm uncomfortable enough on the podium without my nasty bits show-ing, so I had a jacket tied around my waist and looked like a grunge ski racer.

Twenty years to the day before this, my uncle Mike had won the same race at Sugarloaf. It was a big day for the family both times. By U.S. Ski Team rules, the top three finishers at Nationals get a berth on the development squad. One was mine; I'd made a career quantum leap.

My placing took many people by surprise—frankly, because I was seldom a good bet to finish. But I did, and I was fast. Now the ski team honchos were asking themselves, Who is this guy? Was this a fluke?

That race, on my adopted mountain, wasn't my last chance to make it happen, but it was cutting it close. I was eighteen; I hadn't bothered to apply to college because I'd made the decision to join the U.S. Ski Team (without consulting anyone in a position to make that happen, other than myself). At the time, I felt that a fallback plan, while a good idea, would be a dent in my armor. No options, no excuses, never complain, never explain, just make it happen, and so I did. I can be a clutch player. And I can ski up my own ass. It depends on the day. People say I skied onto the team, and my question is: How else are you supposed to get onto the U.S. Ski Team? I'd be offended if people said I waltzed on—or worse, that I snuck on—but skied onto the team sounds like an honest day's work.

I skied a NorAm Cup in early April that year at Mount Bache-lor and got fifth in the giant slalom. It sealed the deal with the team for me; at least I didn't look like a one-race wonder to them anymore. Now I was a two-race wonder.

Despite my becoming a top skier, making friends, and maturing, CVA was not an entirely joyful time in my life. I had a few bumps in the road with the administration, but nothing like the blanket party they'd thrown me my first year. Until my senior year.

As many boarding schools do, CVA holds monthly birthday dinners. It's a way to recognize everyone's birthday, because we're a bunch of kids away from home and need to feel like someone gives a damn. We eat and dance, and it's always a very good time. In my senior year, I was headed to just such an affair, wearing my finest plaid three-piece suit and a pair of beach sandals. It was a look. People (my mother among them) will tell you that I'm not much of a sartorially minded guy. But the truth is that I have fashion guts, and I was showing them that night. Go to any clothes store that caters to the under-thirty crowd, and the jeans and shirts on the racks will look like the last guy who wore them slept in a freight car from New York to Anchorage. I invented that look.

But this was prep school in northern Maine, not a photo shoot in SoHo. My aesthetic sense went underappreciated at times, and I'm afraid this was one of them. As I approached the dance, hearing and seeing my friends inside made me anticipate fun, which got my head bobbing and my feet moving.

Then she was there, as if from nowhere—my English teacher, hovering at the door, a stygian dog waiting to pounce. She looked down at my feet as if I'd stepped in shit and ordered me back to the dorm. "Put some socks on," she told me. She was very dismissive of my fashion sense.

Ever the obedient and cheery pupil, I did as I was told. I went upstairs to the dorm, put on a nice pair of fuzzy wool socks under my sandals, and returned to the dinner. She stopped me on my way back in, and I could see from the look in her eyes that she was angry. Not miffed, not annoyed, not weary of my smart-ass attitude, but actually angry. She blocked the door with her arm and shook her head. I was confused. She'd said to put some socks on, which I'd done, and I told her so.

"I meant put some shoes on," she said. Well, what the hell, I thought. You have to be more precise with your language, say what you mean, teach. She was a stickler about language. "Wicked," for instance, meant bad, not good, in her lexicon. Figure that out. And to us, "phat" and "stoopid" were compliments, but to her, they were Orwellian. Our Newspeak was ironic, and sometimes snotty, but not sinister. We spoke a prep school patois, the language of the extracurricularly oppressed.

She spoke in a very deliberate manner, used only approved adjectives and adverbs, and made everyone around her sit up just a little straighter. Fine. I can do old school. I can speak like Prince Charles if you need me to. Still, she was outraged at my attire. This struck me then, and still does, as unnecessarily uptight. She ordered me back up to the dorm to put some shoes on.

I can follow orders when necessary; I'm a team player. But I don't truckle, so don't expect submission. I kiss nobody's ass. Everybody meets me at least halfway or they get nowhere. The first piece of paper this teacher had passed out to us in September was a list of "Classroom Expectations," number one of which was: "Appropriate language, behavior, and dress." Again, I don't want to put too fine a point on it, but we were standing in the hall outside the cafeteria at the time, not in the classroom. And why should her sense of what looks and feels good supersede mine?

So I said, and I admit this might have been a smidge over the top, "You must be fuckin' kidding me." There was a six- or seven-year period in my life when this was my standard response to everything my ears couldn't believe.

Her eyes bugged and she bristled, her face flushed red. I can only imagine how tingly she felt as her autonomic nervous system kicked in for a fight. You'd have thought that she'd never heard that word before, and maybe she hadn't. I don't know. I didn't actually mean to say it to her; it was more of an editorial comment on the moment.

Anyway, the distinction between insult and exasperation was lost on her, and she ejected me, banished me, threw my ass out of there. And that was just the beginning.

Monday morning, John Ritzo had me on the carpet, and I admitted to my part in the whole ugly deal. I was troubled by how little John seem to care that she'd given her orders so inexactly, then made it my fault when they weren't carried out the way she'd envisioned.

Not only that, but in her report to the headmaster she said I'd used a "four-letter word." I realize she taught English and not math, but "fuckin'" has six letters, or seven if you count the dropped *g*. I told this to John, but he was unmoved, and insisted I apologize. He walked me down to her classroom.

I looked her in the eyes and said, "I'm wicked sorry." As things played out, I can now see that the left-handed apology did little to improve my situation. This was just a bump in the road compared to what was coming.

Despite our tensions, she taught, and I learned. I don't want to leave anyone with the impression that I didn't get anything from our paramilitary-style relationship, because I did. I wrote this poem under her tutelage:

> *The leaves scattered on the ground,*
> *Quilting the moss and dirt,*
> *They are the life of trees.*
> *Now on the ground they are pointless,*
> *Dead and dry, they leave the tree lifeless,*
> *The trees stand somber and still,*
> *Staring blankly at the sky,*
> *Their eyes are closed to me as*
> *I run by hundreds, thousands of*
> *Trees in this rigid,*
> *Depressing state.*

Whether my "depressing state" was Maine or ennui brought on by too much *Ethan Frome,* I don't recall. But I would like to point out that I was seventeen when I wrote that and an upbeat guy, sometimes to a fault. I've always been comforted by nature on an elementary level, especially its deciduous beauty.

I owed this teacher, as we all did, a senior thesis. You know what this is like: a big writing project, with many built-in steps— thesis statement, note cards (a minimum of two hundred!), outline, rough draft, first draft, second draft, third draft. . . . It was all designed to short-circuit the impulse to procrastinate, thus taking the fun out of schoolwork.

I thought I'd compensate for the rigid schedule with an interesting topic. My title, "Sex and Violence as Narrative Practice in Toni Morrison's *Beloved* and *The Bluest Eye,*" was meant to keep me on task. I was, after all, seventeen and living in the sticks and got horny reading cookbooks.

Actually, my English teacher had assigned the topic; why, I do not know. No one else got their topic dictated to them. Just me. I was reading Toni Morrison when I should have been listening to Jim Morrison. Other kids were studying skateboarding (considered a cultural stretch into unknown intellectual territory for a skier) and writing about it, or about fly-fishing or What-I-did-on-my-upper-middle-class-summer-vacation or other can't-lose topics. But I was somehow saddled with a foray into psychosexual literary criticism. It was a challenge and a half.

I did the work, read the books, thought hard about it all, and, given my limited exposure to the world, did what I thought was a pretty good job. On the due date, after months of drafts, meetings, notes, and readings and rereadings of the text, I passed in my final draft, twenty pages of my best badly spelled work, which she branded "Unsatisfactory." Not, reportedly, up to my level of achievement. Her comments in the margins said things like "Reword to make a point" and "Odd statement." I was a seventeen-year-old boy who'd grown up in the Great White North; I'm not sure what insights on race, sex, and violence she'd expected from me.

She informed me that she was going to flunk me if I didn't call some expert she knew and interview him for my paper. Have a chat with some dweeb who'd done his doctorate in sexual metaphor? No thanks. This was payback, her exerting undue influence over my life and education, so I refused. And, true to her word, she flunked me—or I flunked me, however you want to look at it. Neither of us would concede defeat, although I took a bigger hit than she did. She said I flunked for outstanding work. No shit, I thought; everything I do is outstanding.

Anyway, not long after that she left teaching and went into politics full-time. Big surprise.

CVA sent my diploma to my mother last fall, and last Christmas she gift-wrapped it and sent it to me in Austria. CVA didn't have to do it, though I was a good student. They might have done something years earlier, but to intervene with a teacher who had overstepped her bounds would have violated her academic freedom, I suppose. This is the same academic freedom that encouraged my Asian studies teacher to assign essay questions such as "What is China doing in the manufacturing sector that is pissing off the United States so much?"

In the margin of my paper on China (which I began, "The diversity of China is totally apparent") he wrote, "You have some interesting thoughts, but you throw out a lot of non-factual bullshit." The comment strikes me as a redundancy more apparent than China's diversity. Maybe he was being ironic.

I was trying to navigate through the uptight and the laid-back. Schools spend a lot of time teaching teachers about different kinds of students, but no time at all teaching students about the different kinds of teachers. You're on your own, kid.

Maybe giving me my diploma was CVA's acknowledgment of my academic freedom. Or maybe they want some help with their capital campaign for that new campus. Hard saying, not knowing. Either way, CVA can legitimately refer to me as an "alumnus," which is defined as someone who simply attended a school, not necessarily a graduate. I'm glad I went there.

I have many personal theories, such as one concerning the many similarities between skiing fast and driving fast in the snow, and another about how underachievers rise to the top of bureaucracies, but I have very few private theories. If I've worked something out, I spread it around, like it or not. For instance, I used to use PowerBars inside my ski boots, behind my calf, to shim me up. I'd put them in my boots while I was still inside the lodge, where it was warm, and let them mold to my shape; by the time I got up the mountain they'd have firmed up again, nice and high in the back. Worked like high-test gas. I told everybody about it because I thought they should try it. I even told my coach, Chip Cochrane, that he should recommend it to the team. He didn't. But that was then. I swear, now if I told people to wear their underwear on their heads for extra stability and speed, you'd see lots of tightie-whities stretched over helmets plummeting down the course.

Chip was a great coach, as well as my academic adviser; he ran a shuttle-diplomacy mission for me with the dreaded English teacher, trying to iron out our dispute. But with no luck. When he first met me, I was a kid claiming a new technique that required a lot of falling in training, and a lot of DNFs in races. Right, kid, whatever you say. It was not the stuff that makes coaches happy. But he could see that I was different, that I didn't want to be Tomba or Stenmark, as everyone else did—I wanted people to mention my name in the same breath with theirs someday. I was an innovator and a pain in the ass. These, in my mind, are inseparable traits.

It never occurred to me that it took balls to buck the conventional wisdom—especially in a sport where the tried-and-tested method of nearly everything was a long-settled matter. I did it the only way it was fun for me, and that went back to ditching skiing lessons when I was five. But Chip always gave me enough rope to hang myself, and as far as anyone could tell, that's what I was doing. I knew better. I make the gains in my game long before I can prove it to someone standing on the sidelines. You'd have to get inside my head to believe it.

5

Go Fast

I won my first ski race at the age of ten. It was at Waterville Valley, New Hampshire, about five exits south of Franconia Notch, just a fun run of some sort. My uncle Mike took me down. It was a slalom race, and I cleaned house on that bunch of fifth graders. And then it came time to stand on the podium, and I couldn't do it. I was too shy. And perplexed, frankly, about why it was necessary. The race was over; we all knew who'd won, so it was time to go home. That's how I saw it. I still do. But Mike made me get up there; he said it was part of racing, a part you couldn't avoid. And he was right about that.

In 2003, after I bagged the giant slalom at Park City and ended America's twenty-year abstinence from winning a World Cup race at home, the guys who finished second and third—both Austrians, the Spartan warriors from the birthplace of World Cup ski racing—lifted me up off the podium, onto their shoulders, and carried me around. They meant it as a great compliment, and it was, but all the pomp makes me uncomfortable. I felt like the Elephant Man on display. I like to do my thing and get in and out with as little notice as possible.

The Austrians are serious about ski racing. So they dominate.

Racing Cannon Mountain, 1989

It's common for four of the top five racers every year to be Austrians. To compare ski racing in Austria to the NFL or baseball doesn't do it justice. People aren't just ski fans; it's a sport they participate in, men and women, young and old.

The Austrian team was the first to use objective time trials, which means that everybody on the A, B, and C squads races time trials before every event. It's more than good practice; it's a real race to determine who's going to be wearing a World Cup bib that weekend, to find the fastest guys in the world that week. The roster usually won't vary much, but it does change. The U.S. team started using objective time trials just before I joined in 1996, and they proved to be a new path to success for guys like me. The old-school come-up-through-the-ranks approach was over. It was more like, What have you done for me lately?

Every kind of ski coach and ski racer will tell you that time and speed—all that they do to decrease the former and increase the latter—are what counts. Nothing else. And they're right about that.

So now everybody runs objective time trials, and those with the fastest times race. The reason this works is that überathleticism is an unstable cocktail of talent, health, outlook, and anything else that affects performance; it's understood that somebody skiing this week may not be the guy skiing next week. That's how I rose from unknown quantity to World Cup racer so quickly, completely skipping my apprenticeship on the Europa Cup circuit. I had world-class times in training and time trials, and that was all I needed.

Fast is good—I like speed the way some people like chocolate—but I asked myself, at some irreversible point in my skiing career, Why not tennis, or soccer, or hockey? They're all sports I love, and frankly, there was a time when I had more talent in some of them than I did in skiing. Plus, when it comes to tennis, think about it: warm venues, a single piece of gear to fuss with, not a whole lot of crashing through snow fences. On balance, a much more appealing proposition.

Skiing is what we did for fun, and fun was king. The dorkiest kid in Franconia (which might have been me for a while) was relatively slick on a pair of boards. Everyone up here is. You'd go crazy if you weren't. Still, skiing the East, like surfing the Atlantic, is a challenge many are simply not cut out for.

At first I thought I became a skier because winter lasts a lot longer than summer in the White Mountains, and I skied by default. But I know now that it's the ball-knocking speed, the rime in my face, the slap of the gates across my bruised shins—that's what appeals to me about ski racing.

I love the gestalt of skiing—the integration of biology, technology, and psychology to excel at something that's over long before you can soft-boil an egg. The freedom, the expression, the do-or-die will to win, the high-charged physical and mental challenge, the obscurity, the duplicity, the objectivity, and, of course, the speed. In tennis, only the ball goes fast.

Truth be told, I had something to prove in skiing. Coming up, there was a lot of negative energy around me, telling me I couldn't, telling me I shouldn't. I wanted to fill that space back in with some positive achievement and, if possible, serve up a little crow.

I could never be too serious about a sport that's heavily coach-driven. I'd have to fit into a mold, perform a task, and always play that role to have success. Sorry; I need to step out now and then. And if my crew isn't racking up team points the way the Austrians are, I can still take some private satisfaction in my wins, losses, near wins, and gains.

Just as important, skiing provides a lot of downtime. Six months out of the year, I'm free to do what I want. I'm free as a bird in an extremely large cage. I don't mean to imply that I'm not free to do what I want during the season; I'm always weighing the balance between what I have to do and what I want to do. I'm actually quite good at squeezing as much fun out of a day as humanly possible. It's not a special talent—it's my life's work.

I can use my time off exactly as I please. Ski racing isn't like bike racing, which requires you to race and train and do practically nothing else. To be competitive with the best guys in the world, either you're on your bike six hours a day, every day, including Christmas, or you're doing performance-enhancing drugs. In skiing, you need to train, and to have an unshakable commitment to winning, but you can also have a life outside all that—warm summer days and hammocks, friends, family, cold beer, chicken on the grill, fast cars—that's what I'm talking about.

I also need a sport without limitations. When coming down the mountain on a pair of boards, I'm restrained by the law of gravity—the friction burn between ski and snow—and nothing else. Where I take all that power is up to me.

Consider bowling. I bowl at a place in Innsbruck where on Wednesday nights they shut off all the lights and use glow-in-the-dark balls. Every strike you hit when there's a colored pin up front gets a round of shots for your table. As fun as it is, once you've hit 300 points, what do you do next? Become an extreme bowler? Doing a 720 and then bowling a strike might be interesting, but probably not practical for most people. So you just keep bowling 300 over and over, and it feels less good each time. For me, that has all the makings of a shallow and doomed relationship.

Despite the downside, skiing is as fast as a human can go without mechanical assistance. I like that, and it's something to work with. I always knew my technique would develop if I could just practice it enough. But what does practice really mean? It means getting bludgeoned by gates, booting out, plowing up the course with your face, catapulting ass-backward through snow fences, all on a daily basis. It's a full-time job. I couldn't be a casual skier and prove anything to anybody, not even to myself. I had to join the national team.

Nothing in top-level competition comes easily. In the progression from J5 to J1 (junior racing eight to eighteen years of age—the road to the Junior Olympics), the average skier can shave 20 seconds off his or her time. That's seven or eight years of race training, so you'd expect some gains. But it's not that 20 seconds that makes the difference. It's the last .05, then the last .01.

My first year on the team, I missed getting cut by one guy. The next year, I showed them my real chops, my speed, and my occasional ability to finish. They wanted me to be a racer they could be comfortable with. It worked in my favor. Quota spots—the number of racers a team is allowed to enter into a World Cup race—are always tight. So I didn't race World Cup that first year, and all the guys who did race but didn't get results got cut at the end of the season. The suits said "they'd had their chance," and that was it. In hindsight, I wasn't ready to make good on my chance until the next year. So it went well for me. A certain amount of luck is always necessary.

A lot of racers trained and developed by the team make very few mistakes: they hit every gate and pitch perfectly, they look good—no sitting back, no arms waving wildly on the course—but they still don't have winning times. They do everything right except go fast. And when neither they nor the coaches can figure out how to peel any more time off, they fade away.

It's sketchy, figuring out when to push harder and when to temper. I could make individual turns faster when I was in high school than I do now most of the time in World Cup. When I first made those turns, I knew they were so fast that no one could beat them. It was an incredibly valuable discovery, like finding a scrap of paper with the meaning of life scribbled on it, or getting bitten by a radioactive spider. The problem with those superhuman turns then was the same as now: they can be played like wrong moves in a game of chess. They look slick and create a short-term advantage, but in the end, no matter what, the game won't go the way you want it to until you play those turns perfectly, in perfect order. This takes time.

I've always known that I could make my fastest turn get around every gate, all the time. That's the top of the game, right there. That's what I was working at while everyone else was at 60 FIS slalom points and looking to get down to 50. I thought about the way they did it: How do you get down to 50 slalom points from there? Well, first you get to 59, then 58, then 57 . . . ughh. I couldn't do it. Too linear, too tedious.

What appeared to the untrained eye to be blowing out over and over was actually my experimentation with making a hyper-space jump from 60 FIS slalom points to 2. Whoever runs the fastest time in an FIS-sanctioned event has zero points in that event. After that, everybody else's points grow as their time expands. So young racers have to chip away at that wall. That's the system. I was sure there was a way to sidestep it in favor of more fun and less drudgery. Actually, it wasn't such a leap; it seemed that way to my coaches and teammates, but it didn't feel that different. I could go faster. A lot faster. All that falling and skiing off-course gives the coaching staff the ammunition it needed to tell me to back off, so a little success created some goodwill space to explore.

I heard it every day: if you don't slow down, you won't get any results on the board, and with no finishes, there's no place for you on the team. When the big zipper opens and out you go, it makes no difference what gains you were on the verge of making—it's over. Your program is finished, and there's no effective argument against it. So be smart about it. I actually found it a stimulating mental and physical challenge to work my own deal, to develop my flavor *and* keep my coaches happy. It takes time, but you'd be amazed at what you can learn.

Besides, they're right: you do have to finish, because until then you just think you're fast, but you can't say for sure until you have an official time. I didn't finish enough for my liking, or anyone else's, but just enough for a discernible outline of improvement.

During that time, I also had to learn not to overestimate the equipment. It wasn't designed to take the punishment I gave it. Skis broke and delaminated, boots cracked, bindings completely fell apart.

That's why, during my senior year in high school, it was so thrilling when George Tormey, the rep from K2, gave me a pair of K24s, a recreational "shaped," or "hourglass," ski. These were the first of their kind; no one had ever raced on them before. They were wide and short, and designed for weekenders. K2 wanted to expand consumer skiing by putting out a fun, easy-to-turn board. Years before this, I'd tried skiing on a pair of snowboards, to feel the carve under two feet. But they were a little wide to be useful.

George was a no-nonsense Vermont guy, dedicated to skiing and competition. Back when he'd raced, he'd been a contemporary of my uncle Mike's. They were friends because they both liked racers who liked speed.

Tragically, George was killed a few years ago in a freak accident. He was a serious motorcycle racer, and one day in his backyard, as he was putting around on his bike, practicing his balance at slow speed for time-trial races, he laid the bike down on its side, hit his head on a log, and died.

I knew George well. If a race was far away, often my mother would drive me halfway, where we'd meet George, who would drive the second leg of the trip. My mother knew I was in good hands with George; she called him my babysitter. I was too old for a babysitter, but that doesn't mean I didn't need one. George was a good guy who gave me a big break when I needed it.

The first time I used those K24s, it was another eureka moment. I thought, That's what I'm fuckin' talkin' about. Then I raced on them, and for the first time in my life the ski reacted the way I expected it to. It didn't slide, it carved. I dropped down the fall line on a rail. I didn't have to sit back to make the ski bend. I could, but I didn't have to. And with those hot little skis, I scored a spot on the U.S. Ski Team.

The shaped ski is the basis for every ski we race on today. It was a change I needed badly. Of course, I broke them like kindling my first year on the national team. K2 eventually designed a beefier version to take the g-force and torsion I put to them. Ingemar Stenmark, the Swedish superstar—three-time World Cup overall champ, eighty-six World Cup wins in sixteen years, two gold medals at the 1980 Olympics—says shaped skis changed ski racing more than the fiberglass pole changed the pole vault. I don't know how much vaulting Ingemar does, but his point is well taken. Now everybody uses them, so I have to scratch that advantage and keep moving forward.

The final ingredient in my winning formula was actually staying up and getting results. You'd be surprised how many people thought I'd completely overlooked this step. To make that happen, I had to make America's Funniest Racing Recoveries central to my style. I was always working on my technique, quieting my movements and maintaining my balance, but not at the expense of sliding and losing speed. People thought I looked rawboned and scraggy coming down the hill, and it was offensive to them. So I'm skiing and swinging my arms like I have a tarantula on my back, throwing my hips like I'm a coochie dancer. That's what it looks like, but in reality I'm focused on keeping my skis in the snow and carving clean. I never think about how I look. I reduce it all to skis and speed; I send all my energy there. That's the zone everybody wants and seldom gets. I'm going twenty miles an hour faster on a pair of skis than most people ever do in their cars; I'm nearly naked except for a helmet and a pair of ski boots so small they make my toenails go black. People laughed at the way I came down the mountain back then, and they still do. But they seldom step up to give it a try.

When I first realized these turns were possible, and not just images in my mind, I was hopeful. It was a breakthrough, but just a start. If I could do it once, then twice, I'd eventually string together sixty or seventy miraculous carves around gates and ski the ultimate Platonic ski race, as fast as the natural universe will allow, and no faster. That is the dream.

People ask me what's next, and I tell them, truthfully, I don't know. It's hard to race World Cup if you're not completely in it. Planning your next step too seriously is like buying a ticket out. A friend of mine told me about a guy he knows, an antiterrorism official with the FBI. He was a ski racer in college, and now he spends his days tracking al Qaeda. When he saw me go down on my hip in the combined, then get up, finish the race, and win an Olympic medal, he called my friend and said, "That kid is an amazing athlete, and a hero to all of us who wish we were doing what he's doing."

This is a really nice sentiment, but when I heard it, all I could think was: I wish ski racing were that important to me. Not that I'm struggling for motivation or ambition, but I see that intensity in other people, as if they want to live and die with their ski boots on. They're crazy—good crazy, like John Brown or Robin Williams, but crazy nonetheless.

When fans or young racers ask me the Big Question, I tell them: "Go fast." What I should say is that if you want to ski like me, you'd better be like me. Otherwise, ski like yourself, only better. But that takes too long. There's a blogger who wrote that my one rule was to "get down to the valley and get there brisky." I think Google might have translated that.

I could tell acolytes to always defy expectations, which is good general advice, but "Go fast" is good ski-racing advice. It's the whole deal, the only tip worth taking. Otherwise, racing is a lot of practice and getting the small things right, like muscle-specific exercises and equipment adjustments. All this stuff helps a lot, but in the end you either have it or you don't. It's up to you to figure it out.

There are a lot of ways to have fun, and a million ways to make a living, but for the full-body rush of speed and excitement, nothing beats alpine skiing. Not auto racing (not enough athleticism), not skydiving (faster, but not on the ground), and not golf (though a fine sport it is).

If you come to this with little or no knowledge of FIS rules on World Cup alpine ski racing, here are the general facts: there are four disciplines and five events—two technical disciplines (the slalom and giant slalom), two speed (super-G and downhill), and a fifth event that combines the two, the aptly named combined. The technical events are won by the best average time of two runs, raced on different courses, one right after the other. Speed events race one run, and the best time wins. Combined is the best average of two slalom runs and a downhill run, sometimes raced on the same day. Combined is a major workout and, in my opinion, the best event, because it requires all the speed and technical skills that make a great overall alpine ski racer.

World Cup racers are ranked by the points they win: 100 points for first place, 80 for second, 60 for third, all the way down to 1 point for 30th place. The seven best guys draw numbers for racing order; then numbers 8 through 15 draw; that's the first seed. After that, numbers 15 to 30 draw, and lastly . . . everybody else, usually forty or more racers. In technical events, the top thirty times in the first run get to race the second run, but in reverse order of finish. Which means that if you win the first run, you go 30th in the second run.

At the end of the season, the racer with the most points overall is the World Cup champion. There are champions in each of the disciplines, and they all take a Crystal Cup home, too. In addition to that, every two years the World Championships are held in February at various venues, where gold, silver, and bronze medals are awarded.

As originally conceived in 1928, organized alpine ski racing had only two events: the slalom and the downhill, which are the opposite ends of the racing spectrum. Slalom is the quickest; downhill is the fastest. Slalom uses the shortest skis; downhill uses the longest. A slalom run is the shortest distance—between 180 and 220 meters in vertical drop—and has the most turns, somewhere between fifty-five and seventy-five. It generally takes less than a minute.

Consider that: seventy-five turns in under sixty seconds. Think about what you can do seventy-five times in less than a minute; now think about doing it on skis at fifty or sixty miles an hour. Slalom courses are set with single pole gates, which means you can charge them, take them across the boots, and set yourself up for the next one in as oblique an attack as possible. Gates used to be made of bamboo in the early days, and you were supposed to get as close as you could without hitting them.

As skis got faster and were made of different materials (wood gave way to metal, then metal to fiberglass), and as edges got sharper, racers started clipping gates, then banging into them, knocking them down, and snapping them off. New articulated gates, which you can hit head-on and they'll still snap right back up, were a great innovation, and changed slalom racing completely.

Slalom has always been about hurling down the straightest line you can find, but as equipment improves, the line gets straighter and straighter. Over the past decade, shaped skis, big fatties with humongous side cuts, have straightened it even more. So now learning to ski slalom is like running a gantlet, or getting beat into a ski gang. I shudder to think how many hundreds of gates I took in the face, chest, and shoulders until I learned how not to.

A downhill course has a minimum of eight hundred meters and a maximum of one thousand meters of vertical drop, with very few gates—just enough, placed strategically, to slow you down. Downhill racers hit ninety miles an hour plus, which is a lot faster than most people are comfortable doing in a car. With good reason.

The next event added was the giant slalom, in 1946. The GS is both technically and physically demanding because it incorporates slalom and downhill into the same course. It's three hundred meters of vertical drop with fifty-six gates. It's like cruising along on a downhill and suddenly hitting heavy slalom traffic: if you don't hook a tip or ski off-course, you get back in the fast lane and finish. It's a creative way to race, and was originally concocted to reduce downhill speed. The FIS looks for ways to retard speed and keep racers from detonating. Recently they put a minimum length requirement on skis, because with the advent of the shaped ski, it's possible to take corners on shorties at speeds that render human knees structurally unsound. Pop! Hence the need for parameters; otherwise you can count on ski racers to find the boundaries of physical capacity by incapacitating themselves.

The super-G, short for super giant slalom, with six hundred meters of vertical drop and thirty-five gates, is fast and furious. It's a little more technical than a downhill, but not a lot slower. The FIS likes to shake things up now and then, to keep it interesting, so in the 1980s they designed the super-G to attract the slalomers and downhillers, and to discourage racers from becoming one-event specialists. With only three disciplines, it was mathematically possible to win the World Cup overall by specializing in just one discipline. And while getting that good at one thing is impressive, it sort of flies in the face of what the overall champion is supposed to represent to the sport.

Depending upon events and venues, a typical course drops between ten and twenty feet per second. The terrain beneath you falls away faster than the eye can register. You scream by fences, trees, TV cameras, and people at eighty miles an hour plus. For me, this is as powerful and alive as I ever feel. And all I care about at that moment is going to that place where nothing matters and time slows. It's me and the clock. Racing at this level is like a high-functioning form of meditation, or a martial art.

Any given race day carries a list of variables that will produce the winning time. Not the fastest possible time, but the time that wins the race. The other racers are the most complex variables on the course. Who's on, who's off, who's hurt. There are fifteen guys on the World Cup circuit who can win at any time, and their always changing biometrics is more trivia than you could possibly digest. Then there's the weather, and how the course is set, and your equipment, and the other guys' gear. It's all more than a little complicated, and technical events do it all twice in three hours.

We ski these venues all the time, and you'd think that by now someone would have hit the top speed of every course. But it's not likely. Every day, every race, is different. The most unknowable variable is how many racers are there to get the fastest *needed* time, and how many are after the fastest *possible* time. I seldom put the brakes on, and live mostly among the speed demons; other guys know they can win by .02, and that's what they shoot for. That's a trick in itself. Still other guys know they can't win, so they're finagling for a fifth. But everybody's faster these days. You have to walk fast just to stand in place, and run to get anywhere.

Go to a race these days and you'll hear the color commentators yakking it up about the great recoveries racers make. It used to be how smooth he was, or how easy he made it look, like he's floating on air. You don't hear much of that anymore. These days, racers come down the hill like they're delivering live serum to dying babies. Everybody has stepped up his game for maximum velocity; consequently, it's a lot harder to stay off your ass. This is where my history as the "Crash Pilot" comes in handy.

That's the downside of speed: falling. Dumping bothers me—eating shit is never a pleasant experience—but it doesn't embarrass me. I always feel comfortable with my choices. I don't complain. Falling is part of life; I see it simply as a clear marker for where I need to stay up.

I don't master the mountain; I let go of my fear and let my body search for the speed. People call it "dancing with gravity," and if the metaphor holds, I'm more of a clogger than a danseur. I use my Gumby legs and knees to wind down the mountain; if I carve and dip my hip too much, then I use my elbows to stay up, like the outrigger on a sailboat. Whatever it takes. I've skied this way forever; it's in my genes. My grandmother would have agreed that it's better to dump and hike than finish tenth on purpose for lack of courage or imagination. This is how I was raised.

In my salad days, I got used to finishing way out of the money, or not at all. I had a year when I finished four out of twenty. That was DNF, Did Not Finish, beside my name more than three-quarters of the time. If I'd been an Austrian, not only would I have been booted from the team, but they probably would have stripped me of my citizenship.

In the 2000–01 season, I didn't finish thirteen of the twenty-four internationally sanctioned races I entered. I've seen people lose their hair and get religion over less. But I knew I was getting better, I knew I had far more control than ever before. It just wasn't always obvious to everyone else. And explaining myself all the time got old fast. Better to be laconic—the shrug, the smirk, the snort. People hear what they want to, anyway.

The next season, without doing anything differently except having major surgery for an injury, I won four more World Cup races, then two silver medals at the Salt Lake City Olympics. The season after that, I won three medals—two golds and a silver—at the 2003 World Championships. I switched from Fischer to Rossignol skis in the fall of 2002, but aside from that, I'm the same skier I ever was. I'm just better at it.

There's a simple strategy here. It's not ballet or synchronized swimming—it's ski racing. There are no judges at the bottom of the hill holding up style point cards, only a clock ticking off hundredths of seconds. Getting down the mountain the fastest is the only point.

I ski in no style, but when someone else does it persuasively, they'll call it my style. It's inevitable. What I do is lean way back on my skis and carve arcs instead of cutting corners. Also, according to some, I lack sufficient pole plants. I've heard it all: get your hips out over your boots; follow the line the last guy left; take the gates in the shoulder, not the shins; take the gates in the shins, not the boots; get your hands out in front of you; put your hands down. . . .

Before I started winning World Cup races, people said I

scrubbed all my speed every time I flexed a ski, that my line of attack was way too direct and would unravel before I got to the bottom of a race course. One coach way back when told me I'd never win an important race looking like a "Joey." He objected to the whole package—my beat-up gear and hand-me-downs, my drag-ass style, and my occasional tardiness.

As you might imagine, "Joey" wasn't a compliment; it refers to some clod from the flatlands who's clumsy on skis. Not only a beginner but a buffoon. I never consciously decided to ignore much of what coaches said, but it certainly worked out that way.

Learning to ski fast requires falling, as dancing does sweating. Not good or bad but intrinsic, and definitely unavoidable if you're doing it right. Not everyone sees it this way. Falling, at times, has been an issue in my career, especially with coaches who harp about "technique."

By both disposition and point of pride, I'm a fast skier, not a fancy skier. I see it this way: speed is an essential component of the physical universe; technique is not. Speed is what makes it a race; technique gives other people something to talk about while it's happening. Despite these basic truths, in my experience most coaches see speed as the result of proper technique. This is birdbrained, and it puts us at natural odds. They're confusing truth with beauty. Perfect form may be beautiful, but in ski racing, winning times translate as the truth.

I believe speed is something else altogether—not technique with an accent, but a completely different language. Go to any ski area and you'll see gangs of people speaking that language, mostly kids. Put a four-year-old boy on skis and he'll try to get air out of every bump he hits; if there are no bumps, he'll crouch into a tuck and worry about the bottom of the hill when he gets there. Speed is what attracts people to skiing. Not the cold, not the long drive to the mountains, not the high-priced lift tickets, and not the hot chocolate in the lodge afterward.

People want to go fast.

When I was coming up, coaches trained racers with technique regimes. Any gains made were easily quantifiable—shave a second here, a second there, and times get noticeably shorter. They were impressed by consistent improvement, and bemused by bursts of brilliance. You can tick away at the clock literally for years and wind up a half second out of the top thirty time after time. Then you can do one of two things: change the fundamentals, or continue to lose. Most guys choose the latter. At that point in a career, learning to let go and feel the speed is like an old man learning to speak Mandarin. That window is all but closed, brother; better move fast. The change needs to happen at a molecular level: control skiers tame the mountain; fast skiers give it its reins. Tough to coach, tough to learn. But fun.

When I was in J3 up at Cannon Mountain, eleven years old, I complained to a coach—we'll call him Walter—that he had me working too many technique drills (the skiing equivalent of practicing parallel parking). I wanted to ski some gates, and I said so. I wanted the green light to head up the mountain, and I wasn't leaving that room without it. I approached him one afternoon as the JO (Junior Olympics) tryouts rapidly approached; I figured I needed some actual race training. He figured otherwise. He thought I needed to learn how to put my hands forward and plant my poles.

"Miller," he said, his zippered après-ski boots hoisted up on his desk, "when you ski gates, all you think about is going fast." And that was it. His self-satisfied smile said as much. And then he dismissed me with a nod, chumped me off as if there was nothing to talk about. I don't care what your excuse for being lame is, condescending to a kid is like slapping him around purely because you're bigger than he is. At that moment, Walter had proven himself to be a jerk not only as a coach, but as a human being.

My innocent perspective assumed that speed was the point of racing, while Walter believed that not falling was the point of racing. But, I mean, the fastest time wins, right? So that's what I meant to say to him, but it came out: "Are you fucking stupid?"

I don't know how that happened. I was totally dumbfounded; he was pissed as hell. Nevertheless, I'd said what I'd said without irony or regret, and I expected an answer. I felt justified in questioning his native intelligence. It wasn't a rhetorical question; I meant it. I still do.

For his part, he felt justified in kicking me off the team. Which he did.

Walter had a firm grasp of the obvious, but he wasn't much of a coach. I, on the other hand, had a passable mastery of the language, but lacked discretion. Or so I'm told.

This wasn't like getting banned from kickball by the recess monitor—the Junior Olympics were at stake. I needed a berth on the team if I wanted to advance up the ski-racing food chain. Cannon Mountain was my home turf, a ten-minute ride from my house. But I'd been banned by the evil overseer, and I couldn't practice there anymore. Yet the big race was coming up … life was like a damn *Scooby-Doo* episode, and I didn't like it.

Getting expelled from the team just weeks before the JO tryouts wasn't good—around town they tell the story about how I got kicked out of school and off the school bus the same day I got jettisoned from the team. It isn't true, but it's a good story. And even if it had gone down like that, life wouldn't be over, and neither was that race. My path to glory was obstructed, and I was going around.

When I could, I strapped my gear on my back and hitchhiked over to Bretton Woods, where my weekday ski pass was also valid, and where I trained with Dan Cole. It was cold, and half the time I got picked up by skiers, the other half by guys named Claude driving logging trucks out of Quebec.

In addition to being the location of a famous (some would say infamous) post–World War II economics conference that created the World Bank and the IMF, it's also got a good-sized ski area, where they now have a course called Bode's Run. Bretton Woods wasn't the ice monster Cannon was, but it was sufficient to run gates (which I set myself) hard and fast, and not to practice pear turns or J-turns or anything else I could remember from training.

I skied fast and hard for a week, pulling my cuffs tight with duct tape to cut the wind resistance, shaving off the sides of my boots so I wouldn't boot out in deep-cut turns. I fell so hard so many times that week that I knew I wasn't holding anything back. It would be do-or-die come race day, just the way I like it—and there'd be no coach to talk me out of winning.

The day of the last races I showed up at Cannon Mountain, got my bib, and stood around waiting to race. Walter was there, lurking about, shooting me dark looks, but he seemed to have more than me on his mind. He had a stable of young racers to bark at, and strategy to plot. I just relaxed.

I finished first in the slalom that day, and second in the giant slalom, guaranteeing myself a spot on the team. The guy who finished second and first, respectively, was Todd Simones. He was big and strong, with great classical technique. I was fast; we split the day. And I was feeling great.

But at the end, while I stood around confidently, expecting to be named to the JOs, listening to the names of the new team members being announced, I never heard mine—not even in the honorable mentions. *What the hell is up with this?* I thought.

I had my results in black and white, a first and a second, so why wasn't I on the team? I found the race engineer, showed him my results on *his* form, and asked him that very question. He seemed puzzled too. We trekked up to the lodge to find out what was up.

"Apparently," he said, reading a piece of paper he found on a desk in the makeshift office at the back of the lodge, "your coach DQ'd you from the qualifier down at Loon," he said. "Told the judges you hooked a tip on the last gate and felt guilty about it afterward. . . . He said you asked him to disqualify you."

I was stunned. I'd been exposed to a good bit of life at the tender age of eleven, but I'd never bumped up against such black-hearted treachery. "That never happened," I stammered, not knowing whether to cry or kick something. "I don't know what you're talking about."

"There's nothing we can do about it," he said, shrugging. "The team slots are filled. Better luck next year."

It was a plausible story, after all. I mean, I did fall some, didn't I? And hook the occasional tip. At Attitash I fell in two successive races. (So what? I did the same thing in Flachau in 2004.) We raced giant slaloms and super-Gs that weekend—I blew out my binding in the first super-G, pulled it right out of the ski. I owned only two pairs of skis: slalom racers and a pair of trainers. So I was at a distinct disadvantage in the long-board events, but so were a lot of people. That day in the second super-G, I had to use some skis that I think had been nailed to the side of somebody's ski chalet earlier that day. Anyway, I fell three times in that race. I got a DNF and 43rd place for the day.

Then I boned the giant slaloms over at Waterville Valley, too. I totally detonated in both those races, hit huge holes, popped my ski right off once. I DNF'd both.

Walter had to screw me on a qualifier, because, frankly, you didn't need kick-ass results to make the Junior Olympic team. Patch Connors, a great skier I crushed all that J3 year, made the JOs, and he had a sixth and an 18th that day. But he'd finished the races, which is kind of required.

In the ensuing days it became clear to me that no one in my family really knew what to believe, and since they hadn't been there, they'd rather not get involved. Fortunately, my friend Mickey Libby got wind of the story. As it happened, he'd been standing at the bottom of the course, had seen me finish that day at Loon, and knew damn well I hadn't caught a tip. He was more pissed than I was. Mickey is a true-blue skier, was the head of the ski patrol at Cannon Mountain for many years, and has been my benefactor in many ways.

Soon, through Mickey's efforts and outrage, Walter was an excoach, and I was back on the Franconia Ski Club team. But not the Junior Olympic team. That would have to wait for next year.

I did manage to get a spot at the JO invitationals. A racer needs three results to qualify for the JO team. But after Walter DQ'd me at Loon, I had only two results: a second-place slalom at Cannon, and the aforementioned 43rd in the super-G at Attitash, where I hiked three times and was twenty seconds out of first place. The legal point I successfully argued is that a *Disqualification* is not a *Did Not Finish*. And since the requirement is that you have to *finish* three races, I met that criterion—I finished the race, but then I was disqualified. Get it?

Walter wasn't evil, but he was seriously flawed, convinced he was doing me a favor by teaching me the rigors of authoritarianism. I thought then as I think now: screw him and everyone like him. In the end, Walter did teach me a thing or two about life, but nothing about ski racing. In fairness, I was stubborn. I've always been stubborn, and that isn't a trait most adults appreciate in a kid. But I didn't deserve a shiv in the back.

Some kids might have run from such betrayal, found something else to do with their spare time, like snowboarding or writing computer viruses. But I didn't know how to write computer viruses, so I became even more focused on skiing. The next season I was a better racer and a stronger competitor. *Veni, vidi, Velcro:* I came, I saw, I stuck to it.

The JOs that year were held at Sugarloaf. I was determined to make the team. Up to that point, my first J2 year hadn't been significantly different from my last J3: I'd had some good races, but nothing spectacular. I wasn't a favorite by any means. I like it like that, catching people by surprise.

I went out and stuck the slalom both runs, big-time. Then I did pretty well in the downhill and super-G. And then I blew out of the GS. All in all, a great day. My whole family was there, and it was a pleasure to perform well for them. I remember being even more content than usual, which is saying something.

I can be as insouciant as the next slacker, but not when I compete. The mark of a real ski racer is somebody who, come fudge time, knows that there are no substitutions, that nobody's going to hold your hand or give you signals from the dugout or yell audibles at you. Somebody might walkie-talkie up to say that the dusting of powder on the third pitch is sheer ice underneath, but that's it. It's your game to play. Whether it's the Olympics or a ski club meet, you'd better be ready to ski. You don't have two hours of game time to earn your keep or make your mark. You get a minute, maybe two, and then it's over. You better shine.

The 1996–97 season, my first year on the team, I ran a lot of NorAm and FIS races—got some firsts, a lot of top tens, but no great shakes. The point was that I ran forty races—the equivalent of a full World Cup schedule with all four events. Because that's what I knew I'd be doing someday.

In the fall of 1997, my second year on the team, I finished 11th in the first World Cup I ever raced. I was prepared for it; I'd focused on what I would do on the day it came. Focus, prepare, execute. It's like playing baseball: always know what to do with the ball if it comes to you, because it will.

I was psyched to get a starter's spot in Park City that day. I killed the time-trial run, and suddenly, there I was in the big time. I let it all hang out—started 69th, skied the choppiest crud imaginable, and finished 23rd in the first run. In World Cup slalom and giant slalom, the top thirty racers from the first run ski the second in reverse order of finish. So I started the second run in seventh position.

Between runs, the coaches told me to take it easy, to give up a little speed and stay on my feet. All I had to do was finish and I'd chalk up a World Cup point. And so would the team. That was when they learned what kind of competitor I am. I do it all, or not at all. So I finished 11th. Eleventh—not the top ten, but pretty close, and at the time, a respectable finish for a nineteen-year-old American kid.

These were the best results the team had had in eight years, and the one thing coaches won't argue with is success. So this race gave me some credibility with them early on. After that, they were more prone to let me race the way I wanted, and to curb their remonstrations in the short term. The relative tranquillity made it possible for me to grow as a racer.

I didn't have anything going on at the 1998 Nagano Olympics. I skied the slalom and the GS, DNF'd both. It happens. I skied twelve more World Cups that season—got a 28th in a GS at Val d'Isère, four DNFs, and seven DQs. Not a stellar season, but I'd made progress.

The next year was the genuine big time, the Super Bowl of skiing, the World Cup of World Cups: the World Championships. The Olympics are more of a special event than the definitive ski-racing venue. For Europeans, it's all about the biennial World Championships.

That year it was at Vail. I got an eighth in the slalom, and an 18th in the GS. A good weekend, I thought. I skied well for where I was in my game, and I was happy. It, and a couple of fourth-place finishes I'd had earlier in the season, bought me more goodwill with the coaches, got me the space I needed to race and learn.

The following season, 1999–2000, I skied fifty-one races. In twenty-two World Cup venues, I had five finishes, the fastest a 12th at Alta Badia; I also had fourteen DNFs and three DQs. But I stood on plenty of podiums in NorAm and FIS races, and I skied a lot of Europa Cup races. It was a building year for me.

Early in the season I boned a GS bad, hit a gate with only a few to go. I could taste my first World Cup win, and it got away. At the end of the season, I got on the podium twice at the National Championships in Ogden, Utah—a second in the slalom, and a third in the super-G. A little more meat for the coaches, suits, and sponsors to chew on next year. I was happy about stepping up in the speed events, and I also got a 17th in the downhill. I was improving; my results were ascendant, if a little inconsistent. This was true from the time I was a twelve-year-old J3; every year I got faster, added events, learned more and more about how to do it right. It was a steady progression—not picture-perfect, but what is?

Until recently, alpine coaching was stodgy and orthodox. I recently met a guy whose daughter is a young ski racer; her coach says that falling in half your races is okay. Dumping and hiking in one out of two is now acceptable? That's fresh thinking. If I've played a role in this minor mind expansion, this happy inclusion of fast skiers into the mix, I'm glad.

For coaching, this is all a painful departure from spreadsheets and time sheets and technique drills. Now looking for winners is nuanced, a real challenge. It used to be like going to the stockyard and checking hooves and teeth. Now they have to ask themselves, How smart is this monster? What's he capable of? What will he do in ten years?

I fought with coaches most of my childhood. I skied then as I ski now. I understand old-school, and I respect it. I've had it coached, lectured, and pounded into my head from the time I was eight years old. Like an abstract artist who first mastered portraiture or landscapes before he could risk wavy lines, I can side-cut with the best of them. I just don't want to.

The 2000–01 season gave me my first appearance on a World Cup podium: a third-place win in Val d'Isère. I skied 26th in the downhill that weekend, too, which might not have looked like much to casual bystanders, but skiing all four alpine events was at the top of my to-do list, and finishing in the top thirty is where you start a trend. Val d'Isère has been good to me over the years.

The 2000–01 season was a World Championship year, and I love the challenge of a big race. The competition was held at St. Anton, in Austria, and most of my family was there. Some of them stayed with a guy from back home, Herb Lahout, whose family owns a ski shop in Littleton. Herb's folks and my grandparents go way back, and they've always been helpful and supportive of my career.

The night before the downhill, Herb threw a little party at the apartment he rents in St. Anton, and I went by for a beer. My uncles Bill and Mike were there, and Mike was keeping an eye on me. Skiing World Cup downhill is a death-defying act—don't let anyone tell you different. When I ski a downhill race I feel more like an astronaut than an athlete. I'm just doing my job here, but one wrong move and I'm toast. Crashing and burning isn't at the front of my mind, but it is in there somewhere.

I wasn't out late, I didn't overindulge at Herb's party or anywhere else—I'd fess up if I did. I've got no reason to lie. What I've learned over the years is that very few people care why you fuck up; only that you did. It's the crashes you hear about the rest of your life. Wins come and go, but spectacular failure clings like a hobo's fart.

It was a good run, but not for long. I zagged in zig mode, caught an edge, and found myself hurtling through the air backward. It was that fast. It's sometimes difficult to know exactly when it all turned to shit. I'd been doing maybe eighty miles an hour when I went airborne, so I wasn't stopping anytime soon. Then I hit the snow fence and blasted through it like it wasn't there. My left knee was already aching, and I knew there was a toboggan ride in my immediate future.

The initial prognosis in Europe was not good. The Austrian doctor told my uncle Bill that the inside of my left knee looked like someone had stuck a screwdriver in there and hacked around with it. At the time, that was a more graphic description than I needed. All I knew was that my knee was swollen and painful and I couldn't stand on it. Well, I thought, at least it's the end of the season.

When I got to the Steadman-Hawkins Clinic in Vail, things didn't look much better. They told me that I had a complete tear to the anterior cruciate ligament (ACL) and a popped medial meniscus. The meniscus is a crescent-shaped piece of cartilage that functions both as a fitting for the femur and as a strut to give the knee its resilience. The ACL holds the femur to the tibia, and vice versa, and gives it the flexibility and range that make most sports possible.

As Dr. Steadman (the Leonardo of knee surgery) explained it, the knee has two challenges in life: to connect the body's two longest bones and to transfer all of the body's weight to the foot during walking, running, and skiing. Unfortunately, it's at its most vulnerable to injury when bent—which is what knees do. Otherwise, we'd all be racewalkers.

My knee was feeling better by the time I'd been scheduled for surgery. So I went out dancing the night before I was to go under the laser beam. I was with Rob Martin Falvey, an extreme skier who was getting operated on the next day too. At 11:55 P.M., we tossed back three Red Bull and vodkas each because we weren't supposed to put anything in our stomachs after midnight. I don't know how much pain he was in, but I felt fine. Hey, I was out dancing—how bad could it be?

The next morning, when the doctor slipped the arthroscopic lens into my knee for a gander inside, my meniscus had somehow worked itself back into place (I wish I could be so tidy with everything else in my life) and the complete tear to my ACL was now somehow a partial tear.

For the ligament repair, Dr. Steadman used a new procedure called "healing response," which entailed drilling ten tiny holes into my femur. This apparently causes a blood clot, which the ACL gloms on to, causing it to heal back onto the bone, and thereby reattaching itself. I was awake through all this, watching the operation on a monitor, and now I know why Woody hated medical school.

I'd actually already begun to heal. I've always been an accelerated healer—it comes from good nutrition. If I shave with a blade in the morning—which I haven't done in years—and I nick myself, it's healed before lunchtime.

So I was very upbeat about all this. The people around me, however, especially the powers that be on the team, had already assigned me to the bunny slopes of history. Injured knee? How many times have we heard that story? Forget about it, kid, maybe someday you can coach.

The official tea leaves had a dark prediction for my skiing career. The team had sent me to the Steadman-Hawkins Clinic, and after a week of physical rehab officials informed me that they wouldn't be paying for my room anymore, or my meals. I was on my own. Do you know what it costs to live in Vail? I was twenty-three and six foot two, 215 pounds. I had to eat.

But some felt I didn't warrant further investment, and when they say it's over, it's over. I was a dead man skiing. I guess they didn't even care if I limped for the rest of my life, much less skied again. Just a couple of months earlier I'd been on the podium in a World Cup race. But so what? We're talking bottom line here. There's no room to be sentimental about a kid who finally got lucky in a race.

Fortunately, niceness prevailed once again—people took care of me. I crashed on Rob's couch for a few weeks, and then the Van Ness family took me in, and fed me well. I finished my rehab with Dr. Steadman. Within three weeks I was up and completely mobile without a brace. I came back, but with little help from the United States Ski Association.

All that negativity may have steeled me to the challenge of proving them wrong. Maybe that's why I was religious about my physical therapy, and why I trained so hard that summer; hell, I grew another inch. I did what I could do: beef up the muscles around my knees to strengthen any residual weakness from the trauma, and hope for the best.

I met a woman in rehab named Lizzie Hoeschler, and we dated for a couple of years after that. Maybe I was engaging in typical peacock behavior. Everyone has a theory on this, and mine is that I have hot years and I have building years, and they generally alternate. It's no more complicated than that.

In the summer of 2001, the medical staff gave me the okay to train with the team, and then to race. In July, I headed out to Mount Hood in Oregon and worked my ass off. I'd had a building season the year before with limited results, and now I was semi-damaged goods. So no one's expectations were too high. They looked at me and thought, Next! But as I said, I hoped for the best, and that's what I got.

Eight months after surgery, I took fifth in the GS at Sölden, Austria, the season opener. I felt stronger and bigger and more ready to rumble than I ever had in my life. And my knee, the rehabbed knee, now went into the corners better than ever. Injuring myself had actually stepped up my game; could I lead a more charmed life?

A couple weeks later, I got a second in the slalom at Aspen.

Close ones like that suck in a way, but they beat the shit out of 20th place. I knew I was on; I knew the season was going to be a killer.

On December 9, 2001, I won my first World Cup race, a win that ended a nearly twenty-year U.S. slump. It was at Val d'Isère; I edged Frederic Covili, and everyone nearly busted a gut with pride and surprise. All except me. I'd trained for two thousand days to win a race by two hundredths of a second, and as far as I was concerned it was about damn time. I was ready for another.

I didn't have to wait long. The next day, in Madonna di Campiglio, I won the slalom. A couple of weeks later, I got a second in the GS at Kranjska Gora; in January I won the slalom at Adelboden, Switzerland, and I got another win a couple of weeks later at Schladming, Austria. I was pleased with my progress. So were the coaches. Of course, I crashed and burned, literally, right through my speed suit, at Kitzbühel, Austria. And it hurt every bit as much as it sounds like it would.

Then came the 2002 Winter Olympics in Salt Lake City, out west in America's big alpine mountains. It wasn't my first Olympics, but it was on home turf, and there's no place like home. Also, of course, this wasn't long after September 11, and emotions were very high.

February 13 found me at Snowbasin for the combined (one run downhill, two runs slalom). It was windy as hell, and I love this race. It takes the longest and fastest speed event and combines it with the shortest, slowest technical event and averages them into one race. It's a great test of the overall skier, and the toughest race of all. The downhill isn't my strong suit, but I'd had a few top tens. And in Austria they call me Der Slalommeister, among other things. I don't know if I deserve any of them, but I was kicking some slalom ass back then. As always, I was there to win. Not to finish the downhill and try to kill on the slalom, but to kill on both.

It started well. They all do. There I was on the long boards, which I'm not crazy about. If it were up to me, I'd use the ski equivalent of 1970s glam-rock shoes—about sixteen inches long and eight inches high. Alas, the FIS has minimum-length rules now. But I don't think it's a conspiracy.

Anyway, somewhere on this course called Know You Don't, just before a leftward pitch, I lost an edge, slid, and threw all my weight in the opposite direction to compensate, just to keep myself on-course and make that corner. This is how it often goes bad—you move too much one way and then try to get back to where you should be by boosting it too hard in the other direction. I felt like the carpenter who'd cut the board three times and it was still too short.

Even if you do survive a situation like this and don't ski off the course, you're scrubbing speed every time your tips are pointed only slightly off your line. But serpentine skiing wasn't the end of where it went wrong—it got worse. On a leftward drop-off I went down on my left hip. In that frozen moment—I was moving at about sixty miles per hour—I lost control. I realized that not only was I about to die, but I was headed directly for where the coaches were standing, and they were going to die too. This, just when we were all getting along so well. But somehow I stayed up. I don't know how; my eyes were closed. Maybe all that falling I've done has made me good at it, conditioned my body to respond, through muscle memory. I finished 15th, 2.44 seconds out.

A couple of hours later came the first slalom run. It was un-eventful except that I let some speed go to make a gate and went all wobbly. But I recovered and finished. It put me in fifth overall, more than three-quarters of a second out of first place. In ski racing, +.76 is like one of those mile-deep chasms with the sketchy footbridge swaying over it.

And this being the Olympics, fourth meant not much at all, if anything. It was short for "also-ran," the guy with spinach in his teeth standing alone in the corner. Fifth place, my position, might as well be fiftieth. It's not like the World Cup; at the Olympics, you compete against the four best athletes from seventy-seven countries. In the World Cup you compete against the seventy best athletes from about four countries. Well, not really, but it feels that way sometimes. At the 2002 Olympics I skied against Fijians, Iranians, and Irishmen—their grandmothers might all kick my ass on the soccer pitch, but on the piste I, and a few others, have an advantage. So if that edge amounts to nothing and you finish off the podium, it might mean you got beat by somebody from the Tahitian ski team.

A couple of hours after the first slalom run came the second slalom run, and I was ready to go right at it. I skied that course without error, and it put me ahead by a second. When it came down to the end, to the guys with the good times from the first run, Rainer Schoenfelder was +.75, Beni Raich was +1.18, and I had a lock on a bronze. Then Lasse Kjus had a hard second run, and I had a silver in the bag. The crowd was rambunctious; it would be the first time a U.S. man had medaled since Tommy Moe in 1994; and no American had ever been on the podium in the combined. It was pretty exciting. My family was about out of their minds with anticipation.

Because he'd had such a kick-ass first run, Kjetil Andre Aamodt of Norway skied last. Now, consider the internal clock of a master: he runs 30th, skis maybe sixty gates in a race that lasts less than fifty seconds, and modulates his speed to win it with .28 seconds to spare. Very impressive. What can you expect from a guy who, at the time, had 21 World Cup wins, 60 podiums, and 213 top tens? He won the gold and I won the silver; I was happy and proud to shake his hand.

Between the races I flew out to Los Angeles, hobnobbed with Jay Leno, and flew back. The show's producer had asked that I bring the medal, so Rodney Corey, my publicist, had it in his pocket. I was feeling pretty cool coming back through LAX. On the couch with Jay the night before, a private jet ride back to Salt Lake City with all the peanuts I could eat, and I've got my man Rodney traveling with me, carrying my stuff. Hey, I was an Olympic medalist, damn it.

As we went through security, the metal detector squawked at Rodney as if he were wearing chain mail. This was less than six months after September 11, so people were, to put it mildly, still hinky. The security guards pulled Rodney aside, and as a bona fide national hero I stepped over with him to lend my assistance. He dug deep into his pocket and pulled out my medal, swinging it on its ribbon and smiling. The guard looked at it suspiciously— considering its size, heft, and potential as a weapon, I suppose.

"Big belt buckle," he said, squinting at it one more time and waving us through. Belt buckle?

A week later, February 21 at Park City, again with the wind rocking the start house, I raced a good first run of the giant slalom

Jay and me, 2002

until the flats, and then I dumped all my speed. Gliding is tough. It's all in the ankles; you have to finesse the ski's microscopically uneven surface so that it touches the ground as little as possible. Otherwise the time just melts away. It requires feet with the tactile acuity of a brain surgeon's hands. My feet look like a ninth-century Chinese empress's—bound and hopelessly deformed. I wear my boots three sizes too small for the control, have done so for years, and it's a slow torture. By this point in the season, my feet look like cloven hooves.

After the first run, I was in seventh place, two spots behind where I was in the combined at this point, .91 behind the leader, Stephan Eberharter, with one run to go. Despite a nearly one second deficit, I was going for the gold. I love being in this position, the come-from-behind spot, the three-pointer at the buzzer. From this lowly, way-out-of-the-money vantage, the decision to just ski your ass off is an easy one to make. If I'd been in the top three, that nether region of the sustainable lead, I'd have had everyone from coaches to hot dog vendors crawling all over me between runs, telling me to take it easy, to just finish this thing.

Finishing is important, I agree, but not as important as winning. If I were to put in a lackluster second run just to maintain a lead, I'd expect somebody to ski right up my ass. Because that's what I'd do. The problem at hand wasn't maintenance; I had nearly a second to recover. So, as my niece says, easy-peasy. When I'm starting in seventh place, everybody just pats me on the back and says, Go for it. I'm the guy for that job.

I skied the fastest second run, 1.08.30. It was a solid time, and I was happy with it. Then came the waiting game to see if it would hold up . . . and, uhhhh, nope. By the time Eberharter skied last, I knew I had another silver for sure. He skied a great second run, too, only .03 slower than mine, and held his lead. I got the silver, he got the gold, and he deserved it. Stephan had had nine wins that season alone; he's now a four-time world champion. The competition from him, Erik Schlopy, Kjus, Aamodt, Raich, and about ten other guys made winning even more difficult than I'd ever imagined, and raised my game immeasurably.

No American male had ever medaled in the GS or the combined, so the team was stoked. And the happier I make the U.S. Ski Association, the happier they try to make me. It's a remarkably simple relationship. I felt pretty good about my Olympic adventure so far, and I still had a chance for a first place—the slalom, my event after all, was coming up a couple days later. I was ready.

At Deer Valley that Saturday in February, things went a little off-course. Well, I went a little off-course. Three times in the second run, to be exact. My first run was more than enough to put me in position for a win. Hell, I'd come from behind twice previously and won silver.

But it was not to be that day. My slalom had been off all season, the consequence of spreading myself a little thin that first year of four-event competition. So be it. I only have one body and there are only twenty-four hours in a day, so there's a limit to what you can get done. I had a horrible run, and sometimes that's what happens when you push too hard. You fall, you slip, you run into gates, you slide sideways and sidestep up the damn hill when you're supposed

I think my mother put this somewhere for me.

to be skiing down it. But I finished it nonetheless. I had to; I was there, my family was there, and everybody was watching me—unless I went down and was officially out, I was coming across the line.

The week before, I'd skied so hard in that second run of the combined that I'd nearly collapsed in the finish area. I didn't have a ticktack of energy left in me; I couldn't have gotten out of the way of a parked car. But this slalom was different. I finished twenty-five gates in, and any role I might have played in the outcome ended then and there. But I soldiered on. Unfortunately, it was only the first of a string of three mistakes, which is the way things come at you when they go all to shit.

Somebody said later that I might as well have stayed home. That's a bad attitude to take. We'd give up at a lot of things in life if we knew in advance how difficult they'd be, or how badly they'd turn out. But then we'd never excel at anything, or even learn much; we'd be a culture of half-asses and middling wannabes. So thank goodness we can't see into the future. March on, I say. It's our only option.

I read somewhere that a couple billion people were watching that day on television, and there were another fifty thousand, most of them Americans, standing slopeside in the cold too. For me, skiing was over for the day, and for the Olympiad, as the color commentators like to say. But I skied my second Olympics with far greater success than my first—the worst pessimist couldn't complain. Of course, some of the press did. They called me reckless and unpredictable. Jeez, I felt terrible about that. I keep telling them that I'm *predictably* unpredictable, which is a wash. After the race, in front of the press and public, I felt I needed to tone my mood down from relieved and elated to stolid and somber. Too much smiling at a funeral is bad form, even if it's your own funeral.

So that was it. The Salt Lake City Olympics were coming to a close and the ceremonies were as big a show as you'll ever see. Jon Bon Jovi was wrapped in an American flag, and there were enough fireworks to fight a small war—that's the way fireworks have always struck me, as sort of a cartoon battle on the Fourth of July with a lot of prettified noise. But it's never stopped me from playing with firecrackers.

There was clearly an underlying pro-American message at these ceremonies, and that was understandable. But a lot of Europeans weren't happy. I'd been essentially out of the country since before September 11—in and out for a couple of races, but not Stateside for more than two weeks total. But this moment carried the weight of that day for Americans, and it made the athletes from other countries uncomfortable.

They held their tongues while they were here, but when they got back home, they said the Olympics are about international peace and healthy competition, not war plans. Right or wrong, good or bad, making the closing ceremonies a war rally for the Afghanistan operation felt like a hijacking to virtually every other country there. Even though they'd all lost citizens at the World Trade Center and the war in Afghanistan had broad international support, Europeans' long-standing experience with terrorism has taught them to separate it from the rest of their lives. Because when you can't, that means you're terrorized.

It's a matter of perspective. Terror has been an issue in Europe since Guy Fawkes tried to blow up the British Parliament in 1605.

Wearing silver in
Salt Lake City

There were athletes murdered at the Munich Olympics in 1972. It's an issue Europeans cope with on many levels—not just with emotion or jingoism but from long-standing policy. The average European shopkeeper understands terrorism better than the pre-9/11 Bush White House did.

Unlike in the United States in the winter of 2002, European television wasn't bingeing on terrorism and al Qaeda. It wasn't so much a common topic of conversation with people. They followed the story, but not closely. To them, it was just one more tragedy in a long line that stretched out behind us and ahead of us, as far as you can see. Experience has hardened the Europeans against terror, and I guess I picked up on some of that. I fly a couple hundred thousand miles a year and never give it a thought.

In Salt Lake City with Tom Brokaw . . . a cool guy

After the Olympics, it was back to Europe for me. I took second in the slalom at Flachau in March, my eleventh time on the podium and my fourteenth top ten of the season. And this was despite mistakenly wearing GS boots, which are too floppy for the slalom's shorter, sharper turns. It was like driving with soft tires.

So we could probably call this my breakthrough year. And with that objective success, I unofficially gained a technique; my gangly wraparound body rocket had been promoted from Crash Pilot to the American Missile.

I'm not convinced that what I do needs a name. I do see undeniable distinctions between "technically correct" skiers who master gravity and me. But that doesn't mean everything needs a label. We're all simply doing what feels right, or we wouldn't be winning World Cup races at all. It's the same in the arts; Jackson Pollock was making a mess with paint until people in New York started buying his work. Suddenly, he was an "abstract expressionist," using a "drip and splash style." Jack the Dripper proved that a tight leash on one's medium wasn't always necessary, or even desirable.

It's the same in skiing. I don't dispute the beauty in pure control, dropping down the fall line in as few movements as humanly possible. But it's always the same nice tight line that nine guys out of ten would put down. I, on the other hand, am drawn to the untamed side—the full-out, ski-snapping velocity that knocks the wind from my lungs as I turn right and land left; when the skin on my face starts vibrating and moving into the turns, when every joint in my body shimmies, and when things jet by so fast I can't tell what they are anymore. For me, anything short of that feels like holding back, halfhearted, not fast, and not fun.

All that said, I don't overdo this stuff. I'm highly analytical of my technique (I wouldn't call it a style) and how to improve it. I think about the subtle changes I need to make to take it to the next level. And I do the same with equipment; I'm more involved in the design and production of my gear than any racer I know. But once I'm on the piste, I don't analyze; I ski. As I've said before, racing is like sex: you can make all the plans you want, but when it actually happens, it just sort of unfolds the way it wants to.

The best run I ever had was in the 2002 super-G in Val Gardena, Italy. I started first in the dark, hurtling down that sick and twisty course with blind pitches and gnarly turns, a challenge and a half at noon, never mind when the moon is still out. But I bagged it, did everything right—except draw the number one bib the night before. I skied fast and well, but when the sun came out a few minutes later, the snow got slipperier, and I ended up in sixth place. In my mind—all things being equal, and they never are— that was a money run.

I love what I do. I love racing; it makes me happy. I try to be the fastest guy down the hill. If I'm not, somebody else is, and that's the way it goes. When I don't do well, I don't let it bother me, because it doesn't. Not much, anyway. And when I do well, I don't get unrealistic notions about myself. I train smart. I race hard. I win, I lose. What else can happen? No matter how the season goes, I always feel I can ski better next year. And it's that expectation that keeps me sharp.

6

Go Faster

I expected 2002–03 to be a building year, with a flat, probably ret-
rograde success rate. That had been my cycle; I figured it was a
rhythm. I actually liked it. It made time for experimentation and
learning; it kept skiing interesting.

But this year was different. I started with a fifth at Sölden. I lost
a pole halfway down the course, and my then coach, Martin Andersen, claimed it made me concentrate better. Now, that's an upbeat
guy. A couple weeks later I was DNF twice, GS and slalom, at Park
City—walked right out of my ski. Then I had a string of top tens,
including a sixth in the super-G at Beaver Creek and a second in
the GS at lucky Val d'Isère.

Lucky for me, that is, but not for Stephan Eberharter. He went
down in the second run and injured a knee, putting him out for a
month. It was hard on him; he'd been hot before the crash. But
the prognosis was good, and he'd be back.

Then I skied that picture-perfect run at Val Gardena, where I
placed sixth. I was having a journeyman's season—working hard
with respectable results. But I like to win, and the press knows that,
so it wasn't long before they started asking when that might hap-

pen again. Which is a loaded question, because there is no answer until it happens. And then there is no question.

Of course, the subtext to When will you win again? is Will you *ever* win again? They're a dramatic bunch. I think that while they're posing thoughtful questions to me in the middle of the afternoon, they've got their VCRs set to tape soap operas at home. On the other hand, if sports lacked drama, people might find some other way to waste their time. And then where would we be?

I didn't leave them hanging long. My first win that season came on December 22, at Alta Badia, Italy. Something kicked in—time to put down, whatever. It was a good race, and I nailed it by more than a second. I had a great first run, then tough conditions in the second, and it all added up to a win. I was so sick of the question of when I was going to win again that I actually broke a long-standing tradition and put the brakes on a little to win. Davide Simoncelli ripped that run exactly as I would have, had I been him. But it wasn't enough; I had the best time.

This course was the one I'd wanted. I'd boned it the year before—hooked a tip and DNF'd in the second run, after a winning first. But this year was sweet, and its 100 World Cup points put me into the number two spot behind Eberharter for the overall. He'd won the overall the year before, and despite his injury, he was still more than a hundred points ahead of me.

Up to this time, my headgear sponsor—that is, the advertiser that buys a couple square inches of real estate on my helmet—was SoBe. I liked SoBe and they liked me. But they were bought by Pepsi, and Pepsi didn't necessarily want to spend hundreds of thousands of marketing dollars on some skier nobody in America was likely to see. So my agent, Lowell Taub, found me a deal where SoBe was my headgear sponsor in the United States but I was free to do what I wanted in Europe. And then I let Europe know in a fairly creative way that my headgear advertising space was available: I applied some masking tape to the front of my helmet and wrote across it FOR RENT, using a black Sharpie so it wouldn't smudge when I face-planted. It took a couple of weeks, but eventually Kelly's, an Austrian snack-food company, bought the space. I know: Kelly doesn't sound like an Austrian name. People thought it was the supermarket in Franconia, but everybody back home knew better; the spelling is different.

The next week in Bormio, Italy, I got a fifth in the downhill, and it was quickly turning into a good season. Even though the first win was a long time coming, if this was my building year, then things were sturdier than I'd thought. At the start of the season I'd made the commitment to myself to become a four-event skier over the next couple of years. I hadn't done a lot of downhill or super-G training—the speed events I'd added—and whatever I had done was probably to the detriment of my slalom. Being a four-event skier meant a grueling schedule with very little time off for six months, and twice the gear to lug around. So I figured I'd start the season out by running as many races as I could handle and see where it took me. In the end, I was the only racer to compete in all forty races that season.

I also changed ski companies that year, from Fischer to Rossignol. I was girding for another quantum leap, and my equipment was going to be a big part of it. But that kind of transition takes time, and time was precisely what I lacked on the new skis. It was like going back to school: new events, new gear, new people to deal with, and so much to figure out. For me, new skis aren't like getting a new bike; they're like getting a new body part.

My second win of the season was a GS at Kranjska Gora, in Slovenia, where my race tech, Robie Kristian, is from. (He's my technical-event pit crew—keeps my skis tuned.) So that was cool. I took the lead in both the GS and the overall point totals. Then at Bormio the next week I got eighth in the downhill and second in the slalom; it was beginning to look like I could snatch the World Cup overall title, but it wasn't going to be easy. Stephan was back from being injured, and he'd be as tough as ever.

Incredibly enough, on January 14, Hermann Maier, the big dog of World Cup until two years ago, rejoined the circuit. He'd been recovering from an almost fatal motorcycle accident, and now he was stunningly back.

While riding his motorcycle home one day in the summer of 2001, he was turning on to his street when a car T-boned him—and literally almost took his leg off. To walk again after such an accident is a minor miracle. But anybody who saw the fall he took in the downhill at the 1998 Olympics knows Hermann's wearing some kind of organic armor.

So now the Herminator had a full length of rebar holding the tree trunk he calls a leg together and was skiing the World Cup. We gave him a standing O in the finish area that day. The achievement was as if he'd survived lung cancer last year and then finished the Boston Marathon toward the front of the pack. He hadn't raced in two years, but he had finished only .05 off qualifying for a second run. That's an encouraging result *without* the embedded hardware. It was also a great development racewise. Having Hermann on the piste would step up Eberharter's game, which in turn would step up mine.

Because 2003 was a World Championship year, everyone had that extra buzz going in the back of their minds. It's essentially the same as any set of World Cup races, except that only the top twenty-five racers in the first run get a second run. In regular World Cup it's the top thirty.

There are five events in two weeks—a little heavier schedule than usual, but the extra event is more than offset by the fact that you don't have to travel anywhere for those fourteen days. This year it was in St.-Moritz. And other than that, it's just like any given Sunday, except for the let-them-eat-strudel 24-7 partying and the floor-length fur coats in the VIP tent. Most Americans lack a proper appreciation for what wild scenes World Cup races can be.

Not to put too fine a point on it, or carry the fashion metaphor too far, but for World Cup fans, the difference between the World Championships and the Olympics is like the difference between the Miss Universe Pageant and Miss World. I mean, nothing against Miss World, whoever she is, but aside from the *universe* being a tad more comprehensive than the *world,* there's a quality to Miss Universe that Miss World somehow lacks. It's the same with the NFL and whatever football league you'd like to compare it to. What's the point? Or green hemp 420s and Kmart high-tops. You know what I'm talking about.

The first event at the World Championships was the super-G, a speed event I'd had a 12th place, two sixth places, and a seventh in that season. So I wasn't exactly burning up the course. Nonetheless, I planned to win. And I nearly did. I started in the 23rd position and ripped it. Then Maier skied—this is less than a month after he'd rejoined the circuit—and he tore the shit out of that course. I can't imagine skiing faster. In fact, we had the same exact time, down to the thousandth of a second. Then Eberharter scorched down that hill .77 faster than both of us, handily winning the gold. Wow. Hermann and I shared the silver, like poster boys for knee surgery.

Next came the combined, and the weather for the downhill was egregious—all fog and wind, a combination you usually see in horror movies, not skiing. I had a very iffy run and finished in 17th place, +2.95 seconds. That meant I had nearly three seconds to make up over two runs. I was still in the race, but with little built-in advantage considering my slalom results that year. I had a second and a sixth; all the rest were at the back of the pack, or DNF. So there was room for improvement, and today was a good day to start.

Besides, I thought, this was the combined, and anything can happen. People crash and ski off the course—I'd done it myself in Kitzbühel, Austria, in the second run of the slalom just a week before. But I also knew that I was skiing against some tough customers: Raich, Aamodt, and Kjus. I wanted the win; a three-second deficit was nothing, right? I wasn't skiing second or third. I'd had enough of that. I went for it.

I skied two rocket slalom runs, as fast as I could. This was good for two reasons: first, it was nice to see my slalom mojo back in working order, and second, I was in first place. At the end of the second run I watched Aamodt ski out of the money, and I knew I had a bronze. Then Beni Raich crashed, and I had a silver. Kjus skied last and came up .07 behind me, far less time than it takes to blink your eye. And Aamodt was only .13 back. These tiny fractions of seconds define the winners and losers, and make those otherwise unappreciable wisps of time very real, very solid.

That's what I was thinking. Then it struck me as I looked at the board and Kjus's time registered in my brain: I'd won. Only twice before had an American taken this race—Billy Kidd in the 1970s and Phil Mahre in the '80s. I looked at the crowd, and then at Kjus pulling back his goggles; I looked back at the board, squinting because I hadn't had my eyeballs laser-enhanced yet. I remember it all in slow motion. I was in the well of a tornado as everything whipped slowly around me, and I wasn't moving at all.

Then I did something I don't often do. I fell to my knees. Interestingly enough, people will leave you alone when you're in this kneeling position, which is possibly why it's so popular throughout the world. It looks like prayer, and nobody wants to interrupt a spiritual moment. But I was just trying to make the sense of satisfaction last for a while, to remember it as it had happened: the slate sky, the feel of the snow, the sound of the horns and the bells and the yelling. I'd worked all my life for this win, and I knew that as soon as I left the finish area it would no longer be mine. So I took a moment.

This was an incredibly hard race. It lasted all day; three runs means a lot of inspecting, a lot of skiing, and way too many adrenaline rushes. It's a beating. And so was the competition—killer right up to the end. Those guys put some skiing down that day. I feel like we should have had a gang sign to flash at the end.

I was emotionally up and down between the events. I admit it. This was out of character for me, but these were special circumstances. I learned a long time ago that if you're trying to accomplish anything worthwhile, it's not whether you have stress or not, it's what you do with it.

I've learned to channel my tension positively and productively, so that I don't even think of it as stress anymore. But that's what it is. As even-keeled as I am, convincing myself that I could go out and win two slaloms in a row by a second and a half apiece required ninja self-confidence. Which I have, of course, but hadn't needed up until then. I wasn't sweating my situation, but it definitely had my attention.

My family was there in the crowd, hopeful and supportive as ever. I'd wanted to win for them as much as for myself—I always have, for my grandparents and parents, for all the people who've been helpful and kind over the years. But I knew they'd have a good time either way. It was Woody's first trip to Europe, and it would be memorable for him whether I won a World Cup race or not.

Still, being on the podium is what we're there for, and the boss loves it when we do, so I'd run every possible winning scenario through my mind, and had decided to take it in two big bites. Which is what I'd done, and I'd won, and now I was frazzled.

At the finish, I kept my eyes closed and took as much time for myself as I could; then I stood, smiling, still stoked and unscathed, and went out for a great night on the town with my family.

The next race was the downhill, and I skied 16th, which was a significant improvement over the last World Championship downhill I'd run. More progress.

It was the GS in St.-Moritz that brought some of the greatest results in American skiing history. It was an amazing day, the best race of my life, and the most important medal I've ever won.

Like most races, the runs themselves were tough and fast and fun. But it was the grouping at the end of the second run that blew me away. I won it, Hans Knauss at .03 out had the silver, and Erik Schlopy was bronze, .01 behind him. What? Two Americans on the podium? And at the frickin' World Championships. Here was a whole new element. Being on the podium is an honor, but being on the podium with my teammate, my roommate, my good friend Erik, made it a kick-ass day. That day the world got to see Erik ski the way we see him do it all the time. He poured himself down that mountain, and but for an unimaginably small margin, he'd have had silver, or gold. And that's ski racing.

Erik's achievement was overshadowed by my gold medal, and that made me unhappy. Ski racing isn't really a team sport (Gene Hackman says so), but a strong team effort is essential to good morale, adequate funding, team development, and media coverage.

When the Austrians place four skiers in the top five slots, that's a reflection of their resources. Give some, get some. When Americans take two of the top three spots in the World Championships GS, it means we're coming into our own. When Daron Rahlves and I finish fourth and fifth in the World Cup overall, it means the team did some notable skiing that year.

In fact, the U.S. team took six medals at the 2003 World Championships, while the Austrians took five. But no one heralded the U.S. team as the Next Big Thing. I guess I understand that, but the following season, after I'd won the first two races, a journalist asked me if I felt motivated enough to take on the Austrians that year. I don't know what this dude thought I'd been doing. I'm taking everyone on, the Austrians included. I assured him that I wasn't lacking motivation and suggested that he get motivated to write stories that make Americans interested in ski racing. I mean, everybody's got a job to do for the cause.

There were nine more races after the World Championships. I got third in the slalom in Yongpyong, a beautiful place. Then I took sixth at the finals in Lillehammer, Norway. I also had two DNFs and a DQ. I was sick during the Lillehammer series; maybe I got some bad kimchi in Korea—or possibly just the flu, I don't know. What I do know is that you don't dare take anything for it and expect to pass a piss test. So the pitched battle between Stephan and me for the overall title was over before the end. It got to be a mathematical impossibility. He won the super-G in the finals; I was 20th.

At least then people stopped talking about the horse race and got back to discussing the actual races. Or the weather, or the Red Sox, or anything else. I'm only conscious of the points duel because people tend to fixate on those things. And it can be contagious. I see it as an important indicator of what's happening. But it doesn't tell you why it's happening. Just like the unemployment rate or the GNP or whatever number they're using as shorthand for the news that day. It's a single number representing limited variables, creating an incomplete picture. I came in second in the overall behind Stephan Eberharter. Daron Rahlves was sixth. The 2002–03 season was a kick-ass year for the home team.

I'm happy with what I did. Because it was my do-or-die best. I could have done it differently, and maybe I would have won. For example, I could have skied every event to finish fifth. Over forty races, that's 1,800 points, way more than enough to win the overall. But what a bloodless way to do it. I'd get kicked out of my family for something so craven. It's like using cheats in a video game; what's the point?

I won the combined overall title, and what I'd learned by the end of that World Cup season was that I could and would ski a lot better than I just had, that I'd be around a long time if my legs held out and my outlook remained tranquil.

The U.S. Alpine Championships that year were a trip. I won three golds and a silver, and Schlopy got a gold. It was a great few days, with some great races. The following year I couldn't buy a break at the U.S. championships. In the GS, the double gates were actually blowing up the hill. I took bursts of wind in the chest that felt like a hard shove on the basketball court, and came in 30th. I took a fourth in the downhill and didn't do much better in the other events. Somebody else was having the fun. That's cool.

The following season, 2003–04, I didn't know what to expect. If last season wasn't a building year, would this be it? It was bound to happen. The opener was in Sölden, a lovely little Tyrolean skiburg in the shadow of the Rettenbach Glacier, and high enough in the Alps to be a mountain on the moon. It's where they found Ötzi, the "Ice Man" who was frozen for five thousand years after dying in a fierce attack. I have to say, it is a killer course.

I love the Austrians. Nobody sweats too much around here during the week, and the weekend is for drinking and skiing, not necessarily in that order. But do they love to ski.

The night before a race there's always a party for the bib draw. People are outside swilling beer and listening to karaoke rock 'n' roll, wearing beads and funny hats. It's a carnival I wish more Americans could see. It's like spring break with snow; it's like tailgating at the last NFL game of the year.

The year before at this event at Sölden one of the Austrian racers sang a song, and that was fine, though it ate up more time than I'd planned to spend up there. Don't get me wrong—I've got no beef with German rap. Maybe it's bourgeois rap I don't like.

Fortunately, I drew the first bib; then I could get out of there and go to dinner. So out the back door I went, around the rear of the stage, trying to avoid the beautiful Valkyries with BODE written on their foreheads in black felt-tipped pen. Just as I was going over a fence, a German television reporter stuck a camera in my face and asked me what I thought about the song.

Huh? What song? I shrugged. "I don't know," I said. I really hadn't listened to a word.

"You don't speak German?" he asked, his eyebrows raised and his lips pursed in an exaggerated look of television surprise. "You were in the song," he said, amused at my cluelessness.

I guess I should have been listening. I might have thought it was funny, too. I looked into the camera and said, "As soon as I catch myself remembering what a German word means, I put it out of my head immediately." And I walked away. Truth is, I took four years of German in high school and have lived in Innsbruck for half of the last seven years. So I'm not exactly illiterate. If another racer wants to serenade me, or write me poetry, or tattoo my name on his ass, that's up to him. But I'm not giving him the satisfaction of commenting on it. Fuck that—I'll see him on the slopes.

This year I started seventh in the GS at Sölden. I beat Covili by .09 in the first run. Not exactly an insurmountable lead. The course was set straight as white lines on the highway, and the snow was grippy as hell. It was hard to curb your speed around the gates because you could easily catch an edge, and that would be that. I didn't think I'd done that well, so being in first place gave me a boost, made me feel that I could take a risk or two in the second run and really smoke it.

Number two was tight and full of turns, the opposite of the first-run course. I liked them both, but the number two was more my flavor, and I won it by almost a second. It was my seventh win, my fourth GS, and the first time an American had won the World Cup opener. So it was a pretty good day.

The next race was a GS in Park City. My family was there—the whole crew, from my grandmother to my youngest niece. So I had to win a race. Besides, no American had won on U.S. soil in twenty years, and that was a drought I wanted to end.

The weather was off; there were gray skies and flat light. I won the first run by a half second. A snowstorm picked up and dumped hard on the second run, but I won it by nearly as much. I'd done what I'd set out to do, gotten my eighth win, and it should have been a good day.

But it wasn't. Schlopy crashed bad, blew out the ACL in his left knee, and took a toboggan ride down. For him, it was over for the season.

I couldn't believe it. I'd thought the stars had lined up for us: we had a thirty-two-foot, chauffeur-driven motor home waiting for us in Europe to take us in luxury from race to race. We were both in the most unbelievable shape of our lives; we were going to rip it this year. Now, damn. What a lousy time to get hurt. But Erik was cool about it, very stoic, took it as part of the rules and conditions of ski racing. He's such an adult.

The next day, in the closing moments of the first run of the slalom, a run I had a commanding lead in, I hooked a tip and stopped the clock. DNF. Weekend over. Still, I'd won two races so far, and I was ahead in points. It was early to start counting, if you ask me. Tom Rothrock (also known as Roddie) got a top ten that day, which was good for him and the team.

The super-G at Lake Louise, Alberta, put the Austrians back on the map that season. They banged it out, one, two, and three: Hermann, Stephan, and Beni. Daron Rahlves was tenth; I was 19th. Not a stellar performance, but I enjoyed myself.

The first downhill of the season was at Beaver Creek, and I admit to lusting for a downhill win. Since I'd lost that near win at Vail a couple of years before, I'd had the bug, like a downhill tapeworm in my belly. But it wasn't to be for me that day. Daron won, which was great.

It was a ripper run. I was booking, and I cut my line a little late. I always do, because I scrub speed otherwise; but the g-force I was pulling that day instantly delaminated my ski, and I was done.

I didn't fare any better the next day at the second downhill. I caught a gate, and that's all she wrote. Hermann won it, the forty-fourth of his career, and Daron came in fourth. At a press conference later, somebody pointed out to me that I was in fifth place in the overall. Okay, I thought, fine. But isn't it still early? I concern myself with points as a single objective standard. They don't tell you anything; you have to know how to read them.

It was back to Europe, to Italy, to Alta Badia, where my oldest pal, Jake Serino, was waiting with my new thirty-two-foot Concorde land yacht. He'd been down at Barilla HQ loading up on pasta for the season. Jake is the driver and the cook. Truth be known, he cooks better than he drives. He tore the bumper off the rig the first day he had it out. Count the dings on its side if you don't believe me.

We had a great winter together. I'd drive ahead to the next venue in a small, high-powered European racing sedan, while he lumbered along on tiny Alpen roads, squeezing through passes

Jake and me, still on the bus after all these years—he cooks, I mess things up.

and over one-lane bridges. He'd drive to wherever the next race was and park the RV in the same secure area as the television trucks. It was very handy; I could pop in there between runs, soak my dogs, have a bowl of macaroni, and fire up the PlayStation and have at Baldur's Gate. Whatever I liked.

I didn't have to lug equipment from place to place; it was all neatly stored in the rear of the RV. I had a kick-ass sound system, a king-size bed, my comfy comforter, my pillows, my teddy bear. And thanks to Jake, I had what I wanted to eat, when I wanted it. A home on the road, and it was nice. More important, it made running all four events logistically survivable. If nothing else, it was a good place to hide from the press, who were fixated on the past three races, all speed events, and I was DNF in every one.

In Alta Badia, I skied fourth in the GS on a soft, bumpy course that I could feel deteriorating beneath my skis. Not that it made any difference; I've run races with sick times in much hairier conditions. But I also hooked two gates, caught my arm a couple more times, tore a panel off a gate. Not a smooth run, but I watched Kalle Palander win his first race in the event that day. He was kick-ass.

The next week, I was DQ'd in the night slalom at Madonna di Campiglio, which was too bad because that's a fun run. And then I skied 17th and 52nd in a super-G and downhill in Val Gardena. Daron performed, got a fourth in the super-G.

I think I chose a bad line to follow; you don't get much opportunity to recover from that mistake, because the problem compounds quickly; bad angles at the top of a pitch mean impossible angles at the bottom.

Kjus was first in that race; Eberharter and Maier came in second and third. They were locked in fierce battle, like Rock'em Sock'em Robots pounding the crap out of each other. In a civilized way, of course. The Austrians are always tough, but this year they were some bad daddies.

Then it was back to Alta Badia (lots of races got moved around this season, either because of no snow or too much snow), and I got third in the GS. Somebody was nice enough to point out to me that I was ahead in GS points. It was good to be back on the podium. I'd had a lot of rough races so far, but it was okay. I was healthy, I was happy. Jake was cooking me some of the best meals I've ever had. Good friends were staying in the RV with us from time to time. Life was good.

But then came the double whammy of Flachau. I wasn't happy about it. Both races were mine to lose, and I did. But that's the price of education. In the GS, ahead by .7, I lost it in the last split with ten gates to go. I knew I had it won, so I was taking it conservatively around the gate that jumped out and tripped me. It was a mistake; I make them. It's a paradox: I slow down to win the race, and because I'm going too slow, I hook a tip. The same thing happened in Madonna.

I can't improve and be improved simultaneously. I need some ramp-up time. The coaches, predictably, were privately having kittens over my crash-pilot trend; that's their job in situations like this: identify the problem, get it fixed. So they were trying to sign me up for Europa Cup races, to "get my confidence back."

How thoughtful, but I didn't know I'd lost my confidence. In fact, I never have, not then, not when I was in the middle of an avalanche on Tuckerman's Ravine, not when my knee was all lunched out in St. Anton, not even when I realized my car was running on six instead of twelve cylinders and I could have been driving so much faster all that time. Never.

The hand-wringing is amusing in a way. And it was the same old thing; I'm a genius until shit gets tweaky, and then I must come around and do things the way they wanted me to in the first place. The last seven years were a fluke, and it's back to development with me. Which almost makes sense because I'm always in development, always refining, and pushing harder on the accelerator. But at least now nobody blows me any shit.

He still has his point lead in the GS, they tell themselves. Then they make encouraging suggestions, and look concerned, as if somebody croaked. I'm touched by their concern, but it rarely improves things.

The coaches—Phil McNichol, Jesse Hunt, Mike Morin, and Johno McBride—seemed to be huddled over my situation much of the time; I imagined them to be drawing straws to see who had to shoot the downer racehorse. They were, in reality, only a little freaked at my losing streak. The truth was that they knew I was skiing fine—they'd seen plenty in training and knew I'd had some bad breaks, with new and buggy equipment, and the weather sucked. All the things that can go wrong did at some point that season. But the questions they had about my strategy seldom grew into doubts anymore. Still, it was nerve-racking for them at times.

I, of course, was fine. I'm always fine. Which, I'm told, makes me mysterious. But there was no mystery. I was skiing my ass off, because if I didn't there were plenty of guys who'd ski right over me. Guys on my own team, in fact, and I encourage that.

Going faster and faster every season requires a learning curve at some point. My balance, my muscles, my equipment—everything has to ratchet up to the new standard in speed. It's tough to accomplish it all in training; the hard-assed competition on the World Cup always helps juice me to the next level. Compared to the real deal, training runs are dress rehearsals, and the chemistry is different.

So I was learning; it was a building year. I'd had two good seasons in a row and had done some of the best skiing the team had seen in twenty years. But professional sports are like Hollywood—no box office makes you a bum. They wanted podiums and wins. Wins are what the press back home will cover. Even though it's buried on page four of the sports section, next to the volleyball box scores.

People had lots of theories about what I thought of as a building period and everybody else called a slump. Schlopy wasn't there, and they thought that was bothering me. And it was, because he's my friend, and usually a fixture in my life for half the year. But his absence had nothing to do with my skiing.

My girlfriend of two years, Lizzie Hoeschler, and I had broken up. Which wasn't easy, but I don't think my skiing was affected. She'd been in Europe with me quite a bit the season before, and I missed her. According to my mother, she'd been a stabilizing influence in my life. If you ask me, it has a lot to do with the male reptile-brained biological imperative to reproduce, especially when you haven't yet. When there's no woman in your life, it wants to know why, and can be very insistent, even insulting; when there is a woman in your life, it leaves you alone. Of course, I'd never reduce my relationship with anybody to biology. That would be rude.

This was also the first year in a long while without Martin Andersen as my coach; he'd decided to stay home in Oslo with his young family. He'd been replaced by my uncle Mike, who occupies a central role in my life, racing and otherwise. But at the beginning of the season, Mike was headed up the mountain to set a course, and as he got off the chairlift with an armful of gates, he twisted his right knee too much and heard that telltale pop—another ACL injury.

He was sent home to recuperate for the season; it was a damn epidemic. So, in a way, all of these things added up, I suppose. I'd have preferred to have those people all there with me, but I honestly don't think I would have skied significantly better if they had been.

I came back in Chamonix, France, with a third in the slalom (my first finish of the winter in the event) and a first in the combined. It made everybody happy, especially me.

The combined, as usual, was a killer race. It was raining, and I couldn't see anything through my goggles; the temperature was above freezing and the conditions were like skiing in birthday cake. The officials canceled a downhill that weekend because the weather was so warm.

The lousy skiing weather followed us to Wengen, Switzerland, where it was warm and rainy, then cold and blizzardy. When we finally got to it, a quarter of the field, including me, fell. The all-around level of skiing was horrible that day, the snow absolutely unforgiving. Any mistake at all meant falling. Only the guys who skied perfectly made it down at all. Roddie was the lone American to finish, and Beni won it for the Austrians.

On to Kitzbühel for the Hahnenkamm, plus a downhill makeup race from Bormio—a seriously packed weekend. I got seventh in that first downhill and 16th in the regularly scheduled one. Then fourth in the slalom and first in the combined. Three top tens. I also finished 28th in the super-G, which Daron won, plus he got third in the first downhill and second in the second downhill. Roddie got ninth in the slalom—it was a good weekend for the team. I was very happy; it was time to drink some beer.

The combined was the tenth win of my career, and it put me back into the overall points race. Which I was ambivalent about, at best. In my mind, there should be no distinction between winning and points. If I get 60 points for third, instead of 100 for first, it means I finished two places behind where I wanted to be. But that's not true of all racers; some guys play the points game very cute and nuanced, skiing safe when they can, taking risks only when they need to. Some people would call that smart; I call it boring. I'm running races to win, every damn one of them; I'm not paying attention to points. The horse race, which at this phase could have been won by any one of ten guys, was an unnecessary distraction. I decided to ignore that angle and play my own.

If there's no crying in baseball, then you can bet your ass there's no crying in ski racing. Case in point: two days later, the slalom in Schladming, Austria. I smoked the first run by .98. It was boilerplate conditions, and I was all over it. Then in the second run, Ivica Kostelic fell. Nobody knew if or how badly he was hurt; he was on the ground for a long time. He's my friend and I was worried about him, but it wouldn't make any difference who it was. Injuries always take precedence over fun and games.

There wasn't anything to do but wait. I stood in the start house with an unbeatable first run time on the board; I was tranquil. I thought about calling my mother, which is what I often do in the start, while everyone else froths, or jumps up and down, or bangs their head against the wall. Then it started snowing, and the white-out left only a moving mass of flakes backlit by cold, flat light. Under these weather conditions, the world appears two-dimensional. It was a damn blizzard, right in the middle of my ski race.

Twenty minutes passed by, and as the snow accumulated, the vibe around the start grew more and more paranoid. By the time I was finally cleared to ski, everybody around me was all sharp edges and tension. I was glad to leave.

The course felt like a bushwhack; the snow was deep and blinding. The rule regarding stopping and restarting a race is one of the few FIS rules that's clearly written: the course shall be slipped (smoothed out by course tenders) if a race is delayed by more than fifteen minutes. The race had been delayed a lot longer than fifteen minutes, and it had snowed like hell, but it hadn't been slipped. Consequently, I had a torturously slow second run, like I had climbing skins on my skis. My .98 lead dissolved almost immediately, and by the time the race was over, I was fourth.

Everybody who finished ahead of me had great runs and might have beaten me anyway. So what are you going to do? You can't fake a good attitude; you either have one or you don't. Race over, move on.

Besides, jump ahead to the end of the season, the World Cup finals in Sestriere, Italy. I DNF'd in the first run of the giant slalom (I didn't finish eleven events out of forty that season), which put Kalle Palander of Norway in a good position to take the race and the GS championship away from me. I had the over-all GS lead, but with fewer than 500 points, it was going to be hard to hold on to.

Then, by the grace of nature, the point was moot. Between runs it dumped snow so hard that they canceled the second run and, therefore, the whole race. So I won the giant slalom Crystal Cup by default because of a snowstorm. Which is why I never bitch.

It's an outdoor sport, and things happen—sometimes to your disadvantage, and sometimes not.

Before that, I got second in Adelboden in the slalom, after losing it in a squall the day before in the GS, on the second run, too. It was more weird weather: rain, snow, wind; we hadn't had clear weather for a race in weeks, so we were getting used to it, I guess.

Then I had a first in the slalom at St. Anton. Some of my family, including my dad and my uncle Mike, were there. Having family around always makes me ski my best. I was getting tired; I was going so fast I nearly crashed in the finish area, but I tipped over instead. This was all good data on how much stronger I needed to be next year. I had a first in the GS in Kranjska Gora, which was my last podium of the season. I had one top ten after that, a seventh in the finals at Sestriere.

Hermann Maier won the overall with 1,265 points, Stephan Eberharter came in second with 1,223, Beni Raich was third with 1,139, I was fourth with 1,134, and Daron Rahlves, my teammate, was fifth with 1,004. And that's the balls—two Americans in the top five overall. Plus, I won the GS championship—so that's not a good season, that's a great season. And next season will be better. That's the expectation that drives me forward.

In the end, it's important to remember that we all do it for the sport, the bust-out competition, as you do when you play golf or boot up a video game. You don't work yourself to the highest level for the accolades, because there are none. You do it for the challenge, to test your skill and yourself. Everyone on the World Cup circuit would be there if there were no fans, no big sponsorships, no TV coverage. They're there to race against the toughest competition in the world and see where they stand.

The off-season in 2004 was quality downtime: lots of hanging out, a little travel; I played golf or tennis every day, sometimes both. My family and friends were all around me, Tamarack was cranking, the 935 was out of the garage, on the road and banging on all twelve cylinders. A summer of fun always tops off my batteries, but damn if it doesn't fly by.

After some hard-fought passive negotiations with the team's coaching staff, I skipped technical training in New Zealand that year. Don't get me wrong: I love the town of Wanaka, and Treble Cone mountain, where we train, is very cool—especially to drive up and down. And the Kiwis are a great, proud, and independent people we could all take a lesson from. But I wanted to do some speed training this year, and I couldn't do both.

I'd had some results in super-G and downhill in the past few seasons, but I hadn't won a speed race yet. So naturally, the coaching staff wanted me to dial in the slalom and GS—because above all, you reinforce your strengths, right? Even at the cost of developing new skills and expanding your repertoire. Not for me—no thanks.

If I wanted to go to Chile and step up my speed game, that was okay with them. But not in lieu of training for the technical disciplines. And while you're at it, don't get hurt either, and don't lose focus on tech. And run those gates, run those gates. I regarded all this as an excellent and necessary point for the organization to make to one of its athletes. It was like a warning label, or a speed limit in the desert. I pretty much ignore that sort of thing. All the USSA coaches are top-rate, and extremely smart and dedicated, and every one of them is my good friend, but that doesn't mean they're always right. In fact, that's true of all my friends. The team used to fine me for skipping training camp. I don't think they do anymore. But I'm not sure, and I don't want to bring it up.

Anyway, I went to Chile, hoping to polish my long-board racing. The skiing was great. I was on new equipment: skis, bindings, and boots this year, all Atomics. This is not without its irony. Atomic was originally a target of mine, the big dog. Beating that beastie back into his cage would have been sweet. This goes to my taste in fantasy novels—I like slaying dragons. Eventually, though, in the face of consistent and overwhelming results, a rational mind accepts the obvious. After working with three other companies for the previous eight years—K2, Fischer, and Rossignol—I signed with Atomic. When my contract was up and I started looking around, I had ski companies offering to make me the "highest-paid skier ever." But the truth is, I didn't need their money; I needed skis, boots, and bindings that could take the beating I give them and still get me down the hill fast and healthy. Do that, and the money will come from everywhere.

It was a good move. The ski tips were softer than ever, which kept them from snapping. And I was standing right on top of the skis now, so suddenly I had higher-hip and lower-chest control. This meant I didn't have to overcompensate anymore by leaning forward, so I'm much more aerodynamic. And faster than ever. Not only in Chile—when I slapped on the slalom and GS skis in Europe, too, I was hopping through the tightest and turniest courses like they were nothing. The gear was dialed in.

I didn't get around much of Chile—from the plane I saw a sea of tin roofs across the city of Santiago, and then the hotel we stayed at in the Andes Mountains, and the mountain we skied, of course: Termas de Chillán. There's nothing up there but slopes and clouds and a couple hotels, a few restaurants. It's the kind of empty and desolate beauty that drives people to Scrabble. I played a lot of chess and drank beer.

It was around then that it struck me: I'd been at the same gig for nearly a decade. Eight years of essentially the same thing. Holy shit. Sure, I'd programmed a subdirectory for myself into the USSA operating system, a firewall between me and the shit that makes me crazy. But I was only sufficiently content, hardly ecstatic. I asked myself, given my hard-core fun addiction, how long could this go on? Even living in the RV during the season, with Jake making me cream cheese omelets anytime I want, coming and going as I please, pretending not to hear most of what's said to me—and still, it's a damned long trip every winter. The truth is that I'm as peripatetic as a bear cub in the woods, sniffing at this and that, but never for very long. That's my true nature; I prefer to take it all in. For me, eight years is longevity of righteous proportion. Just staying healthy that long in this job is a major accomplishment.

But that's not what I was thinking about on the drive up into Sölden for the first race of the 2004–05 season. It was my third year in a row racing every World Cup event, and I was ready to win races in all five. I won here last year and I liked this course. Before winning, I'd come in fifth twice in a row here, so it followed for some that I might win again here this year. I was feeling good—more fit than ever—and finally I'd been around long enough for experience to start paying off.

An American hadn't won the overall in twenty-two years. I have to admit, I'm generally not moved by such things, but a drought is never a good thing. This wasn't a Bambino-sized curse, but it was definitely getting to feel like some sort of jinx. So I wanted to win the overall partially for my team, but generally not for the reasons people think.

This sounds funny, maybe even stupid, coming from a guy with an autobiography, a movie, and a pile of endorsement deals, but I'm very reluctant to be any more famous than I already am. In fact, if I could un-ring that bell, it would be hard not to. I'd love to ratchet my Q score back a few notches. I was naïve. Who isn't? (Well, besides my mom, who told me this would happen.)

In the towns where we race World Cup, I typically meet a hundred or more people on the street when I go out. It's all semisweet; the vast majority of fans are great people. Skiers! And in a big way. Plus beer drinkers all of them, so these are people I'm at home with. But signing thousands of autographs in the course of a season, posing for thousands of photos, making thousands of chitchats, eats up several hours of my day, every day, if I let it. And that's when traffic is light. At the end of the season, when blood runs high, I need army protection to use the ATM. And then I ask myself, What the hell do I need money for? I can't go anywhere to spend it.

There have been times when I've come as close to freaking out as I ever have, and I've stranded friends who were out and about with me—just left them standing there as I exited stage left up the sidewalk and down an alley, sliding away from a growing crowd as if I were the Flash on my way to a catastrophe.

I was unaware of many things when I started out on this course, but now I understand that no matter what the deal, the back end is always as big as the front end. One of the reasons I became an athlete was to make a pile of dough and be free of the workaday world. I'll admit it. Why not? So I'm not complaining. I went into this with my eyes as open as I could get them. I'm merely observing, thinking out loud, and giving anybody with a desire to be on top of the world a clue as to what's really up there. Bill Murray said it best: "I always want to say to people who want to be rich and famous: 'Try being rich first.' See if that doesn't cover most of it. There's not much downside to being rich, other than paying taxes and having your relatives ask you for money. But when you become famous, you end up with a twenty-four-hour job."

I'm shy, and being in the center of the circle can be excruciating for me. I like to keep life on the downlow, but that gets way more difficult with success, especially for athletes. The role-model Nazis of the left and right, the political- and moral-correctness police who demand that top athletes all behave like the people they wish they'd grown up to be—I say screw them; they're nothing but a bunch of crackpots. I realize I'm not the only one with these problems, and that I've made my own bed, as we all do. But that doesn't make it any more comfortable. Protecting what's left of my privacy, as it steadily dwindles, is my priority.

Still, the overall championship was a key plank in my platform against arbitrary rules and silly bullshit. For me, winning the World Cup off my edges and in the backseat was the most objective standard available to disprove the Lords of the Impossible, the people for whom nothing ever changes but the date; they run the world with their tired playbooks about what can and can't be done. Enough of that.

I wanted to give anyone who was paying attention one more concrete example that bright-lined how seam-splittingly full of shit the powers that be truly are. I hoped an overall victory this season might shout out—to poets and shot-putters alike—to trust themselves, to ignore the built-in limitations that all systems impose. Heat it all up and bend it into any shape you want.

So publicity aversion aside, Sölden wasn't just the first race of the World Cup season, it was also the maiden voyage of SIRIUS Satellite Radio's *The Bode Show,* airing every Thursday night. What could be more anonymous than radio? No pictures, just sound. Very sweet setup. And the studio is crazy; it looks like Dr. Evil's moon base, with satellite displays everywhere and glass-walled rooms. On the radio I get to hold court on whatever I like, run my mouth, play music, tell stories, embarrass people. It's a great way to spend an hour.

The show takes its name from a line the coaches used to describe my performance in the early days when I would come ass-screaming down the course, killing everybody's time, and then eat it on the final pitch—sometimes spectacularly, sometimes pathetically, but always where everybody could see it full-on. The Bode Show was always worth the price of admission. The day after the show premiered, I skied well and won—a combination that never fails to satisfy me. I took the race by a full second. The only Bode show that weekend was on the radio.

After that, we got a three-week shakedown period until the next race, across the pond. While other racers train, hone their gear, and do whatever, I prefer to relax. I work on my game for the last week, but otherwise I go home, get in a last round or two of golf, and fulfill some contractual work for the companies I endorse, which could be anything from shooting television commercials to doing a grip-and-greet at a promotional event.

I spent one day doing a photo shoot for a men's outdoor-life/fitness sort of magazine. It wasn't my first time, so I knew what they wanted. It was in New York City, and I showed up in the same clothes I'd soaked through on the dance floor just a few hours earlier. I'd eaten since then, but I hadn't slept. I was a tad pale, and to call what I had "hat head" does a disservice to hats. For an even greater touch of realism, the makeup artist was late, so what the photographer saw was what he got, and it wasn't pretty.

Fortunately wardrobe took awhile. They wanted me in jeans, and they had twenty-seven pairs, all "my size," except my thighs are too big, my waist is too small, and my butt has bubbled. This is an occupational hazard that they don't tell you about in J3s. So I'm telling you young skiers out there: pants will never be the same. I'm surprised guys like Dane Spencer and Chip Knight, who have legs like bridge abutments, don't wear sarongs.

That weekend was the first time ever that somebody walked up to me on the street in Manhattan and shouted my name. Busted by a fan. I'd have been a lot more shaken by the experience if the guy hadn't been Austrian (thank goodness).

The season started up again in the Canadian Rockies—Lake Louise, near Banff. On November 27, I won the downhill training run, and while winning is usually good, it isn't if the start list is the reverse order of training times. This meant I'd be starting 30th the next day. I prefer somewhere in the middle: 14th or 15th is ideal. This is another example of how I don't even listen to me when I'm in the start house. I go into racing mode, and it makes no difference what anyone has told me to do, or even what I'm telling myself to do: I have an inner racer, and he just wants to rip.

I won that downhill the next day, 30th position and all. It was my fourteenth World Cup victory, and my first in a speed event. The hill was fast—conditions had dealt us a glider's course, and I was putting out more than ninety miles an hour in spots. I'd been working my gliding skills, and won the race by .97. Daron came in fifth, which made it a great day for the team, too.

Ever ride half naked in the back of a very fast-moving pickup truck and stand up to face into the wind? No? Well, downhill is a lot like that—except there's no truck under you, and the turns and pitches are inhuman. At top speed, a racer can pull between three and four gs, just like flying a fighter jet—except, again, there is no jet. Standing on a street corner is one g, the force of gravity, which is plenty for most people. But squeezing down into a bullet shape (and that's the other thing I worked this year in training—a tight little bull), and flying into some sick corner at ninety miles per hour puts my effective body weight at around eight hundred pounds, which is why we need tree-trunk legs and our pants don't fit.

I went out with the coaches that night to the Glacier Saloon and had a few pops. Then I woke up the next morning feeling rotten, but I said nothing about it before the race; Johno would have called me a lightweight. My condition might not have been so bad, but this being Canada and not Europe, there was no RV for me to store my gear in. That meant I had to carry it around from place to place, and there was a lot of it because we were headed directly to Beaver Creek, Colorado, for four events. I had to move it all down to the team van to be taken to the airport that morning, and heavy lifting has never been my preferred way to start the day. Or spend it. Or end it.

But it was another clear blue sky up at the mountain, and I had a super-G to run. This time I started 14th and finished first—a great run. I made very few errors, none worth mentioning. It was my first super-G victory (my best result to date had been a seventh-place finish), and a history-maker, too, because I became the first American to win World Cup races in all five events. On top of all that, I was sitting on 300 World Cup points. I'd been in the lead for the overall since October, and tripled my points that day. Three races, three wins, and in the eyes of some, nowhere to go but down. Of course, there were others who talked as if the season was over. But it was early. Daron represented again with another fifth-place finish, and the Austrians had six guys in the top eight that day, so I wasn't counting my chickens just yet. Not by a long shot.

Beaver Creek, our next venue on this North American stop-over, had more than just the Birds of Prey downhill course, which is a steep and technical run; it was also billed as a mini-Olympics because it ran four events in four days. It was a challenging schedule with not a lot of room for my favorite pastime, screwin' off.

The first race was another super-G, and I broke my winning streak by coming in second. Don't you hate that? I skied well, made a few mistakes, I was happy. The next day I put the downhill in the can, rolling right atop the podium in first place again. Even better, Daron was second, and Bryon Friedman, AKA Freedog, the musician-scholar of the U.S. Ski Team, was seventh. Having three guys in the top ten kicked ass. It was a huge day for the team, very emotional and misty.

After seeing that race, even my mom said she no longer feared for my life when I raced downhill. So now I could do no wrong, right? Wrong. I had a bad weekend, DNF'd the GS and the slalom, and the stories of my imminent demise immediately took root.

Back in Europe, in Val d'Isère, France, the first thing I did was get DQ'd from the downhill training run for wearing a GS suit. The DQ had no adverse effect on anything, including start numbers. Is there anything more meaningless than rules without purpose? If the FIS, or the race organizers in Val d'Isère, weren't taking this run any more seriously than a course inspection, then neither was I. The GS suit has padding to protect against gate-crashing, which makes it more aerodynamic than a downhill suit. And warmer, which is why I wore it. I came in fourth in that downhill the next day, December 12.

The day after that, in the first run of the GS, I maneuvered my way down the race course in a nuanced way, skidding through turns easily when I needed to, and taking them clean where possible. Not because I suddenly wanted to, but because I suddenly could. Up until now, my attack had typically been all or nothing—not always, but generally. Today I temporized. It wasn't easy; in fact it nearly short-circuited all the hardwiring in my body. I don't see the point of skiing as if I were waiting to make a move. There's no one else on the course, what the hell am I waiting for? And what's the move?

I wanted a time from the first run to determine how hard to charge in the second. This was radical thinking for me. But with more control, I didn't have to constantly attack; my approach was more measured and consistent. And of course, my time sucked. But I had a time.

So in the second run I yanked out the stops and, as I've been known to do, made some bad moves. But as luck would have it, a couple other guys, Raich and Christoph Gruber, also made some mistakes. Next thing I knew, I was on the top of the podium again; I had 630 World Cup points to Maier's 291 (who came in third). The beauty part was that, in addition to the race, I won my weight in wine. I sat on this big wooden scale as they loaded case after case of local wine until we were even.

So everything was good, except Freedog, who, after he crashed in training in Lake Louise and punctured his leg, landed in the hospital with a blood infection. When we headed out for Sestriere, Italy, we had to leave him behind, a World Cup casualty. We'd hook up again in Val Gardena.

On December 13, the night slalom in Sestriere—a beautiful and demanding course, steep to start and flat at the end—was memorable not only because I won it by 1.27 seconds, which is pretty fast; it also marked the moment when I'd won events in all four disciplines in the same season. It took sixteen days. Only a couple other World Cup racers—Marc Girardelli and Petra Kronberger—have done it. They also won combines in the same season, and we hadn't raced one yet.

I'll tell my kids about my speedy record setting, but beyond that, records don't mean much. As I say, there are so many variables in alpine ski racing that records are valuable only for rough context. The length and breadth of a racer's career provide a much better barometer of success. Today was a snapshot, a moment that happened because a lot of gears clicked. Case in point, I didn't even finish another slalom until March 13, three months to the day, the last race of the season. I placed sixth.

One objective measure that did rise that day was my overall point total, to 730. That was when everyone wanted to know if I planned to win the overall. I didn't know what to say that results can't say better. "We'll see?" If the question was, "Would you like to win more races than everybody else this season?" then the answer was definitely yes. And is that a goal of mine? It sure is. But mathematically, I could win more races than everybody else and still lose the overall. At the end of the season, when we add up everybody's points, we'll see who won the overall. But we won't know until then. I guess that's not great copy, because nobody ever seems satisfied with it.

Val Gardena, Italy, high in the Dolomites, is what World Cup considers one of its "classics." The rest of the big four includes, Wengen, Kitzbühel, and Val d'Isère.

I like Val Gardena. My results there can be middling, but the mountain is slick. The downhill has a nifty feature called the "camel humps," which are two significant jumps, one after the other, and they can hit you like big waves in a cold ocean.

The next day after the super-G, it was all Austrians on the podium: Michael Walchhofer, Hermann, and Beni. I came in fourth. Mistakes were made, not terrible ones. Walchhofer is big, six-five, built for downhill. A four-discipline racer, too. So I had my eye on him, and Raich. Strangely enough, Beni was the only Austrian in the top fifteen, but this game of musical chairlifts was far from over.

The downhill the next day was a slightly different deal from the super-G; I came in 14th. If you ski your best, there's nothing wrong with placing 14th, 24th, or 64th. What I like about skiing 14th is that I get to skip the press conference and go back to the RV to relax. Those are great days. But the days that you're on the podium, you get marched around from interview to interview until you begin to wish you'd caught a gate. So when my results aren't stellar, I remind myself that the downtime is precious.

But as always, you should be careful what you wish for. The next day in Alta Badia I missed a gate, hit a rock, broke my favorite GS skis, and DNF'd in the second run. Sometimes, when you attack, the mountain attacks back. What was cool about that day was that Tom Grandi, an Italian-born Canadian who had raced World Cup since 1993, won the first race of his career. Now, there's a determined and patient brother if ever I've known one.

He didn't have to wait another twelve years for his next win; three days later he won another GS in Flachau, Austria. I was third. From where I sat, I skied a great race, but he was simply unbeatable that day, greasing me by more than a second. Didier Cuche, who came in second, killed it, and me, too.

The next day, in the first run of the slalom, I plummeted down that course and crashed, DQ'd. Not much else about that, really. Back to the RV, boys.

A week later, after Christmas, I came in 14th again in the downhill, this time in Bormio, Italy. It was a long haul up that medieval cow path it's at the end of, just for a single race. But that's all there was. Getting into Bormio, and nearly every other World Cup venue, in a thirty-two-foot rig is world-class driving. Jake hadn't cracked up the RV in more than a month—hadn't torn the bumper off or tap-tap-tapped the guardrails in the Alps for a good while. We'd be back here in a few weeks for the World Championships. I still had a pretty commanding lead in World Cup points over Beni, 858 to 546. I was 14th, but he was 17th.

The next week, back in France, in Chamonix, Freedog crashed in the downhill training run and broke his right tib and fib and his left hand, which sidelined him as a racer for the rest of the season, and as a musician for who knows how long. Really sucky day for him, for the team competitively, and moreover for all of us personally, who are like family.

I came in eighth in that downhill and skied off the course the next day—my third consecutive unrealized slalom race. It was Giorgio Rocca's second slalom win in a row. Should I have spent more time sharpening the slalom last fall? Is skiing every event not without its consequences? Okay, fine. That still doesn't mean the story doesn't have a happy ending; it just means the narrative trajectory is a little uneven. What do you expect?

The following weeks moved by like a blur. I got second in the GS in Adelboden, where I lost a pole in the first run and nearly pulled my groin inside out in the second; I skied like crap, but I had a great recovery, which I count as a component of great ski racing—so I was conflicted but happy. The Chuenisbaergli is one of the toughest courses, and that day it was dark, literally near-zero visibility at the bottom. Daron had a superhuman backward-somersaulting crash at very high speed—many bumps and bruises, but otherwise okay. And second place got me the GS leader's red bib back from Grandi.

I was third in the downhill in Wengen, a race that Walchhofer won, his first this season. He was already wearing the red bib, because he'd been on the podium in more downhills than not this season. It's a long and grueling course, 2.8 miles of pure sport—invigorating, challenging. When you're done, you're done for a while.

The next day I boned the first slalom run of the combined, a true disappointment. I was being cautious—always a huge mistake. I hated the way I was skiing; it was slow and uninspired, purely designed to get me down the hill without a mishap. Then—oops—while pondering how little fun I was having, I straddled a gate like a distracted J1. Actually, I didn't know it had happened until I got to the finish and saw the star next to my name. Holy shit, I thought. What did I do? I looked at the training films later, and sure enough, I humped a gate halfway down the hill. Beni won the race, which put him less than 200 points behind me, fueling the horse race.

Daron was second in the super-G at Kitzbühel, and I was fifth. I was late on every turn; I played it all way too round. They canceled the downhill because of weather: too much wet snow. Usually a cancellation is no harm, no foul, but that was one of only two combines scheduled for the whole season. Plus I took time out of my slalom training to race in a downhill training run, because I thought it determined start placement in the race. Wrong. But how would I know the rules? They change every week. I took valuable time from something I should have been doing to get no number in a race that was canceled anyway. Because otherwise I'd just have been DQ'ing and DNF'ing my way across the Alps until I arrived back at Bormio for the World Championships.

The training-run confusion is a good example of what pisses me off about the FIS: it has a bad habit of allowing house rules to take precedence from race venue to race venue. This is some kind of stupid for a sport that would like to be taken more seriously. The criteria for how and when a course should be slipped, when a race should be stopped, when a training run counts—I could go on and on—is a local call. I say you can't act like a pickup game and expect to be treated like the NBA. If you're playing World Cup strip poker, either socks count as one article of clothing or two. It can't be yes in Wengen and no in Kitzbühel.

What if the designated-hitter rule in baseball varied from ball-park to ballpark, instead of league to league? Or if a first down in football meant the offense had to move the ball ten yards in Boston, twenty yards in Buffalo, and five yards in Miami? Tyrolean idiosyncrasies are charming, but the World Cup has outgrown provincialism; it's raced on three continents and speaks a dozen languages. *World* Cup, get it? Time to step up.

Around that time, the conventional wisdom was that the over-all was slipping away from me once again, that I was going to screw it up. Truth is, I hadn't lost my point lead once. It fluctuated all right, but that's ski racing. And who cares anyway? The idea is to go as fast as possible in every race, not to finesse an overall win with clever strategies and modest tactics. Nevertheless, I was developing a peevishness toward all the speculation regarding the end of the season. When I'm racing, I'm focused on the now, not the when; the present, not the presently. That's the way to keep it pure.

The acceptable answers to questions such as "How much energy will it take to win the overall?" are total flash: "I'm here to give it my all" (obviously), "I'm focused on a Crystal Cup. My strategy is blah blah" (shows character and basic math skills). "I work hard at this, day and night; it's my only interest in life; I've avoided all non-racing fun since my eighth-birthday party" (shows commitment and a serious personality disorder). I know it's hard not to concentrate on the one thing that's concrete, such as a point total, but that's just the lowest common denominator, the tangible thing that people who know nothing at all about ski racing can grasp.

People digest predictability well, but it's all watery oatmeal to me. I tire of repetition, which is good for my creative impulses but bad for those activities that benefit from a lot of mindless rote. I'm uncomfortable saying this to people who ask "What's it feel like?" I don't want to disappoint them, burst their bubbles about the nature of competition. But the way you get good at most things is by doing them over and over. And when you're as good as it gets, you start to get bored with it. At least I do. Some guys are as stoked the hundredth time they succeed at something as they were the first. Not me.

When all else fails, I have the power of the shrug. I'll say that a gold medal, in and of itself, doesn't feel like anything in particular (shrug), that it's just another day in a yearlong conga line (shrug), and that's the truth (shrug, tug cap visor).

When I win a race, I could thank my coaches, my equipment, and the snow fairies. I could also be wearing a purple wax poultice, sacrificing goats for good weather, and thinking only happy thoughts. But I'm not. The truth is, when I win it's because there wasn't anybody faster. It's as simple as it sounds—a lot simpler than back in the day, when a World Cup season was a seventeen-move chess game. But it's a six-month season now, and nothing much out of the ordinary ever happens, except on the piste.

Life is short, and it goes by fast. When I'm working my game, I like to take big steps. As you get to the top of your ability, the steps get smaller and smaller. All that's left for me in World Cup is baby steps, but everybody should have such problems. I mean that: imagine if every individual realized his or her potential; consider a world where failure is defined as not trying your hardest, and the worst it ever gets is the faint sense of anxiety brought on by stunning success.

In the 2004–05 season we raced forty-one times (plus five at the Nationals in April), and the variables—the weather, the equipment, the number of guys who can take care of business—are never fewer than the year before. Different courses set by different people every week, all run under different conditions for every snap of the wand. There is no even playing field in ski racing; like no other sport, it's a multileveled crapshoot, a changing constellation of possible outcomes. Anything can happen. As confident as I am, there's no escaping the X factor that determines whether things go your way more than they don't. Anything can happen, but not anything you couldn't have predicted, or shouldn't have expected.

I love the World Championships. They're a minivacation in the middle of the season every other year. For me, anyway. It's two weeks of partying and big crowds (albeit crowds that I can't participate in), and some very fast skiing. I don't care where you go or what you do, it doesn't get better than that.

I won two medals at the 2005 World Champs: a super-G (despite some bad skiing on my part) and a downhill. That, apparently, was expected. Then I DNF'd in the other three events, and while that's always half expected, it was not welcomed.

Easy come, easy go. I lost the super-G medal that night. It was in my jacket pocket and some shithead swiped the jacket out of the bar where we celebrated. Fortunately, he or she returned the medal to the bartender, but unfortunately the jacket was gone for good. It wasn't the first gold medal I'd lost. I'd put my combined medal from the 2003 World Champs to a utilitarian purpose, and like so many widgets in the machinery, it went missing. Make a long story short, the toilet seat in my apartment in Innsbruck was one of those that unexpectedly leaped out at you while you were peeing. I have a low tolerance for that. Turned out the medal was the perfect weight to anchor it, and all was right with that little part of the world. Then one day, I was using the toilet and bang! Down came the lid. Someone, it seemed, had relieved me of the medal. Oh well.

The next week in Garmisch, Germany, we ran two downhills (I got a third and a fourth) and a super-G (I got third). So again, a good weekend, inching me ever closer to what everyone else thought was the climax of my career, the unbeatable sense of hard-won victory. But I could feel the anticlimax coming, like hearing too much about a movie before you see it.

I didn't grouse about the undue focus on what hadn't happened yet, because people would write it off as burnout, or early-onset midlife crisis, or ennui. But I'm no fool—I know "ennui" is French for "whiny asshole." And if anything I'm lachrymose-intolerant. So I shrug when I do well, I shrug when I don't, and anybody who cares to speculate on what it all means can be my guest.

I was unhappy with my showing the next week in Kranjska Gora, Slovenia. We raced a GS and a slalom, and I DNF'd them both in the second runs. Problem was, it's where Robie Kristian, the ski technician I've worked with for years, is from. He's a great guy, so hometown props would have been nice. On top of my bad weekend, Raich had a good one, so the overall race tightened by 160 points. There were now just 31 points separating us.

We went to Kvitfjell, Norway, for a couple of speed events, and I got a fourth in the downhill and a fifth in the super-G, and added 20 points to my lead. You don't have to hang around there long to understand why the Vikings were such badasses. Then it was off to Switzerland for the finals. And they'd be finals in the strictest sense, deciding the season-long chase for the overall.

My family came to Lenzerheide for the end of the season, a bunch of them like a tribe from the faraway mountains. My cousin Chance Stith traveled ahead of them, alone, and overshot his stop on the train. When he learned they were going to charge him for the extra distance in the wrong direction, plus a ticket to get back where he belonged, he leaped off the moving train and disappeared into the Swiss countryside. He eventually found us, and we had a great time.

Expectations were running pretty wild at this point; my winning the overall had become the object for a lot of people. Under such circumstances, it's harder and harder to hear my own voice, to rely on my own motivations, and to keep them purely about speed and ability. In the past few years, I'd become a midsized cottage industry, and a lot of people had time and resources invested in my success. But I can't be thinking about that. In the end, happiness is running the best race possible. Nothing else. Should I be more conservative because I have others' fates in my hands? I don't get into it with myself, never mind anyone else. I just race my race. But this is out there in the ether, and it's impossible to avoid 100 percent.

The weather refused to cooperate in the Swiss Alps, and the races kept getting rescheduled because of whiteout conditions. So to the extent that I could, I shunned the world for a week. I stayed cloistered with my family or holed up in the RV alone, and chilled.

When we finally got to run, I came in second in the downhill;

Walchhofer won it and the title. Beni came in 24th, so now, with three races left, I was 90 points ahead. Winning the overall was a solid goal of mine, but it represents such an abstract concept to me that I wasn't even extra-stoked. I just skied my races. There is no real competition in World Cup, no "I'm running the field with this soccer ball, let's see if you can catch me," no one-to-one matchups, like in tennis. In skiing, no one ever competes against another skier; the clock is our adversary. Time.

The next day I won the super-G, along with the title, which was gratifying because it meant that my gold at the World Championships was no fluke. It also grew my lead over Beni to 184 points.

It was a great team day. Daron gave me an A-plus race report, and armed with his expert information, I laid down a killer run. We tied again, Daron and I, this time for first place. So that was all cool, and more proof that anything can happen in ski racing.

The clamor of "Is it over?" began in earnest. Despite the fact that there were still two races left, and 200 points on the table. Many of the people asking were Euros and were never steeped in baseball wisdom, but still, you have to know that it ain't over till it's over. I needed to be on my game for the remainder of the season. End of story. I had to be in the top fifteen the next day in the GS in order to mathematically cinch the overall. The operative phrase in that sentence being "the next day."

So the next day, the GS, and I had trouble on the top of the run; it felt sticky, and though I had the best time for a while in the second run, I knew it wasn't likely to hold. Eventually Stephan Goergl zoomed by me; I got second. And Beni got third, which meant he got the GS cup. And I won the overall. That was a good night.

Twenty-four hours later, with the overall wrapped and the curse lifted from the U.S. Ski Team, I messed up and came in 13th after the first run of the slalom. But in the second run, I ripped, despite the fact that I hadn't finished a slalom since that night in early December in Sestriere, eight long slaloms ago. But I finished this one, coming in sixth—a redemptive end to the season, a good way to go into the next. If I were so inclined.

On the way home, the airline broke my trophy: a twenty-six-pound cut-crystal globe on a broad stem. It was swathed in bubble wrap and encased in a carry-on bag with CRYSTAL embroidered on the front. But the plane from Dulles to Manchester was small and they insisted I check it.

When I claimed the bag, it was jangling. My, my, said the customer service representative when I opened it for them to see. They suggested I file a claim. What was its value? they wanted to know. A very good question, I thought. I'm sure it has inherent value, it's a beautiful thing. But total value? It's just a trophy; an artifact of the actual event.

Exactly, my mother said when I got back to Tamarack. It's an artifact. Somebody might actually want to see it someday. She'll ask the FIS for a replacement, and because she's so nice they'll probably give her one. So the airline is off the hook, but I'd like to know why it's such a mystery to them that they're all going bankrupt.

I used to think that the best thing I could do for racing was to race. Golds at World Champs, win the overall—that sort of thing. But this season convinced me that the best thing I can do for ski racing is to mix it up a little. In interviews I suggested I might form a new pro tour funded by factory teams, where all the racers and coaches—not just me and a few others—would get a piece of the action; everyone would make a good living, have plenty of time off, and get basic benefits, such as health insurance, a 401(k). After all, Erik got hurt last year, Bryon and Marco Sullivan both broke bones and were out this season, and Daron could have gotten creamed in Adelboden. This isn't volleyball.

So if it's possible for me to help create a more exciting and dynamic ski tour that rewards racers, coaches, and techs at the level they deserve while at the same time leaving room for full-blown lives off the slopes to raise families, race cars, or raise hell, then I feel like I should pursue that. It's not a new feeling. I had the idea long ago that the ski team ought to be unionized. Now I realize a separate competitive tour would be so much sweeter.

I also said I might not go to the Turin Olympics in 2006, because fame simply doesn't become me; I'm not the famous-for-being-famous type. I realize, of course, that maybe I want to be anonymous in the same way World Cup skiing wants to be a club sport. We live in the era of the grand spectacle, and I have no problem with that, as long as I'm not the one expected to fill in the blanks for those who prefer watching to doing. I like *The Matrix*, but I prefer meat space.

These days, everything from sex to golf to politics is a spectator sport, and anyone lolling on the sidelines of life is losing out in ways I can't begin to explain (so I won't). And since I no longer have to imagine skiing ninety miles an hour, or whacking a golf ball 350 yards, I don't. But even if I did, I doubt sufficient language exists to properly convey the difference between reality's rock-hard kick and the wispiness of even the best simulations. Just like a raucous crowd is only fun if you're part of it, there isn't even the slightest comparison between watching the greatest race ever run and actually running one yourself.

7

Have Fun

Race preparation is simple: unless you're injured, your body is ready—that's a given, and if it's not, get back to work. Make your mind ready, too. Lose any baggage, personal or otherwise, go ninja, and wipe your mind clean of negative thoughts. Conditions, equipment, and the other racers are variables you can't control, and that's enough. Don't add to the list of unknowns. I'm a very even-tempered person, and this isn't a problem for me. I just go and race. I'm actually more relaxed racing than in most things. I don't go up to the start house until it's my turn. The antics up there look like a Japanese game show—people growling, primally grunting, exorcising their slow-demons. That's because in those clutch moments when you need to recover from a bad move or go faster than you ever have, the little voice inside your head better be saying *Yes you can,* because if it isn't, prepare to die.

I don't mean to sound like a late-night self-help infomercial, but to stay focused you need standards—something to measure your day-to-day progress by. And in this, as in all things, happiness is my yardstick. You can use what you like, by all means, but I highly recommend happiness. If I'm happy in a comprehensive, contented way, then I'm doing things right. If something is bad for my skiing but good for my general happiness, I give more weight to the latter. I recognize that there are things I enjoy—certain people, beer, and fast cars—that are not directly beneficial to my sport. Still, they make me happy. And that's all there is to it.

I live exactly the life I'd choose for myself if I could go to the hardware store and buy one off the shelf, and I got it by maximizing my fun. I'm convinced that in the end, it's that very pursuit of happiness that makes me ski better. It's like the old bumper sticker: THERE IS NO ROAD TO PEACE—PEACE IS THE ROAD. Same deal with happiness. Exactly the same.

Your folks may never tell you this—especially if they're ripping a check for $28K every year so you can attend a ski academy—but I'll tell you: don't exert yourself too far past your misery threshold for too long. Boredom coupled with rote exercise leads to unhappiness and poor performance. Then you're susceptible to any number of adolescent gripes, mishaps, and psychological conditions, which can't be good for your game either.

Dry-land training is one of those things, like sexual abstinence and multivitamins, that purport to be good for your racing. It is, but not much evidence backs up the claim that endless amounts of it pay off endlessly. It's like wearing skis: if two make me go fast, will four make me go faster? I don't think so.

Let's face it: running through tires makes you good at running through tires. Everybody knows that. Running an obstacle course, scaling a ten-foot wall, leaping over a water hazard, and, of course, running through tires—I did all that in high school. In fact, my team once won an intramural competition because I climbed the wall without touching the rope. I just walked up it, like Spider-Man. Actually, there was a seam between the two pieces of plywood, an ever-so-subtle toehold, and I used it for all it was worth. That's the lesson there. It was fun, but it never made me a better skier.

It did, however, come in handy at the CBS SuperStars in Jamaica just after the 2002 season. I did my Spidey act again, beat LaVar Arrington of the Washington Redskins over the wall, and won the big check with the fastest time ever. CBS now holds the SuperStars a month too early for skiers to compete—largely, I think, because we dominated it. Guys couldn't live with getting taken down by ski racers year after year: Hermann had won it the year before, and Johnny Mosley took second two years in a row. I mean, why show up just to get shown up? You guys in the NFL know who I'm talking about. Kidding, kidding . . .

CBS SuperStars, 2002

I don't run through tires; I play myself into shape. I run a soccer ball up and down the field, or whack a golf ball or a tennis ball, ride a mountain bike or a unicycle, walk a slack wire. Whatever I like. I use my mind and my body, which adds a dimension to training that running tires is never going to match. And it's not that I don't want to do traditional dry-land stuff, but rather that I find it difficult to pass up all the golfing and wakeboarding I do. I have time for both, but I eventually wear myself down; my physical exertions become counterproductive from a training perspective. Recovery and rest are just as important as whatever it is you need rest from.

I joke about it a lot, maybe to my detriment, but I take ski racing very seriously—including the training. In fact, training is more important than results. A hundred different things can happen in a ski race to affect the results. So I endeavor to control the things I can control. That includes thirty-seven full days of training before the start of ski camp in New Zealand every August, or in Chile in

September. Some of it is muscle-specific work, some of it is grueling stamina building, and some of it is redlining up Butternut Hill on my Cannondale.

I invented, and my uncle Mike welded together, the E-centric Machine, the tummy-trimmer of my dreams. It also works the precise upper- and lower-body parts that a racer needs, without wasting an ounce of energy on some other muscle that contributes nothing to skiing fast. Your eccentric muscles are the ones that control the weight coming down. Watch a power lifter clean and jerk a quarter ton of plates and bar into the air above his head. Pretty impressive, but as soon as it's up and the judges say, "Clear," the guy drops it. How much more impressive (and difficult) would it be if he put it down slowly and smoothly? How much stronger would he be if he could? So I train every muscle that needs training. Nobody eats without working around here, except for Cam and Chelone, but they're *snowboarders,* so we expect that. Cam actually skis on a mono-ski, which is a snowboard with a seat.

Primarily, the E-centric Machine is designed to improve my eccentric leg strength, which is the ability to turn. At eighty miles per hour, tucked in a crouch, and beating feet over the uneven crud left behind on the racecourse, making your moves and holding your line is what wins races. And you can't do that without X-Men-strength mutant legs, all the result of a welding experiment gone terribly, terribly right.

I'm an economical exerciser, always searching for that fine line between training and not-training. My patented method involves working as hard as you can—pump iron, ride a unicycle five miles with your cousin on your shoulders, push an abandoned snowmobile up a logging road, whatever—until you puke. And puke hard. This has to be a good gut-wrenching retch so that your eyes bug out and your navel is flush with your spine. Next, have a nice big drink of water and throw that up too. Be as sick as you like.

Now quit for the day, and go play any combination of soccer, golf, and tennis until it gets dark. Go out that night and drink enough to dance your ass off so you have to get half naked to avoid passing out from the heat, play some pool to cool down, then get up the next morning and do it all over again.

The reality of my wild life is embellished by the tellers, and encouraged by me as a way to needle coaches who say I don't train hard enough. But that's me; I can be a ballbuster. And the truth is that when I'm in St. Anton and I hang at the Funky Chicken drinking beer until after the dishwashers have gone home, like I did last year, it's only because that's what I want to do. I had friends and family in town, and I was enjoying myself. I skied eighth the next day in the downhill, and I won the slalom the day after that. When the job prevents me from living life as I see fit, that's when I'll be too old for it. That's when I'll take up fun as a full-time concern.

Truth is, I ski and train or both for four events ten months of every year. So forget the hype that I don't train, because I train my ass off. I just don't respond well to orders to do so, summonses from afar to be in some foreign place where it's winter, while I'm still enjoying the ridiculously short summer we get in the North Country. I ignore them because you can never do enough for some people, so why start? Everybody from the publicist's assistant to brainless ski association vice presidents to adoring fans would be barking orders at me, telling me what to do. Not to mention the coaches—nice and helpful as they all are, it's in their genes to micromanage. I don't want to be bothered, and I follow advice only if I ask for it, and I never ask for it. People call that arrogance, but I've gotten so little good advice in my life that it's not worth mentioning, and certainly not worth following.

When I was young and I'd miss a turn or bang a gate, my coaches would have tips, such as "Get on your edges and make the turn." Duh, no shit, I would if I could. I knew what I needed to do; I just didn't have the chops to do it yet. I was small and hadn't developed the muscles necessary to carve out a turn at fifty or sixty miles an hour, then link it up with sixty or seventy more arcs. So months later, when I'd gotten closer, I'd start bending my knees, or getting my tips pointed downhill, or dipping my hip and popping back up, and they'd say, "See, if he'd only listened to me three months ago . . ."

I train on my own quite a bit. In fact, I do everything on my own. When I inspect a course, I like to get there first and see it for myself. I don't want another human in the picture if I can help it. I like it barren and tranquil.

Sure, I'm unorthodox, but I try to keep an open mind. It

serves me well. For instance, back when I'd been on the U.S. Ski Team a year or so, I was looking to bulk up that summer. I did my regular sick regimen religiously, and I felt like I'd been kicked down a flight of metal stairs most of the time. My uncle Bill raised organic cattle, so I beefaloed up.

One day in August I was relaxing on my skateboard, and in order to keep myself properly hydrated I was drinking a bottle of SoBe. Somehow—because this never happens to me—I fell, but this time on the bottle, and crushed it under my hand and laid open my right palm, from pinkie to thumb. The result was pain, and puddles of blood, and then a small drama involving the emergency room and emergency major surgery to reattach my tendons and repair the nerves in my hand. Not the mellow afternoon I'd planned. So a bad move, right? I mean, you need your thumbs to hold on to your poles.

Fast-forward to later that year, later that season: my hand was healed (though my middle and ring fingers are partially numb to this day) and I was racing in the World Championships at Vail. A television reporter asked me what I'd done this summer, so I told her I'd cut my hand. And then I stuck it in front of the camera and delivered a somewhat didactic explanation of what was severed and where, and how it was all reattached. I find this stuff interesting, especially when it happens to me.

I also mentioned that it was a shattered SoBe bottle that had sliced me. As it happened, the founder and then CEO of SoBe, John Bello, was staying at the same hotel as the team and saw the story. He thought it was all pretty cool stuff, and asked to meet me in the bar. We had a good palaver, by the end of which we had a nice endorsement deal. Chance had come out with Jo for the races, and he and I stayed up half the night designing a SoBe logo out of cardboard and tinfoil to paste on my helmet. This was long before I'd done anything sufficiently athletic to warrant a sponsorship—except cut myself skateboarding, so you never know how things will go. And though he's no longer involved with SoBe, and SoBe's no longer involved with me, John and I remain good friends. And I still drink a lot of SoBe.

I have a lot to say about certain things, but that's no reason for you to listen. There's no shortage of unbidden advice out there about working hard, not sweating the small stuff, paying attention to your feng shui, never playing cards with a guy named Doc, whatever. Well, here's my small bit: everything you need to succeed is inside in your head; listen to yourself.

8

Be Good

When I do good, I feel good. When I do bad,
I feel bad.

—*Abraham Lincoln*

I follow a simple plan: go fast, be good, have fun. It isn't a mantra; I don't have it tattooed anywhere, or on my license plate. It's just what I live by, how I was raised. My mother said it to me every time I left the house. Well, she said the "be good" part. The other stuff was always implied.

I was good at going fast and having fun and didn't need a lot of encouragement to do either. Go with your strengths, right? Isn't that everyone's secret to success? The secret sauce of happiness— and spread it thickly—is living life fully and honestly in the context of something greater than yourself. When we're young, it's teams, gangs, role-playing games, the glee club, whatever. For adults, it's power, prestige, and income—to be happy, we need a certain amount of all three; whichever you put at the center of your life determines that life.

Not that anything is ever set in stone. The second ingredient to a full life—being good—is always a work in progress. We can always be nicer, can't we? I can, anyway. For instance, I love fans. It's nice to be appreciated, but I'd race if there were no fans. And I've got to say that people banging on my RV in the middle of the night or writing love letters in Sharpie on the door do not make me happy. Same with the eighty-seventh person in the course of an average day who asks me to sign their kid's forehead; I could do without that at times. Not that I begrudge them the autograph, but it can get to be a big part of the day, and I have things to do too. Still, I'm nice anyway, because to be anything other than civil and accommodating to a fan who's being reasonable is an act of absolute tin-pot villainy.

Sustaining fun through circumstances that in themselves aren't fun—making the best of jail, school, an IRS audit, knee surgery, alien abduction, whatever you've got—is central to finding true happiness, which is the meaning of life. I know it sounds stupid. So what?

Plenty of people believe that there's no meaning to life, and their own lives are probably perfect examples of this pointlessness. It's existentialism, but it's also resignation, and it doesn't get you far. We can't all sit in cafés smoking clove cigarettes and arguing that a beggar's life and a king's are no different from our own. Maybe to appreciate your own life you have to improve the beggar's, overthrow the king, or both.

Early on I understood my gifts; I knew that they'd lead me to something more important than simply doing them. Skiing fast can't possibly be the entire point of a person's life. But skiing introduced me to the Special Olympics, and since high school I've been involved with them, and I hope to be more involved someday. Makes me happy to help.

Skiing fast made me famous; if I use it to do more than sell junk food or financial services, then I'm tapping into something larger than myself. And that makes me profoundly happier than my Porsche ever will. Not faster, but happier.

We all know people who mask their unhappiness with drugs,

prescription or otherwise, or with acquisition, or with other pleasures of the flesh—all of which can be momentarily satisfying. But in truth, they only make you temporarily less miserable. When you've dialed into the life you ought to be living, all the other games you play to lighten your load will seem like wasted time. Thomas Jefferson understood this; that's why he listed the pursuit of happiness, along with life and liberty, as essential elements of a free society. This isn't hedonism I'm practicing; it's good citizenship.

It all seems straightforward: go fast, be good, have fun. I've been stepping up to the "go fast" and "have fun" side of things pretty regularly: money, cars, jet-setting around the globe, playing golf with the pros, riding in the Indy 500 pace car, making movies. Believe me, it's hard not to have fun.

The "be good" component is easy to slack off on, and sometimes I do. Always have. But on the last day of the 2002–03 season, circumstances converged to sharpen the focus of what it means. Call it an epiphany. Somehow my perspective on ski racing was developing, becoming more seasoned. I wasn't tired of winning (that'll never happen), but I was sick of beating Schlopy. And I'm not usually that way. Ninety-nine days out of a hundred I'm more than happy to kick his ass.

This is what happened: it was the final race of the U.S. Nationals, the last day of a great, grueling season. I was the new combined and GS world champion, I'd won silver in the super-G, a new event for me, and I'd never felt stronger or more confident. I'd battled the greatest skiers in the world all season long and done well. But now it was spring and I wanted to play golf, go for a run in my shorts, ride my bike, drive my car. Pretty much anything but ski.

I'd won three of three races there in Lake Placid, New York, three gold medals, and I was in line for the second run of the GS, two seconds ahead of my closest competitor—Schlopy. So it looked like another gold. It wouldn't be a sweep because I was fourth in the downhill, and I started wondering, yet again, What the hell is the point of all these medals anyway? Is there a point?

So unless something happened, it looked like Erik was in line for the silver. And things always happen. Erik's a great guy, five years older than me, very experienced. In November 2003, he got hurt in the first race at Park City, Utah—blew out his ACL, down and out for the season. I missed not having him around, not having the camaraderie we share. It took some getting used to. During the season, he's not only my teammate; he's been my roomie for the last four years. We met in 1998, the year Schlopy returned to the team from a couple of years on the pro circuit.

We decided to find a place in Europe where we could live when we weren't racing or training with the team. We found a shepherd's shack, essentially, in the hills above Innsbruck, in Austria: no running water, no central heat, and at the literal end of the road. The mountain was behind us, straight up into the sky, and nothing else. We had a couple of rooms, a place to cook. Sheep ran everywhere, and guys in little green hats smiled and waved; they were nice people who liked having us around purely because we were ski racers.

I had the idea to find a crib first; Schlopy swears he came up with it, but that's total bullshit. He did live in a van for a couple of years with a guy he paid $500 a month to be his driver and equipment tech while he skied. So he may have come to feel the need for a home base sooner than I did, but I mentioned it first. I think.

Living there and skiing European mountains, with their different conditions and snow types, was a huge leg up for us as American skiers. Not traveling home or living in a crappy hotel when we had downtime was a step toward humanizing our lives. Getting off the institutional eating and sleeping program and onto a regime that seemed more like what we'd be doing if we were home was healthy on every level imaginable.

It was Paul Fremont-Smith, once again, who helped us pay for that place. A year later, when we had some results to back up the talk, he rented us an apartment down in Innsbruck. At the time it was the killer app of ski racing, the program we needed to take our act to the next level.

Anyway, I'd been on the team for a couple of years when Schlopy returned. He'd been on the pro circuit, basically skiing freelance for a few years. It had made him tough, and he was already smart. I knew immediately that this was someone who would contribute greatly to my racing education. I was only partly right; he turned out to be a good influence all around. He turned me on to some great books and ideas; he encouraged me to stand my ground when others accused me of obstinacy. When I was injured, he's the guy who stayed in touch. In some ways, if not for Schlopy, I might not have been standing there that day with three gold medals. He's a brother.

It's true that no one had won four golds at the U.S. Nationals since 1959, and that getting to the bottom of the hill fastest is what ski racers live by. But in the greater scheme of things, what was more important: winning this one race or being generous to someone close to me? I realized that I wanted Schlopy to win that race. He's a great skier, and he hadn't gotten the notice that he'd deserved that season, partly because the press was fixated on me. In a way, I'd robbed him.

There's also a practical side to winning and losing. The financial incentives put on gold medals by the companies racers endorse are significant. I added up in my head what I thought Schlopy's sponsors would pay him for a gold as opposed to a silver for that one race. It was a nice piece of change.

My mother and uncle Mike were standing in line with me, and I told them what I was thinking. Never in my life have I considered not winning, and how good it might feel. But when I pictured myself doing it I felt unburdened, elated even.

They weren't so convinced. Jo brought up the 1959 record, and I just looked at her like, When did you start reading books with lists in them? She eventually came to agree with me.

When they can, people do for friends; people sacrifice for friends. That's the deal. That's what was going through my mind. Up until now, when it came to ski racing, the only win-win situation I was interested in was when I killed both runs of a slalom or GS. Magnanimity on the racecourse was so out of character for me that it was definitely worth pondering. Maybe not then and there, but I did anyway.

Schlopy winning was a bit of a pipe dream because I'd have to fall or ski backward to lose a two-second jump on him. I knew it, he knew it, everybody knew it. So what was the point?

Uncle Mike, a U.S. Ski Team coach and a former national skier, quizzed me in his Obi-Wan Kenobi way, making sure that I knew the implications of doing such a thing. His Socratic reasoning helped me realize that not only did Mom and I think it was a good idea, but Socrates was on board too.

Mike eventually concluded that it was a case of me exerting my dominance in an evolved way; that now not only could I win, but I could make someone else win. That's some deep sports psychology, and it actually sounded devolved rather than evolved to me. The only eternal truth here is that simplifying one's life is very complicated.

I thought that if it were possible at all, I could take a hard dogleg where anybody could have a bad turn; I'd take it too wide and scrub the time I needed and then some. But once I started racing, my body, as usual full of muscle memory, was more in control than my conscious mind. I went shooting right through that dogleg; I carved it so hard and fast that both my left cheeks nearly scraped the piste. Schlopy was no longer on my mind. Evolved? I don't think so, not in this altered state.

I came through the finish not thinking I'd lost much time anywhere but aware that I'd been having a conversation with myself all the way down that my body had tried to ignore. I'm always cognizant of what transpires in a race, and I can describe in exquisite detail every one of them from the time I was a J1. But I couldn't remember much of what had just happened; my mind had been elsewhere. I looked up at the clock, and lo and behold, I was second. Schlopy won the race, took the gold. Cool, I thought.

The woman standing next to my mother turned to her and said, "Wasn't that nice of him!" But it wasn't. I'd only been thinking about it; I hadn't actually done it. There's no virtue in being absentminded.

I got a silver, and a good time was had by all. Erik got some of the attention that he richly deserved and I had that warm feeling of having done something nice without actually having done anything at all—a great way to end the season.

I'll give you another example of where good finds the sweet spot. A few years ago, in the local men's soccer league I play in with the Easton Aliens, I took a penalty kick against Hanover—in truth, I fired a meteor against their line of defenders, sure that they'd step out of the way when they saw black and white with sparks flying off it coming at them. I wanted to put it just over their heads, so there was nothing they could do to stop it, and low enough so it retained the proper trajectory to land in the back of the net. But, best-laid plans and all, some brave player put his mug in the way to block it, or maybe my shot was slightly off—I don't know. It wasn't pretty; he crumpled, and howled, and I didn't like it—not as much as he didn't like it, granted, but I'd hurt that guy and that's the last thing I ever want to do. And what made it suck even worse, I didn't score. And they won.

The Easton Aliens, 1995. I am standing at the far left.

The next year, we had a big play-off game down in Merrimack, New Hampshire, against Hanover. The Aliens met at my uncle Mike's, and just to get all ginned up, we watched a soccer game from Europe on ESPN. A so-so game, but there was a penalty kick that the guy booted from a slightly oblique angle, spinning junk all over it, and it boomeranged out around the line of defense and popped into the high right corner of the goal as if it were an open net. Money shot.

With that for inspiration, we jumped in our cars and cruised to the game. It was uneventful, 0–0 until halfway through, when the Aliens had a penalty kick. Just like last year. In keeping with tradition, I stepped up to take it, and I could see that their memories remained fresh. Half of them had their faces all scrunched up like they were sucking lemons; the other half looked like their asses were about to explode.

I scoped up and down the line, choosing my shot, and they waited breathlessly for the cannon to fire. Finally, I ran at the ball from a hard angle and launched it out over their clueless heads so that it arched back in and around them and slid into the high right-hand corner of the net. The goalie found it about the same time everybody else did. We won that game 1–0. So the question is this: Which kick would they prefer? If you ask me, everybody wants the shot they can stop.

And, of course, being nice doesn't end at the piste. I bought a house a couple of years ago. Not just any house, but my grand-mother's house, the one she'd built across the road after Jack went to the veterans' home down in Tilton.

When she moved there, we moved into my grandparents' old place. Despite looking like the monolith in *2001: A Space Odyssey,* it was home sweet home to us. It's off the road but not in the woods, and up a hill you need a tractor to plow snow off in the winter. Every evening, the black bears treat the compost pile as if it's their appetizer, and the deer always get as much of the garden as we do, if not more. But it's accessible by car and has running water and electricity, so we're talking twentieth century.

Anyway, below that house and across the road from mine is a cabin that Tamarack bunks tennis instructors in. It's sketchy but fine in the summer. Half the people in the North Country have "camps," which are small cottages on a lake or in the woods some-where, usually no more than ten miles from their regular house. People move into these places for the warm months as a way of doing something a little different—roughing it, fishing every night after work, seeing a whole different group of neighbors—a lot of reasons. So the cabin below Jo's house isn't a bad place to live in the summer.

In the winter, however, it sucks. It's cold and drafty, not insu-lated, and the windows fit like somebody else's dentures. Keep in mind, this is the heart of the Easton Valley—the wind tears through the place at all times, quickly carrying away what little heat the green wood barely burning in the tiny stove can throw. My sister Wren's partial namesake, the local big wind known as the

Bungay Jar, sometimes blows like it's going to pick the whole place up and flip it over like a dish of ice cream—which is what it feels like inside. The drains and pipes freeze regularly; ice in the toilet is not unheard of.

The winter of 2002, my friend Cam was living in the cabin. Now, that's not so bad. He grew up deeper in the woods than I did, but he's in a wheelchair now, paralyzed from the chest down seven years ago. Frozen pipes and splitting wood are a challenge for him. And he has a hard time living at his folks' place because they have an outhouse.

I remember the night of Cam's accident too well. It was 1997, just before the start of the ski season, and I was home. Worm was visiting, and a party was in play. We were on the horn, trolling for friends, but no one was around. I told Worm that this was strange because those guys were always somewhere, and I knew all the somewheres. I started to get a bad feeling; Lars and Chelone had gone for pizza and weren't back yet. My Spidey sense told me something was up, so Worm and I jumped in my car to reconnoiter.

Not far from my mom's house we saw red and blue emergency lights. As we approached the scene, the strobes filled the dark sky, fire foam covered the road, and we could see a car in the ditch. One front tire slowly turned as if someone had just bumped into it or the accident had just happened.

The Franconia Fire Department is a volunteer outfit, so I knew them all, and I could get up close. In the flash of a blue light I saw a red Jetta off the soft shoulder, on its side. The firefighters used the Jaws of Life to cut it open, and I realized it was Cam's ride I was looking at. I went closer, and a cop yelled at me. I was angry and anxious because they wouldn't tell us anything useful, just gave us a bunch of shit. So, of course, I yelled back at him. Worm got us out of there. We went home and stayed put.

Chelone and Lars showed up at the house much later, both shaken. Chelone is not easily ruffled, but he was tweaked that night. They'd been at the hospital until somebody there had made them go home to sleep.

Cam had been right in front of them when he'd crashed. It just happened, they said. One minute he was on the road and the next he wasn't. They pulled over, and it was just them there for a while, huddled over Cam. Outside, the hood of the car was on top of Cam's legs, while his upper body was twisted and stuck up through a window. They tried everything to move the car off him, but they couldn't budge it. All they could do was talk to him, and try to keep him conscious.

Cam was terrified and wailed in pain, "Get this car off me, get this fuckin' thing off me!" Mickey Libby was right behind them and went for help. "I'm dying in here," Cam told them.

When the state police arrived, the trooper looked closely at Cam and told Chelone he was dying. "He's going," he said, and they pulled Chelone away. But Chelone shook them off and made a stink, so they let him stay, figuring what the hell, Cam was dead anyway. As the firemen cut the car away from Cam's body, Chelone held on to his hand and talked to him, telling him to breathe and to focus, to squeeze tight and stay alive.

Emergency workers had taken Cam away by the time Worm and I arrived. Chelone rode in the ambulance with Cam. I can't tell you how many times Cam should have been dead or badly injured already, but it comes when you least expect it. An incubus lurks in the night sky, and he's a bloodthirsty asshole.

That's the hell of it—there's no moral to the story. He wasn't speeding; he wasn't doing anything stupid. Cam doesn't remember—maybe he was reaching for a tape or playing with the heater. Who knows? It doesn't take much on a back road with a deep drainage ditch along the side. You could flip a Bradley armored vehicle without much effort.

Fortunately for Cameron Chedley Shaw-Doran, he doesn't recall any of it. His brain mercifully secreted a megadose of the neurochemical that blots out bad memories and erased the night from his mind. He didn't come around for nearly a month and spent more months in the hospital. The last thing he remembers is eating pesto and pasta with his folks. It's a nice little homeostatic device my body has used more than once, too. The Eliminator. Some terror is best not relived. But it only removes the incident from your memory, not from your life.

Cam had a rough few years after that. He was not the happiest guy in town for a while. He never took well to the chair, and had a hard time getting back to life and normalcy without it. So Chelone and I got him thinking mobile again—both literally and figuratively—by learning to use his wheelchair as extremely as possible, crash testing it in oh so many ridiculous ways. We fell on our heads a lot, but we fall on our heads a lot anyway, so we didn't care. In the end, we knew the chair's top speed both frontward and backward, as well as its tipping point in all directions, its turning radius, its turning radius on one wheel, and so on.

When Cam saw what could be done in his chair—dips, spins, fake drops, dead stops—he began to see the possibilities, and eventually it looked different to him. It wasn't necessarily a wheelchair—maybe it was a slick little chariot made out of aircraft aluminum and rubber. Fun, fast.

A couple of years later he got a handcycle, which is a long-nosed tricycle that he can nearly lie down in while he pumps the pedals with his big Arnold arms. One day I saw Chelone going down the Easton Road doing a wheelie on it; later that week, Cam was seen driving it up on its side, on two wheels, headed into town.

Last summer I passed him in my Porsche on Three-Mile Hill, the road from Cannon Mountain into town. As I went by, I slowed and beeped to say hi; he immediately fell in behind me and drafted down the mountain six inches off my rear bumper at sixty miles per hour. Later he said the Porsche was too low to the ground to create a decent vortex, and that the wide tires kept bouncing gravel off his forehead. According to him, Kenworths have what's needed for cadging a magic-carpet ride: a big wind tunnel and mud flaps.

All this might sound reckless, but we don't see it that way. Cam believes he shouldn't avoid danger and fun because he's in a wheelchair but rather should seek it out, especially because he's in a chair. Either way, life goes on with or without you. Cam knows that to get anything done, he has to work twice as hard as you or me. He accepts that. And it makes it no more central to his life than his red hair is.

Anyway, he was getting booted from the cabin because Tamarack needed it for the summer, so I had him move in with me. He was reluctant at first, because my girlfriend would be living there too. Cam didn't want to be a third wheel, so to speak. But it was either that or ice in the toilet again next winter. I assured him that there'd be so many people around all summer that it would be hard to tell who lived there and who didn't—other than he'd have a room and would theoretically load the dishwasher once in a while.

So he moved in. And so did my cousin Chance, who'd been burned out of his apartment downtown. He'd lived in a building with a lot of our friends. On the scanner, the police referred to the place as "the Rat's Nest." I have no idea what they meant by that.

We had a great time living together that summer; we still do. We have simple deals—call them living arrangements. I buy the hot tub; Cam keeps it clean. I pay for the addition to the house; Cam finds a contractor. That kind of thing.

Now Cam splits his habitation between my place and his apartment in Plymouth, where he goes to college. So I have to find somebody else to clean the hot tub. Not that Cam ever did, anyway. Or load the dishwasher, for that matter. He did, however, on August 1, 2005, become the first person in the 144-year history of the Mount Washington Auto Road to make an ascent in a wheelchair—all 7.6 miles of it, straight up. He didn't tell anybody what he was up to; he didn't even train for it. He just got it into his head to go try, and fourteen and a half hours later, through rain and two miles of gravel, his hands numb and elbows aching, Cam succeeded. Now *that's* cool.

I bought a house in Park City, and Cam will be moving out there; they have one of the best adaptive-skiing programs in the world, and there's a University of Utah campus there, too. I couldn't figure how the hell else to get rid of him. And Chance? I've decided to double the size of my house and move over into the new and improved half. My cars can live there with me, downstairs. They're quiet, unless they're running, and they never use all the toilet paper.

I like it at home; I like having roommates. And nothing's changed much. That's good, because normalcy brings out the best in me. By normalcy I mean having my mother chew my ass out once in a while, and fixing broken windows because nobody else will, and having my friends treat me regular. The fuckers do call me "Superstar" behind my back and don't think I know it. But I have my sources.

At the end of the 2003–04 season, my buddies all pitched in and bought me a ticket on a cruise out of Florida. Of course, they all came too; there were nine of us. All those shaved heads and tattoos—we looked like an escaped chain gang out for some fun. It was a great time, and damn nice of them boys. We swam, ate, drank, played water polo, ate more. Then we ate again. I don't gamble—not with money, anyway—but I believe there was a bit of that going on too. I was eating at the time. So that was nice, and I appreciate nice. Truly. Especially in the face of all the not-so-nice one encounters.

I don't like not-so-nice. I offer unconditional indifference, so my bar for socially acceptable behavior isn't that high. But some things are just too much. For instance, on the road with the Aliens a couple of summers ago, there was an incident in a town that will remain nameless because not everyone there is an asshole. Actually, there are many nice people there; I've met them. But the soccer team, for the most part, was a bunch of thugs in cleats, and somebody had done a lousy job of raising them. So we'll leave it at that. Anyway, we were kicking their fat asses one evening when some inbred on their bench started yelling, "Break his leg! Break his leg!" Since I was doing most of the running with the ball, I assumed he meant me.

Now, I take my sports seriously, but wishing harm on another person, especially a guy you're playing in a town soccer league with, is not mentally healthy. A few minutes later, the Bigmouth Dickhead, as I'd come to know him, finally got in the game. I was a little worried about my legs, but there was no reason to be. He hadn't even made a play when a guy on his own team cocked his head back to skim a ball and caught the Bigmouth Dickhead over the left eye, splitting his Neanderthal forehead open like an over-stuffed sausage.

As he lay bleeding on the ground, waiting for the ambulance, we all stood dutifully about, looking at our feet, trying to feel bad. All I could think was that if this dude didn't straighten up, he was screwed. I mean, instant karma like that must mean your ticket is all but punched out. Cut the hooliganism, already.

But who knows? People talk about karma, and I don't claim to be an authority, but it seems to me that if you're going to accept that concept, you also have to accept its consequence: caste. This means people deserve their bad luck and misfortune for something they allegedly did in their last life. And that doesn't sit quite right, either. So maybe karma is bullshit. I say always err on the side of good; things never go badly with good—that is, simple niceness, a smile, a nod, a gracious reply. Even if you'd really like to just choke the bastard, niceness will always pay off. It's pleasing to other nice people and disarming to assholes.

Cam and I were out in my car a couple of years ago, just tooling around, when we saw a friend of ours who had a little Japanese sports car. (Which he has since sold to pay for medical school; where have people's values gone?) Dr. Kildare and I had the same thought: it might be interesting to test the relative velocities of our fancy little overpowered foreign machines. And so we did.

We were on a winding road going up Sugar Hill, and I got out ahead of him quickly, letting him ride me but not letting him pass. It was all looking like a fun way to spend the morning until a police officer, sitting just over a blind hill with a radar gun, clocked us at about a buck and a quarter. What the hell, I figured; I was headed to Europe in a few days for six months, so I didn't care if I got a ticket. Well, I cared, but you know . . .

So I waved our not-quite-fast-enough friend by me, and he zipped up over the hill and out of sight like George Jetson. I pulled over, figuring the cop would pull in behind me. But he didn't; he flew by us and chased the guy we'd been beating instead. I had mixed feelings about this. I mean, if anybody had been breaking the speed limit here, I had. So I waited about fifteen seconds for the cop to come back, and when he didn't, we went home.

This being a small town, it hadn't taken long for Officer Radar to learn who was driving fast enough to go airborne on a road that twists like a large intestine. Plus—again, this being a small town— he'd seen the car the day before while giving Dr. Speedy's roommate a speeding ticket of his own. He'd had to chase him home, too.

After some brilliant negotiations on our racing pal's part, the officer graciously agreed not to give him a ticket, but to let him pay his roomie's freight from the day before instead.

I say, Bag med school; he should have gone to law school. Or bag it all and become a sports agent. In any case, I stood down to take the rap and then didn't get caught, and he basically skated anyway. I was nice, the cop was nice, and the roommate was tickled. That sounds like primo karma. That's the zone you want to live in. Share the love.

If we'd have both run from that patrolman, they'd have called out the National Guard and run us down like dogs. If we'd both stopped, we both would have been written up, and I would have lost my license. (Points!) One good deed begets another—I see it too often to doubt it. Call it viral niceness.

People ask me for advice all the time, and I really have nothing to tell them about skiing that they won't learn on their own if they work at it. In addition to "Go fast," I'd like to say this: Be good, give respect where it's earned, don't waste, and have fun wherever you find it. But who's got the time to say all that?

9

The Essential Raw Material

There's a lot to be learned in the forest, and in mountain snowfields—especially about snow. If you're a skier, or just live
north of anywhere, you have to pay attention to snow. You can't
help it. I've heard that the Inuit people have a hundred words for
it, which might be bullshit, like being able to see the Great Wall of
China from space. But it actually sounds about right to me. Where
I grew up, the first snowfall of the season usually comes before Halloween and lasts until after Easter. Because it's with us so much of
the time, we develop a certain relationship with snow, as people do
with smog in Los Angeles and hungry lions on the Serengeti.

My grandparents prayed for snow to fill up their ski lodge with
guests. And I openly longed for snow—it always gave me something to do. People who live with snow tend not to take it for
granted. I'll admit that by the end of the season, I get sick of it.
Bubonically sick of it sometimes. But that doesn't mean I don't
love it. It just gets to be too much of a good thing.

And that's the point: we're acutely aware of what kind of winter it is, every winter. New Hampshire, for instance, has had three
cold, nasty, and snowless howlers in a row. I wasn't even there for
them, but I know they sucked because everybody bitches about a

bad winter as if it were the drought that killed their crops and starved their families. I hear it all the time from people.

What you learn here first about snow is that there are lots of varieties. I like spring snow; people call it sugar snow—not because it comes at maple-sugaring season but because its individual ice crystals are about the size of a grain of white sugar, like tiny hailstones. A handful curls over on itself like a wave and produces very little friction; it seems almost fluid and rolls around in your palm like quicksilver. This lack of friction makes it the fastest possible snow to race on, and that's why I like it.

It comes late in the season, as the weather gets warmer and water molecules rise up through the snowpack, surrounding each individual snow crystal, rounding it off, and making it impossible for it to latch onto the one next to it. It's also called "old snow," and meteorologists refer to it as "depth hoar." It can make for good avalanches and extra-hard icy snowballs, if you know how to pack them right.

That's three names for just one type of snow; I probably missed at least one more, so I doubt the Inuit have anything on us linguistically, snow-wise anyway. On the other hand, if they distinguish between snows that take either one kick or two to get it all off your boots, or if a dusting of powder and a big dump of the stuff have completely different names, they might have us beat.

The science of snow was invented here in New England, in Jericho, Vermont, not far from where my father grew up. A man named Wilson Bentley, who came to be known as Snowflake Bentley, made a lifelong study of one thing: snow. That's intense. He was naturally fascinated by it, and it became the passion that finally ended his life.

At first, when he was still a little boy, he observed snow crystals under a microscope and hand-drew them. Painstaking stuff. When he was sixteen, he began photographing snowflakes with a camera with a built-in microscope. It was 1882, and this specialized gear came in a wooden case the size of a dorm-room refrigerator; it had a long, accordioned Snuffleupagus aperture hanging off the front, and three skinny legs to stand on.

Bentley's parents were farmers, not wealthy by anyone's standards, but they really dug their son's passion and commitment to what, as far as they and everyone else could tell, was common as dirt. They spent their life's savings to buy Bentley his camera, and he held up his end of the deal by discovering that no two snowflakes are alike. *Big* payoff. He traveled widely, lecturing on snow to scientists everywhere, and published his photos in magazines all over the world. In 1931, the scientific community collaborated to publish Bentley's images in a book, *Snow Crystals*.

He concentrated primarily on snow crystals—that is, the individual, usually six-sided little miracles of nature that make my profession possible. In addition to ski snow, there are several other kinds of falling snow, most of which I first encountered in the woods. The most common are snowflakes, of course—big piles of snow crystals interlaced with one another like Legos Gone Wild, all locked and eventually melting into each other's arms. Snowflakes come in everything from small, dry, and powdery—not much more than a frozen puff of dust—to big and moist, as if sheets of wet toilet paper were floating out of the sky. So Bentley had his life's work cut out for him.

The snow family also includes graupel, which looks like frozen beads of Styrofoam, and rime, which is made up of nano-iceballs; it's also a form of frozen Velcro that sticks to everything it lands on, and coats the world in ice sometimes inches thick. It's pretty until you picture your car as an ice sculpture. Or yourself. And when you get up over seventy miles an hour on skis, rime in the face is like taking a sandblasting.

I understand Snowflake Bentley's love for snow. People use it, appreciate it, curse it—some of us even make a living from it. But snow has no use for people, and would be an awesome force of nature even if we'd never existed. Since the last ice age, billions of cubic tons have fallen year after year, millennium after millennium.

People laughed at Bentley when he was a kid, but he didn't care. He had a whole different beat going. He was homeschooled by his mother until he was fourteen years old, and self-educated after that. Bentley was an innovator, a genius with an eye for beauty and mystery in the obvious—and there's nothing more obvious than snow in Vermont.

When Bentley was sixty-six, after taking some photographs of snow, he walked home six miles in a blizzard, toting his camera. He died of pneumonia less than a week later, a couple of days before Christmas. The man loved snow with a passion very few of us ever have for anything. That's pure. He loved it from the time he was a child, and so have I. We developed radically different uses for it; he was a scientist and photographer; I ski on the stuff. But that's a brother.

My true interest, clearly, runs more to ski snow than ice crystals. But I'll take what I can get and like it. Powder snow is the holy grail of skiing for a lot of people. Deep freshies as light as air. Powder is, in fact, mostly air. All snow is. The wettest, slushiest snowflake imaginable is only 25 percent water; the rest is atmosphere.

Because there's so much air in powder, it rarely hurts when you fall, making all your mistakes inconsequential, which is what we're all really after in life. When I was a kid, I'd climb rocks and trees, as high as I could, and jump off into the deep powder. It's like flying and landing safely.

For me, the beauty of powder is that you have to go fast, because if you don't, you'll sink like a warm brick. And depending upon how deep the snow is, that can be a major suck because you have to dig yourself out. And I do mean yourself. Nice or not, only a moron would stop to help; he'd sink too.

At the right speed, you skim across the soft pack like a snowmobile on a thawing pond in April. Lean back, but not too much or you'll fall on your ass; keep your tips up, flex those calf muscles until they go into tetanus, avoid the big rocks hiding in the fluff, and you're skiing powder.

Then there's crud. There's a lot in a name. It's what's left of a nicely groomed course when you've had your fun with it. It's broken and bumpy, slippery where it wants to be, crusty and treacherous otherwise. But still full of fun if you know how to play it.

Start a race well out of the pack, and you'll see a lot of crud. Watch ski racers starting in about fortieth position come down the course: their knees are popping in fast forward, taking a piston pounding over the uneven surface. That's crud. Most guys don't like it much. Hermann Maier says he prefers it, and that the courses these days are overgroomed. But he's more of a machine than a Sno-Cat is, even without that metal rod in his leg.

Crust is completely different from all other types of snow, and generally not much fun. Thankfully, the conditions and timing have to be just right for it to form. The sun must lightly melt the top of a new snowfall, and then you need a nighttime freeze to harden it. How much it melts and how hard it gets depend on a lot of variables, but the result can be unskiable crust—the kind you break through without warning and get locked into place, then face-plant through it on the other end. Not fun. It can be potentially funny if it happens to someone else, but only if they don't get a bunch of those little ice cuts all over their face and bleed in the snow. It would be in bad taste to yuk it up too much under those circumstances. Not nice.

There's slush, of course, wet and slow. You could ski in a Jules Verne deep-sea diving suit and still get soaked in this stuff. Go home, be dry and warm, ski another day.

Last, there's boilerplate—as hard as dry ice on Pluto and slicker than Canada goose shit on a dewy putting green. Even people who have never been out of Los Angeles County can imagine why ice isn't the optimal surface to ski on, unless you want to see how fast you can go and have a Ph.D. in falling, and maybe a cast-iron ass for insurance. Otherwise, again, go home and live to ski another day.

There are a lot of subsets to these categories, too. There's chalky snow, there's grippy snow (a sub-subset of which is Styrofoam snow), there's chunky snow and sloppy snow, all in varying gradations. You have to get out there and check it out for yourself. Pick it up and feel it, like a hunter fondling fresh deer shit for the clues it holds. Do this, in particular, before a race, and see what you learn; then put it to use.

My favorite snow condition is corduroy—just after the groomers have finished with it. But there's more to snow than skiing. There's color. In New England, late in the season, we get streaks of orange in the snowfields. Its color comes from algae; same with the "watermelon snow" they get in the Rocky Mountains—it's bright red. Then, of course, there's yellow snow, which gets its pigment from a couple of sources, one being algae. In the fir and spruce forests in the mountains where I grew up, you can find green snow in the spring—again, algae.

The coolest snow, I think, is red snow. It falls in Europe, in the Alps. To me it looks pink, and it's very different from the others. The color comes from the red dust off the Kalahari Desert in southern Africa; it travels on the wind all the way north to Europe, where it attaches to the water molecules in the air, staining them red before they freeze into snow crystals.

It's interesting, even enlightening, to run a ski race in the Alps on sand from Africa. Weather patterns are a clear indication of how tightly wrapped the world is, how deep into one another's shit we are—dust from one side of the planet coloring snow in the other hemisphere. But it's not all skittles and beer. For instance, the decade-long drought in China has covered the west coast of North America—from Canada to Mexico—in a layer of dust. Nothing against the Chinese, but unless you're an asthmatic looking for something to choke on, it's really unusable dust.

You can't see the Rockies from their foothills anymore. That's like not being able to see home plate from the outfield. All because of a Chinese dust storm caused by desertification, another symptom of global warming, the problem at hand. And so the diseased circle closes and we all start to choke. Scientists claim that the damaged rain forests of the world may soon start to produce huge amounts of carbon dioxide instead of oxygen, and that the oceans are absorbing so much of it that their chemical compounds are changing—all of which would exacerbate the problem exponentially, like gasoline on fire.

I know it's touchy to talk about the environment—with all the fast cars I drive, I'm a lukewarm environmentalist myself. Oh, I've got my bona fides: I recycle, compost, and pee off the porch whenever possible. But ignoring global warming, it seems to me, is like ignoring Hermann. Even if you could, it wouldn't make him go away.

In the summer of 2003, the glaciers in Switzerland were melting; twenty-six thousand people died from the heat in the eight European countries that were counting. The real death toll might be three times as high. That same season in America, we had more tornadoes in one month than ever before—an average of sixteen a day. And record heat waves, too.

A Brit named Ben Saunders tried to trek across the North Pole solo last spring and got mired down in slush; he had to be airlifted out when he reached open water that should have been a permanent ice pack. He says no one will ever cross the North Pole again without a boat.

Anyway, it was the hottest, most weather-twisted summer in the past ten thousand years, and it got my attention.

We're just beginning to appreciate the effects of global warming; rising sea levels, for instance, are just getting started and, if not corrected soon, will continue to rise for another five hundred years. At that rate, Tamarack Tennis Camp in the White Mountains will be beachfront property someday. We could be well on our way to the next Great Extinction, which, according to climatologists, will be the sixth in the earth's history. So it's not like it can't happen; geologically speaking, it happens all the time.

The good news is that until the Alps are actually underwater, there'll be no lack of snow to ski on—harsh winters and record snowfalls are also consequences of global warming. If we're not careful, the world in the future will be all boats and ice hotels. So I say it's time for each of us in our own way to turn it around. For my part, I'd be real interested in a hydrogen-powered 450 horsepower race car, if anyone has a mind to invent a nice one. I need it, and the world needs it too.

10

Running My Mouth, Ain't I'm a Dog

M y family taught us that the best way to protect your own freedom is to watch everybody else's back. That's the essence of
community. I don't make a habit of airing my political ideas, but I
was raised in a political household, rode on my mother's shoulders
in antinuclear demonstrations at Seabrook from the time I was
two. We lived a hundred miles from the ocean on the survival side
of the prevailing winds, but we marched at Seabrook because the
people in the evacuation zone needed our support.

We were also once in a Washington-to-Moscow peace march—
that's Washington, Vermont, to Moscow, Vermont. Took two days;
we camped along the way and met a lot of nice people.

Anyone with kids knows you can't just drag them off to this
stuff without some serious explanation. So I was schooled early on
in the delicate balance between security and freedom, and made
aware of the good and bad governments can do; I completely understood why we leaned toward the freedom side of that equation.
Way toward it.

So when a French journalist asked me what I thought of the
impending invasion of Iraq in the winter of 2003, it wasn't as if I
hadn't thought about it. All my life this had been exactly the kind

of thing that would energize the adults around me into action, or at least cause them to talk about it a lot, and get all worked up and drink extra beer.

When this dreaded Frenchman asked me what I thought of the war, I had to answer him. Anything less would have been cowardly and unpatriotic. So I said, as simply as I could, that I felt I was representing my country better than my country was representing me. I still can't think of a better way to put it. I've spent half my life in Europe since I was a teenager, and I benefit from a well-traveled perspective that certain people running the world lack.

It's important to speak your mind now and then; it's also essential to good citizenship. Read your American history and you'll find that dissent is patriotic. It's gotten a bad name lately, but that's politics, not patriotism. History teaches in no uncertain terms that when shit goes bad, it only gets worse until something makes it better, puts it back in balance—the yin and yang, the Dark Side and the Force. Dissent. The civil rights, gay rights, and women's rights movements were all positive responses to negative energy. Everybody knows that.

And that's why I said what I said about Iraq. I even tried to put it in neutral terms. I didn't attack the Iraq policy directly, I didn't mention anybody by name; I merely implied that the image I projected in Europe was better than the administration's was at the time, and that there was a reason for that. Every American president has to earn his chops with the Europeans: they liked Clinton's charm, they loved Kennedy's wife, and they were amused by Carter's dweebishness. But from what people tell me, they haven't taken to a Republican president since Eisenhower, and they preferred him as a general.

Anyway, I could easily have sidestepped the question, and certainly not have mentioned it in this book, but war deserves our attention. It isn't an abstraction; it isn't the war on drugs, or the war on inflation, or the war on poverty. Think of the dead and wounded, the billions spent on destruction, the museums from the cradle of civilization looted and destroyed—there's nothing intangible in any of that, nothing ephemeral about bodies and devastation everywhere. If I have nothing to say about that when asked directly, then my brain needs a jump start, maybe a new battery.

In Europe I saw BODE FOR PRESIDENT signs at races, but at home there were only scolding editorials implying that because I'm an athlete, I've relinquished my right to an opinion. I get the sense that they think I'm a skier with no interior life. That's an ugly stereotype: dumb jock.

To its credit, *The Union Leader*—my home state's very conservative statewide newspaper—was editorially pissed off about my war comments, yet still named me its Athlete of the Year that year. *The Union Leader* has always been gracious to me, even when it was mad. Which means that either we really can all just get along or, as far as they can tell, I am just a dumb jock.

Many Americans thanked me for voicing what they were thinking. And that made any grief I took well worth it. Besides, if you believe in self-governance, this is pretty basic stuff. Everybody's got to shoot their mouth off every now and then, and under the most inconvenient circumstances if necessary. Otherwise, may the best war chest win.

So let me say it again: personally, I hate talking about politics; I'd rather have a stone in my ski boot. A big sharp one. But if there's one thing in the world I wish I was wrong about, it's the government. I didn't talk about the war because it's my hobby, or because my view carries more weight than the average Joe's, but because I was asked. And not enough reporters in the United States were asking that question at the time; now it's too late.

In the end, had I been supportive of the president and his war, no one would have said boo about it. He probably would have invited me up to the White House to play video games. So that's the problem: I should either be mute or be a mouthpiece for war? I'll pass. Aside from funding the antidoping Gestapo, the U.S. government doesn't contribute a pisshole in the snow to my livelihood, and I like it that way.

And while we're on the subject of piss, let's discuss the World Anti-Doping Agency. I know—it sounds like the DEA run by Vince McMahon's Goody Two-shoes brother. Actually, it's run by a guy named Dick Pound. It and its national chapters test athletes for a variety of substances, only some of them relevant to sports. They are the International Pee Police: "Have Dixie cup, will travel." My experience with them has taught me one basic truth: we can have a free society or we can have a drug-free society, but we can't have both.

On the one hand I believe that athletes who use performance-enhancing drugs are cheaters and ought to be caught for the sake of the sport. That part of what the World Anti-Doperators do is needed and appreciated, so job well done. But on the other hand, this is ski racing—NASCAR without the car—so if a guy feels he needs to use some designer chemical to beat me, then he profoundly doubts himself, and that's his real problem as a ski racer. You can't do this sport without absolute confidence.

Doping is more apparent in some sports than in others. Weight lifters will obviously get more out of human growth hormone than Ping-Pong players will. Nonetheless, a national table tennis champ tested positive for steroids not long ago. Figure that out.

I have no problem with busting the guilty, but Alain Baxter lost his Olympic medal over some Vicks he used. As I write this, a World Cup skier is on the hot seat for taking cold medicine. And actually, the table tennis player says he was banned for two years over a weight-gain powder that he bought at a health-food store. If that's true, it sucks worse than cheating does. Especially since there are baseball players who need the Periodic Table of Elements to explain their stats and asterisks next to their X-Men titles. Once baseball gets serious about drug testing it's going to be a long time before any mortal breaks those records.

In World Cup races, everybody who finishes in the money gets tested, and everybody else is subject to random testing. Which occurs regularly. And that seems adequate. You'd think. But I've had them appear at my house, unannounced, in the middle of the summer, a little bag of tricks in hand, demanding my precious bodily fluids.

I'm supposed to inform them about where I can be found at all times, and I've been in trouble twice for not being at my designated location. Both times I was at my girlfriend's instead of home. This was in July. As if I'd tell them where I was going so they could burst in on us at an intimate moment, demanding a specimen. I don't think so.

The antidoping regimen is worse than an electronic anklet,

which I know something about because I have a cousin wearing one. I've decided that if the inspectors show up and I'm not home, I hope they had a nice trip. Really. I can think of far worse places to be stuck with some time on your hands. There's a hot tub and a Kegerator on my deck—help yourself. Bring your clubs, a fishing rod, a tennis racket, a mountain bike, and have a blast. It's not disrespect, it's self-respect. For me the question is simple: If my mother never needed to know where I was, then why does Dick Pound?

The reason there are so many antidoping rules that have nothing conceivable to do with performance enhancement is pure politics. The war on drugs is an industry now, in both the public and the private sectors, and like all powerful, multibillion-dollar concerns, it has lobbyists in Washington whose job it is to ensure that next year's tax break and/or subsidy is bigger than last year's. Consequently, we live during the New Prohibition—a society that's officially puritanical and unofficially always juiced on something. Some of it is hypocrisy, the rest is cognitive dissonance, and it all sucks.

I've been invited to the White House more than once. Pass, again. Smiling in photos with people you don't want to hang out with may be second nature for politicians, but not for me. I don't raise the issue to be rude to the president; I'm sure he cares far less about meeting me than I do about meeting him. But I think his administration is wrong about important things, and I'm not about to pretend otherwise.

I'm a citizen of the United States of America, and to me that means that life's purpose is the pursuit of happiness—"pursuit" being the operative word. Happiness isn't an excuse to slack; it's an opportunity to be your best, to create a life's work, to make your mark. If this is news to you, then it's definitely time to get off your ass and do something extraordinary. Happiness awaits.

Acknowledgments

The authors give many thanks to Susan Raihofer at the David Black Agency for her unerring navigation, Bruce Tracy for seeing what we saw, and Adam Korn for being on top of things. Thanks to Lowell Taub at SFX for his always considered advice, and thank you, Maja, for permission to reprint your interview with Woody.

ABOUT THE AUTHORS

BODE MILLER is an Olympic medalist and World Cup champion. He lives in Easton, New Hampshire.

JACK McENANY has a master's degree in writing from the Johns Hopkins University. A former Washington, D.C., reporter, he lives in Franconia, New Hampshire, with his wife and two children.

ABOUT THE TYPE

This book was set in Baskerville, a typeface which was designed by John Baskerville, an amateur printer and typefounder, and cut for him by John Handy in 1750. The type became popular again when The Lanston Monotype Corporation of London revived the classic Roman face in 1923. The Mergenthaler Linotype Company in England and the United States cut a version of Baskerville in 1931, making it one of the most widely used typefaces today.